Bruno Taut's Design Inspiration for the Glashaus

Bruno Taut's seminal exhibition pavilion, the *Glashaus* (literally translated as Glasshouse), is a formative exemplar of early architectural modernism. However, the historical record of the *Glashaus* is significantly skewed toward a singular notion of Expressionism as it was primarily established by the art critic Adolf Behne. The result is that the official history of the *Glashaus* surprisingly excludes Taut's diverse motives for the design of the building. This building is therefore logically part of the important debate that rethinks the origins of modernism.

In an effort to clarify the problematic historical record of the *Glashaus*, this book exposes Bruno Taut's motives and inspirations for its design. The result is that Taut's motives can be found in yet unacknowledged precedents like the botanical inspiration of the *Victoria regia* lily; the commercial interests of Frederick Keppler as its client and as the Director of the *Deutsche Luxfer Prismen Syndikat*; and imitation that derived openly from the Gothic. The outcome is a substantial contribution to the re-evaluation of the generally accepted histories of the modern movement in architecture.

David Nielsen graduated from the Technikon Witwatersrand and the University of the Witwatersrand, where he earned Diplomas, Bachelor's Degrees and a Master's in architecture. While resident in Johannesburg, he both taught architecture at the University of Johannesburg and practiced as an architect. In 2006, he migrated to Brisbane, Australia and subsequently took up an appointment within the architecture discipline at the Queensland University of Technology. Here he currently teaches in the spheres of architectural technology and design. David's research interests are focused on architectural history and he has also previously undertaken research in Building Information Modelling. In 2015, he completed his PhD, from which this publication derives.

Routledge Research in Architecture

The *Routledge Research in Architecture* series provides the reader with the latest scholarship in the field of architecture. The series publishes research from across the globe and covers areas as diverse as architectural history and theory, technology, digital architecture, structures, materials, details, design, monographs of architects, interior design and much more. By making these studies available to the worldwide academic community, the series aims to promote quality architectural research.

An Architecture of Parts
Architects, Building Workers and Industrialisation in Britain 1940–1970
Christine Wall

Towards an Articulated Phenomenological Interpretation of Architecture
Phenomenal phenomenology
M. Reza Shirazi

Architectural System Structures
Integrating Design Complexity in Industrialised Construction
Kasper Sánchez Vibæk

Space Unveiled
Invisible Cultures in the Design Studio
Edited by Carla Jackson Bell

Architectural Temperance
Spain and Rome, 1700–1759
Victor Deupi

Assembling the Centre: Architecture for Indigenous Cultures
Australia and Beyond
Janet McGaw and Anoma Pieris

The Films of Charles and Ray Eames
A Universal Sense of Expectation
Eric Schuldenfrei

Intersections of Space and Ethos
Searching for the Unmeasurable
Nikolaos-Ion Terzoglou, Kyriaki Tsoukala and Charikleia Pantelidou

Ars et Ingenium: The Embodiment of Imagination in Francesco di Giorgio Martini's Drawings
Pari Riahi

Kahn at Penn
Transformative Teacher of Architecture
James Williamson

Designing the British Post-War Home
Kenneth Wood, 1948–1968
Fiona Fisher

Drawing the Unbuildable
Seriality and Reproduction in Architecture
Nerma Cridge

The Idea of the Cottage in English Architecture, 1760–1860
Daniel Maudlin

Cut and Paste Urban Landscape
The Work of Gordon Cullen
Mira Engler

Wooden Church Architecture of the Russian North
Regional Schools and Traditions (14th–19th centuries)
Evgeny Khodakovsky

Mid-Century Modernism in Turkey
Architecture Across Cultures in the 1950s and 1960s
Meltem Ö. Gürel

Bruno Taut's Design Inspiration for the Glashaus
David Nielsen

Bruno Taut's Design Inspiration for the Glashaus

David Nielsen

LONDON AND NEW YORK

First published 2016
by Routledge
2 Park Square, Milton Park, Abingdon, Oxon OX14 4RN

and by Routledge
711 Third Avenue, New York, NY 10017

Routledge is an imprint of the Taylor & Francis Group, an informa business

© 2016 David Nielsen

The right of David Nielsen to be identified as author of this work has been asserted by him in accordance with sections 77 and 78 of the Copyright, Designs and Patents Act 1988.

All rights reserved. No part of this book may be reprinted or reproduced or utilised in any form or by any electronic, mechanical, or other means, now known or hereafter invented, including photocopying and recording, or in any information storage or retrieval system, without permission in writing from the publishers.

Trademark notice: Product or corporate names may be trademarks or registered trademarks, and are used only for identification and explanation without intent to infringe.

British Library Cataloguing-in-Publication Data
A catalogue record for this book is available from the British Library

Library of Congress Cataloging in Publication Data
Nielsen, David, 1968–
Bruno Taut's design inspiration for the Glashaus / David Nielsen.
pages cm. -- (Routledge research in architecture)
Includes bibliographical references and index.
1. Glashaus (Deutsche Werkbund-Ausstellung, 1914, Cologne, Germany)
2. Taut, Bruno, 1880-1938--Criticism and interpretation. I. Title.
NA6750.C65G59 2016
720.92--dc23
2015014487

ISBN: 978-1-138-88754 -1 (hbk)
ISBN: 978-1-315-71403-5 (ebk)

Typeset in Sabon
by Fish Books Ltd.

Contents

	List of figures	ix
	Preface	xi
1	Introduction	1
2	The client: Frederick Keppler	10
3	*Victoria regia's* bequest to the *Glashaus*	68
4	Bruno Taut and the Gothic	125
5	Conclusion	159
	Index	163

Figures

1.1	Bruno Taut's *Glashaus* at the Werkbund Exhibition of 1914 in Cologne (Bildarchiv Foto Marburg).	2
1.2	The interior staircase of the *Glashaus* that led upward to the Dome Room (Bildarchiv Foto Marburg).	5
1.3	The Dome Room in the *Glashaus* (Bildarchiv Foto Marburg).	7
1.4	The Cascade Room in the *Glashaus* (Bildarchiv Foto Marburg).	8
2.1	A 1903 advertisement for Luxfer Prisms (Page, 1903).	13
2.2	An aerial view of the 1913 *Baufachausstellung* in Leipzig (SLUB Dresden/Deutsche Fotothek).	19
2.3a	The Crystal Place at Sydenham (Unknown author, 1872).	28
2.3b	The Exhibition Place at the London International Exhibition of 1862 (Science Museum/Science & Society Picture Library).	28
2.4	The entrance to the Vienna *Weltausstellung* of 1873 with the *Rotunde* in the background (Josef Löwy for the *Wiener Photographen Association*).	34
2.5	A birds-eye-view of Paris' *Exposition Universelle* of 1878 (Bitard, 1878).	40
2.6	A view of the Midway Plaisance at the Chicago World's Exposition of 1893 showing the Moorish Palace directly to the left of the Ferris Wheel (Arnold & Higinbotham, 1893).	44
2.7	The Horticultural Hall at the Chicago World's Exposition of 1893 (Arnold & Higinbotham, 1893).	47
2.8	The *Chateau d'eau* at Paris' *Exposition Universelle* of 1900 (Neurdein, Neurdein, & Baschet, 1900).	53
2.9	The *Salle des Glaces ou Salle des Illusions* at Paris' *Exposition Universelle* of 1900 (Neurdein *et al.*, 1900).	55
2.10	The *Palais Lumineux* at Paris' *Exposition Universelle* of 1900 (Agence photographique de la RMN-Grand Palais).	56
3.1a	A period illustration depicting the flower of the *Victoria regia* lily (Fitch, 1851).	70
3.1b	A period illustration showing the anatomy of the *Victoria regia* lily (Fitch, 1851).	70

x *Figures*

3.2 Joseph Paton's 1850 *Victoria regia* glasshouse at Chatsworth (Lindley, 1850). 74

3.3a John Claudius Loudon's proposal for an Accumulated Semi-Globe glasshouse (Loudon, 1822). 93

3.3b John Claudius Loudon's proposal for an Aquatic glasshouse (Loudon, 1822). 93

3.4 Interior of *Victoria regia* glasshouse designed by Eduard Ortgies for Louis van Houtte at his Gentbrugge nursery (van Houtte, 1851–2). 104

3.5a The *Victoria regia* glasshouse at the Botanical Gardens of the University of Leiden (Leiden University Library Collections). 110

3.5b The *Victoria regia* glasshouse at the Berlin Botanical Gardens in Schöneberg (Landesdenkmalamt Berlin). 110

3.6 A section through the *Victoria regia* (left) and main palm (right) glasshouses at the Berlin Botanical Gardens in Dahlem (Sarrazin & Schultze, 1909). 117

4.1a The original aisle vaulting in Stuttgart's *Stiftskirche* (Bildarchiv Stiftskirche Stuttgart). 126

4.1b The structure of the Dome Room in the *Glashaus* (Bildarchiv Foto Marburg). 127

4.2a Bruno Taut's 1904 illustration of Stuttgart's *Stiftskirche* (Akademie der Künste). 143

4.2b Bruno Taut's 1904 illustration of a *Tannenwald* (Akademie der Künste). 144

4.3a The preliminary plan of the Glashaus that was first made public on 1 January 1914 (Taut, 1914). 148

4.3b The final plan of the Glashaus as submitted to the Cologne City Authorities (Historisches Archiv Köln). 149

4.4 The initial 'Geometric seed' that was scaled according to the square root of two (By author). 152

4.5a Overlaying the 'geometric seed' onto the plan of the *Glashaus* (By author and Historisches Archiv Köln). 153

4.5b Overlaying the 'geometric seed' onto a section of the *Glashaus* (By author and Historisches Archiv Köln). 154

4.5c Overlaying the 'geometric seed' onto an elevation of the *Glashaus* (By author and Historisches Archiv Köln). 154

Preface

This book seeks to offer an alternative explanation for the design of Bruno Taut's seminal *Glashaus*. However, if it were not for coincidence, this work might have offered an account of glass façades. During the process of researching these façades, I discovered the botanical glasshouses that were constructed for the cultivation of the *Victoria regia* lily. In particular, it was reproductions of two 19th century images in John Hix's book *The Glasshouse* that made a lasting impression on me. The first of these images was an aquatic glasshouse by John Claudius Loudon. While the second, was an photograph that depicted a *Victoria regia* glasshouse which was constructed at the University of Leiden. Both of these images impressed me because of their timeless aesthetic of smooth curved-glass shells; an aesthetic that could easily be connected to contemporary glass facades.

If it were not for my attendance of a student's architectural design presentation in 2009, this information might have remained one of those semi-interesting discoveries that demonstrated the logical progression of glass façade development. In this presentation for the design of a theatre building, the student saw fit to include an image that depicted a section though Bruno Taut's *Glashaus*. I immediately recognised similarities between this *Glashaus* section and the above mentioned reproductions of Loudon's aquatic and Leiden's *Victoria regia* glasshouses. In all three buildings there was an uncanny convergence of aesthetic and planning. My *Eureka* moment arrived, when I discovered that Bruno Taut had explicitly mentioned *Victoria regia* in one of his writings. From this point onward, all thoughts of producing a work that explored glass façades were abandoned. Further investigation of Taut and *Victoria regia* revealed that both shared a strange convergence of space and time that was centred in Berlin. This line of investigation also exposed more curiosities concerning the *Glashaus*. For example, reading Taut's writings also exposed the unique role that both the *Glashaus'* client and Gothic thinking had played in its design. Synthesising these new facts destabilised the long-held notion that the *Glashaus* was the singular product of Expressionism. This manuscript instead proposes the design of the *Glashaus* as an architectural product which cleverly married the prescriptive desires of the client to the creative processes of the architect. Therefore, what

xii *Preface*

this book hopefully contributes to the understanding of the *Glashaus* design is a unique interpretive narrative which is largely based on available sources.

Rather than reflecting on each chapter individually, I would instead encourage the reader to consider the narrative of this work in its entirety. Likewise, due to publishing constraints numerous buildings mentioned in this book are not illustrated. Considering the adage that 'a picture tells a thousand words', I would strongly advise that the reader find images of these.

1   Introduction

Bruno Taut's *Glashaus* was an extremely influential example of early modern architecture. As such, it is widely discussed in architectural history and extensively referenced (Ching, Jarzombek and Prakash, 2007; Colquhoun, 2002; Curtis, 1996; Frampton, 2007; James Chakraborty, 2000; Richards and Gilbert, 2006; Sharp, 1966; Sharp, Scheerbart and Taut, 1972; Thiekotter, 1993; Watkin, 2005; Whyte, 1982). Constructed for the *Werkbund* Exhibition in 1914, the *Glashaus* is generally classified as Expressionist in its style. Although the purpose of the building was to showcase the products of the glass industries, the deeper 'theoretical' intentions of the building encompassed a complex mix of cosmic mysticism and utopian ideals.

But given the passage of time, why should anybody care about Bruno Taut's *Glashaus*? After all, it was only a small exhibition building at a relatively obscure exhibition, which existed as a physical object for a few short weeks during the summer of 1914. To answer this question, one needs to view the *Glashaus* as a powerful and seductive metaphor. With the story of the *Glashaus*, architectural history has been written, contested and reinvented numerous times. Even at its 100th year anniversary, the *Glashaus* still taunts and disturbs architectural history.

The parameters of debate concerning Taut and the *Glashaus* have been largely established through the writings of Reyner Banham (1959), Dennis Sharp (1966; 1972) and Iain Boyd-Whyte (1982; 1985). In his 1959 article, 'The Glass Paradise', Banham was the first English-language author to expose the unique relationship between Taut and the bohemian poet Paul Scheerbart. Banham (1959) contended that there was a hitherto-overlooked prophetic ancestry of odd personalities, myths, and symbols. He argued that events in Germany immediately before and after World War One demanded further study. To this end, Banham first proposed two key, but previously overlooked, personalities who emerged from this period that needed to be added to the list of key modernist figures: Paul Scheerbart and Bruno Taut. By linking Scheerbart and Taut to the *Glashaus*, Banham presented an argument that countered the accepted history of the modern movement by introducing a light-mysticism as well as the cultures and practices of the Orient and Gothic Europe, which he believed ultimately, influenced the design of the

Figure 1.1 Bruno Taut's *Glashaus* at the Werkbund Exhibition of 1914 in Cologne. Photo by permission of Bildarchiv Foto Marburg.

Glashaus. Banham suggested that it would be appropriate to enquire as to the *Glashaus*' origins as the building was both vastly dissimilar from and yet exceeded any of Taut's previous designs (Banham, 1959: 87). In doing so, Banham (1959) concluded that the history of the modern movement required rewriting because of its narrow linear perspective and thus its exclusion of an important literary influence like Scheerbart.

Although 'The Glass Paradise' first appeared in 1959, it is a valuable resource for any study on the *Glashaus*. Numerous authors have subsequently accepted Banham's argument, and, through their research, uncovered key facts concerning the *Glashaus*.

In 1966, Dennis Sharp accepted Banham's interdisciplinary challenge by documenting the Expressionist origins of modernist architecture in his publication, *Modern Architecture and Expressionism*. Rosemarie Haag Bletter (1973) published her dissertation, *Bruno Taut and Paul Scheerbart's Vision: Utopian Aspects of German Expressionist Architecture*, in which she systematically explored the Taut–Scheerbart relationship. Haag Bletter (1981) further developed her initial argument in, 'The Interpretation of the Glass Dream: Expressionist Architecture and the History of the Crystal Metaphor', in which she traced the mystic and historical associations of crystal and glass. In the early 1980s, Iain Boyd Whyte also responded to Banham's call with two publications: *Bruno Taut and the Architecture of Activism* (1982) and *Crystal Chain Letters: Architectural Fantasies by Bruno Taut and His Circle* (1985). As a result of these publications, which formed part of the debate to revise the accepted history of modernism, Scheerbart and Expressionism are now included in most contemporary histories concerning Bruno Taut and the *Glashaus* (Colquhoun, 2002; Curtis, 1996; Hix, 2005; Thiekotter, 1993).

It was the generally accepted view that the *Glashaus* constituted an Expressionist exhibition pavilion, which resulted from the mutual efforts of Paul Scheerbart and Bruno Taut. In the 1990s, there was a resurgent interest in Bruno Taut. During this period, numerous additional German publications became available on Taut. These included Angelika Thiekotter's 1993 publication *Kristallisationen, Splitterungen: Bruno Taut's Glashaus (Crystallisation, Splintering: Bruno Taut's Glasshouse)*, and Leo Ikelaar's 1996 publication *Paul Scheerbart's Briefe von 1913–1914 an Gottfried Heinersdorff, Bruno Taut und Herwarth Walden (Paul Scheerbart's 1913–14 Letters to Gottfried Heinersdorff, Bruno Taut and Herwarth Walden)*. In 2005, Kai Gutschow published his dissertation, *The Culture of Criticism: Adolf Behne and the Development of Modern Architecture in Germany, 1910–1914*, in which he re-established the importance of art critic Adolf Behne's contribution to the *Glashaus*. Manfred Speidel (1995) also called into question Scheerbart's contribution to the *Glashaus*' design, revealing that Scheerbart only met Taut a few months before its construction – after Taut had finished his preliminary sketches. Kurt Junghanns (1983) had earlier asserted that the *Glashaus* design was complete before Taut and Scheerbart ever met.

Gutschow (2005) proposed that the *Glashaus* was a collaborative result of Taut, Scheerbart and Behne. He argued each of them played a distinct role: Taut was responsible for the overall design of the *Glashaus*, including the circulatory experience, the geometry, the reinforced concrete structure of the dome, the water cascade, and the stained-glass artwork; Scheerbart's role was that of a theorist; and Behne was the official historian of the *Glashaus*. However, Behne's inclusion into the official history of the *Glashaus* was not without significant implications. Gutschow (2005) argued that his inclusion was problematic because he over-emphasised the Expressionist link to the *Glashaus*. Behne was actively seeking to link Expressionism to architecture, a link that did not exist before the *Glashaus*. It was through Behne's involvement with the *Glashaus* that the enduring link with Expressionism was first forged. It was through Behne's prolific writings, and not through Taut, that the *Glashaus* was initially labelled as Expressionist. According to Gutschow (2005), this labelling was particularly troubling considering that nobody contributed more to the original literary record concerning the *Glashaus*, Bruno Taut, and Expressionism than Behne. As such, Behne's original writings could be argued as having unduly influenced the secondary sources of Banham (1959), Sharp (1966) and Boyd Whyte (1982; 1985).

4   Bruno Taut's design inspiration for the Glashaus

Although it is not possible to 'experience' the *Glashaus* anymore, a close interpretation is still feasible due to the existing black-and-white photographs and the technical documentation that was submitted to the Cologne City administration. This is despite the fact that Gutschow concluded his reassessment by stating:

> Unlike permanent buildings that are more readily reinterpreted by later generations of viewers, Behne's reviews, his panegyrics on Scheerbart, and the few remaining photographs, became the lens through which all subsequent interpretations have been made.
>
> (Gutschow, 2005: 270–1)

Following Banham's initial provocation, all of the authors mentioned above have sought to explain the *Glashaus'* origins in a wider cultural context. Yet, if one takes into account the gradual marginalisation of Taut's own motivations and the influences upon him as the architect of the project, as well as the questions raised over the level of Scheerbart's and Behne's input, the outcome reveals that an architectural historical analysis remains as important and pressing as ever. It is still appropriate to question the current understanding of the *Glashaus*. Has the historical record not been misled into believing that the *Glashaus* is Expressionist? Furthermore, on the basis of the subsequent research, it is fair to question whether Scheerbart's role has been overstated. While Taut was responsible for the overall design of the *Glashaus*, it was Expressionism that provided much of the theoretical basis for the design details of the building. Indicative of this tendency, Regine Prange (1991) credited Scheerbart as having been responsible for the 'details' of the glazed floor of the Dome Room, the kaleidoscope, electric lighting and glazed internal partition walls of the *Glashaus*. Speidel (1995) credited Scheerbart as having been responsible for the 'details' of lamp fittings and double-glazing. The Expressionist focus has effectively ignored Taut's central motives, while concentrating on the contributions of Scheerbart and others in the design of the *Glashaus*. This book proposes that an alternative explanation for the origins of the *Glashaus* needs to be formulated that returns to re-examine the sources that influenced the central contribution of Taut.

This task is not as easy as it might sound as Taut left nothing that identified his design motives for the *Glashaus*. He did however leave certain key writings, that when combined with insight into his life, reveals tantalising clues as to his formulation of the *Glashaus*. Key amongst these writing are a pamphlet that he prepared for the opining of the *Glashaus*, 'Glashaus: Werkbund-Ausstellung Köln 1914, Führer zur Eröffnung des Glashauses' ('Glashaus: Werkbund Exhibition in Cologne 1914, A Guide to the opening of the Glasshouse') and little known film script 'Die Galoschen des Glucks' ('The Lucky Shoes').

This book addresses these limitations in understanding by revealing some crucial motives and inspirations behind the design of the *Glashaus*.

Figure 1.2 The interior staircase of the *Glashaus* that led upward to the Dome Room. Photo by permission of Bildarchiv Foto Marburg.

6   *Bruno Taut's design inspiration for the Glashaus*

These have not yet been fully accounted for in any previous study. This book will therefore contribute to the re-evaluation of the generally accepted histories of the *Glashaus* and, in the process, the modern movement. Yet, this work is not a comprehensive account of the careers of Scheerbart, Behne, or Taut – or even the term Expressionism; numerous authors have already undertaken these studies. Equally, this thesis does not totally dismiss the roles played by Behne and Scheerbart in the *Glashaus*. Instead, this work accepts that they played a role, albeit a more limited one than outlined in various prior studies. What this book establishes is an alternative account of the original collaboration that informed the *Glashaus* design more directly.

Dietrich Neumann (1995) first alluded to the relationship between Bruno Taut, as architect, and his client, Frederick Keppler, of the *Deutsche Luxfer Prismen Syndikat* (German Luxfer Prism Syndicate). This is an important aspect of the commission that has not been fully researched. From an architectural perspective, this would seem the logical starting point for an investigation of the *Glashaus'* origins because all architecture can be argued as having both a commissioning client and a designer to creatively develop the brief. Importantly, the relationship between the two is often filled with varying intentions (and thus tensions) on the path to a final outcome.

In the three chapters that follow, this publication will argue that Keppler mandated a prototype building for the design of the *Glashaus*. It will be demonstrated that by 1914, this prototype was *tried and tested* because it derived from similar buildings at earlier exhibitions – in particular the World's Fairs of 1893 and 1900. Given the detailed stipulations of this brief, it will be proposed that Taut's design response for the *Glashaus* was interpretive; that is, it only allowed for the 'artistic clarification' of the requirements of the brief.

This work will establish a number of new insights into this well-worn analysis of the *Glashaus*. First of all, Taut's response offered a vivid interpretation of his client's requirement for a building that presented his products in the best possible manner. The requirements were that the building had to be structurally expressive, and that it had to contain a glazed dome, electric lighting, a fountain and a cascade. Second, the work establishes that Taut's design drew from earlier architectural precedents in order to fulfil the brief, namely the Gothic. Third, it shows that Taut was also attracted to the design inspiration offered by the *Victoria regia* lily. To satisfy Keppler's brief, Taut subsequently extracted the myths and symbols associated with these two precedents and reworked them in the design of the *Glashaus*.

This book concludes that the *Glashaus* was the result of a particularly focused client–architect relationship: Keppler, as the client, sought a particular type of building to best display his new building products, while Taut, as the architect, designed a building that was firmly based on earlier architectural precedents. This work therefore establishes the collaboration pivotal

Figure 1.3 The Dome Room in the *Glashaus*. Photo by permission of Bildarchiv Foto Marburg.

Figure 1.4 The Cascade Room in the *Glashaus*. Photo by permission of Bildarchiv Foto Marburg.

to the *Glashaus* design that has been largely overlooked. In the process, it establishes the previously overlooked importance of the *Victoria regia*, the *Deutsche Luxfer Prismen Syndikat* and the Gothic in Taut's design.

Bibliography

Banham, R. (1959). The Glass Paradise. *The Architectural Review, 125* (February), 87–89.
Ching, F., Jarzombek, M. and Prakash, V. (2007). *A Global History of Architecture*. Hoboken, NJ: John Wiley & Sons.
Colquhoun, A. (2002). *Modern architecture*. Oxford; New York Oxford University Press.
Curtis, W. J. R. (1996). *Modern Architecture Since 1900* (3 edn.). Oxford: Phaidon.
Frampton, K. (2007). *Modern Architecture: A Critical History* (4 edn.). London; New York: Thames & Hudson Ltd.
Gutschow, K. K. (2005). *The Culture of Criticism: Adolf Behne and the Development of Modern Architecture in Germany, 1910–1914*. (Doctor of Philosophy), Columbia University, New York.
Haag Bletter, R. (1973). *Bruno Taut and Paul Scheerbart's Vision: Utopian Aspects of German Expressionist Architecture, Vol. 1*. (Doctor of Philosophy), Columbia University, New York.

Haag Bletter, R. (1981). The Interpretation of the Glass Dream-Expressionist Architecture and the History of the Crystal Metaphor *The Journal of the Society of Architectural Historians, 40*(1), 20–43.

Hix, J. (2005). *The Glasshouse*. London Phaidon.

James-Chakraborty, K. (2000). *German Architecture for a Mass Audience*. London; New York: Routledge.

Junghanns, K. (1983). *Bruno Taut, 1880–1938*. Berlin (West): Elefanten Press.

Neumann, D. (1995). 'The Century's Triumph in Lighting': The Luxfer Prism Companies and Their Contribution to Early Modern Architecture. *The Journal of the Society of Architectural Historians, 54*(1), 24–53.

Prange, R. (1991). *Das Kristalline als Kunstsymbol: Bruno Taut und Paul Klee*. Zurich: Georg Olms.

Richards, B. and Gilbert, D. (2006). *New Glass Architecture*. New Haven, CT: Yale University Press.

Sharp, D. (1966). *Modern Architecture and Expressionism* London: Longmans.

Sharp, D., Scheerbart, P. and Taut, B. (1972). *Glass Architecture by Paul Scheerbart and Alpine Architecture by Bruno Taut*. New York: Praeger.

Speidel, M. (1995). *Bruno Taut: Natur und Fantasie 1880–1938*. Berlin: Ernst & Sohn.

Thiekotter, A. (1993). *Kristallisationen, Splitterrungen: Bruno Taut's Glashaus*. Basel: Birkhauser Verlag.

Watkin, D. (2005). *A History of Western Architecture* (4 edn.). New York Watson-Guptill Publications.

Whyte, I. B. (1982). *Bruno Taut and the Architecture of Activism*. Cambridge: Cambridge University Press.

Whyte, I. B. and Taut, B. (1985). *The Crystal Chain Letters: Architectural Fantasies by Bruno Taut and his Circle*. Cambridge, MA: MIT Press.

2 The client
Frederick Keppler

2.1 Introduction

This chapter will argue the significant influence exerted by the client, Frederick Keppler, on the design of the *Glashaus*. Starting with a discussion of Luxfer Prisms, their marketing strategies and the key personalities associated with them, it will then be reasoned that the *Glashaus* was by no means a unique Expressionist conception. Rather, the *Glashaus* is alternatively proposed as the latest iteration in a longer tradition of glazed exhibition architecture. The result is an understanding of the *Glashaus* that dramatically dissolves some of its prior Expressionist associations, and instead argues its exhibition pedigree and the commercial interests of its client.

2.2 The Glashaus' client

Taut's article 'Glashaus: Werkbund-Ausstellung Köln 1914, Führer zur Eröffnung des Glashauses' was published to promote the *Glashaus* and the important contributions of the individual firms that were involved in its construction. The articles started with Taut stating that the *Glashaus* had no other purpose than to be beautiful exhibition architecture, which through its use of glass, would provide inspiration for the future development of architecture. After praising the efforts of the company that executed the reinforced concrete structure to the *Glashaus*, Taut then detailed the involvement of the *Deutsche Luxfer Prismen Syndikat* (German Luxfer Prism Syndicate) and its crystalline glass products. Taut stated that the enclosing terrace walls to the *Glashaus* were constructed using Luxfer Prisms that were joined together through the use of a patented Keppler System that used reinforced concrete. He also stated that Luxfer Prism products were also used for the stairs, dome glazing and the floor to the dome (Taut, 1914b).

While the importance of the *Deutsche Luxfer Prismen Syndikat* and its glass products are evident in the Taut's article (1914b) what is not apparent is the fact that *Deutsche Luxfer Prismen Syndikat* commissioned, majority funded, donated the building materials and supplied many of the exhibits to the *Glashaus*. Likewise, the Keppler System referenced in the article (Taut, 1914b) was patented by Friedrich Keppler who was the Director of *Deutsche*

Luxfer Prismen Syndikat (Neumann, 1995). Accordingly the interplay of these aspects will be explored in detail.

2.3 Luxfer Prisms

Early in the 17th century, light-redirecting glass products began to be used to illuminate the darker areas of both ships and mines (Neumann, 1995). With the advent of industrialisation and associated urbanisation, the need to light the darker areas of buildings, especially basements, arose. This task was initially achieved through the use of open grates, using a system that was generally termed as vault lighting. However, early applications of open vault lights proved unsatisfactory, as they admitted precipitation and were non-trafficable. The open frame of vault lighting was soon in-filled with glazing. Initially, the glass in-fill was housed in an iron or steel frame. Later, reinforced concrete was also increasingly used as a structural material. At first, the glass in-fill was a rough bull's-eye product, which simply allowed light to pass through. With the advance of technology, they evolved into more sophisticated prismatic-shaped devices, which directed the light to the required location (www.glassian.org). However, the majority of these vault lights were only suitable for horizontal, load-bearing applications.

With the introduction of the Chicago skyscraper in the late-19th century, the need to light deep plan spaces arose. Before the widespread availability of electric lighting, prismatic glass was an architectural product that was placed on the façade of a building to precisely redirect natural light to interior spaces through both refraction and reflection. Thus, a vast number of prism glass manufactures originated on the east coast of the United States of America, among them the American 3-Way Prism Company of Philadelphia; the Solar Prism Company of Cleveland; the Condie-Nealle Glass Company of St Louis; and the Jupiter Prism Company of Davenport, Indiana (www.glassian.org). The Luxfer Prism Company, established in 1897, was an amalgamation of the Radiating Light Company and the Semi-prism Glass Company. It was established to commercialise the prismatic glass tiles initially invented by the British inventor James G. Pennycuick in 1885 (Neumann, 1995). These tiles were correctly referred to as Luxfer Prisms. However, today 'Luxfer tiles' is a common term for all forms of prismatic glass, regardless of manufacturer (www.glassian.org).

In 1881, Pennycuick and Peter Collamore were granted a patent for the improvement of vault lighting tiles through the use of semi-prism, or 'star shaped' vault lights, that would increase the amount of light for reflection (Pennycuick and Collamore, 1881). Following this initial patent, in 1885, Pennycuick was granted a further patent for the improvement of window glass (Pennycuick, 1885). This 1885 patent proposed a vertical or inclined window system, composed of a number of glass tiles, which would dramatically increase the light reflected into a room without increasing the size of the window. The proposed tiles consisted of a small pane of glass that had a

12 Bruno Taut's design inspiration for the Glashaus

regular surface on one side, and of a series of parallel prismatic projections on the other side; thus, Luxfer Prisms were invented. To commercialise his 1885 patent, Pennycuick together with a group of Chicago entrepreneurs founded the Radiating Light Company in October 1896. Two months later, its name changed to the Semi-prism Glass Company, which later changed in March 1897 to the Luxfer Prism Company (Neumann, 1995). The financial power of the Luxfer Prism Company's investors, combined with an astute marketing strategy, resulted in Luxfer Prisms being perceived as a grand concept rather than a simple product. Luxfer Prisms were clearly marketed to address the concerns of both the thriving and sophisticated Chicago environment and the wider west-coast American context. In its marketing material, Luxfer promised substantial savings to downtown businessmen and their architects. These savings were to be achieved through an increase in the available space and improved working conditions. Luxfer also claimed that its new and expensive prisms would contribute to the development of modern architecture. Fortuitously, the advent of Luxfer Prisms coincided with a period of both widespread passion for modern technologies and a growing awareness of a more simple life in agreement with nature. As such, Luxfer Prisms were marketed as both a product of scientific progress and as an antidote to modern civilisation and urbanisation. Luxfer Prisms negated the need for artificial lighting during the day by providing healthy natural light through scientific means. In turn, this negated the need for open windows and the subsequent exposure to the heat, noxious vapours, dirt and disease of the modern city (Neumann, 1995).

As stated above, Luxfer Prisms were architectural products. As such, unlike traditional windows, which did little to enhance the architectural scheme of a building, Luxfer Prisms aided and created the architectural ornament of a building façade: 'When looked at from the outside they do not have the appearance of glass, for they lend themselves to the scheme of exterior treatment as to become a part of the whole surface' (Crew and Basquin, 1898: 5).

To turn the marketing concept of progressive modernity into scientific reality, the Luxfer Prism Company hired the prominent physics and optics expert Professor Henry Crew and his assistant Olin H. Basquin of Chicago's North-western University. Luxfer's brief to Crew and Basquin was threefold: they were to further develop Luxfer Prisms; explore potential applications; and, most importantly, establish the scientific merits of the product. The basic principle of light reflection, through the use of prismatic glass, could not in itself be patented, as it was very common and by no means new. Crew and Basquin alternatively developed the scientific ability to predictably and precisely control light reflection through the use of Luxfer Prisms. Crew claimed that this notion was derived directly from August Fresnel's mathematically exact system of prismatic lenses that had been in common use in light-houses since the early 1820s. Through directly observing Chicago daylight conditions, Crew and Basquin subsequently developed precise

Figure 2.1 A 1903 advertisement for Luxfer Prisms.

mathematical formulas to exactly calculate the specific lighting requirements of buildings, predictably using Luxfer Prisms (Neumann, 1995). These formulas were subsequently published by the Luxfer Prism Company in January 1898 and firmly established the scientific merit of Luxfer Prisms (Crew and Basquin, 1898). Additionally, by 1897, the Luxfer Prism Company had submitted 162 patents for production equipment, technical details, supporting frames and canopies for prism tiles. Of these, 96 were for particular design of Luxfer Prisms, and of these, 41 solely concerned so-called 'Iridian' prisms. Interestingly, it has been claimed that it was Crew and Basquin, and not Pennycuick, who invented prismatic glass, and supposedly exhibited their invention at the 1893 World's Colombian Exposition (Neumann, 1995).

Initially, patented Luxfer Prism glass tiles were 100 millimetres square and approximately 4.75 millimetres thick; larger sizes became available as manufacturing technology and techniques evolved. At first, Luxfer offered four grades, or types, of glass prisms ('Cut', 'Commercial', 'Factory' and 'Iridian') and nine degrees of refraction in accordance with different lighting conditions (Neumann, 1995). Cut prism were the very best quality glass, individually tested by polariscope, and exactly polished and ground to within 1/100th of an inch. Furthermore, Cut prisms were only intended for assembly using the patented technology of electro-glazing or electro-deposition, a technology patented by William Winslow of Chicago in 1897 (Winslow, 1897). Significantly, electro-glazing was the most significant of the 162 patents filed before 1897. Interestingly, the original Winslow patent makes no assignment to the Luxfer Prism Company, despite the fact that Neumann listed Winslow as one of Luxfer's directors (Neumann, 1995). The process of electro-glazing further made the supporting structure as light and as strong as possible, as well as making the finished pane of prisms both wind- and water-proof. Commercial prisms were considered as an inferior class of Cut, because they were not tested by polariscope or polished. However, they were ground, and thus suitable for electro-glazing. Factory prisms were rejects or 'second' prisms that were neither suitable for Cut nor Commercial grading. However, like Commercial prisms, they were also ground and appropriate for use in electro-glazing. Iridian prisms had the same features as Cut, but with the further application of an ornamental pattern to the regular surface of the prism tile, i.e. the side not occupied by the parallel prismatic projections. Iridian prisms appear to depart from the strictly scientific intentions of Cut, Commercial and Factory prisms in that they also embodied additional 'architectural qualities' since they interacted in a peculiar manner with the surrounding building façade (Crew and Basquin, 1898). Through the use of Iridian prisms '...a design may be inwrought upon the face of the prism plates in variety and beauty only limited by the capacity of the designer' (Crew and Basquin, 1898: 5). The resultant harmonious effect created by Iridian prisms was described as extremely opulent, taking its colour from the surround materials and context. Iridian prisms therefore produced '...a fine textile-like effect...' with the '...appearance of the product is that of a highly interwoven crystal fabric, as delicate and brilliant as the most exquisite of cut glass ware' (Crew and Basquin, 1898: 6). Furthermore, all of Luxfer's initial 41 Iridian prism designs were conceived by the young architect, Frank Lloyd Wright, who, on behalf of the Luxfer Prism Company, filed the majority of their Iridian patents during October 1897. At the time, Wright occupied an office in the Steinway Hall on Van Buren Street in Chicago. This initial commission created a subsequent relationship between Luxfer and Wright; in 1898, Wright occupied office number 1119 of the Rookery Building and moved to office number 1104 in 1899 (Twombly, 1987), while the Luxfer Prism Company occupied office 1129 from 1897 to 1901 in the same building (www.glassian.org).

Luxfer Prisms were traditionally assembled into regular metal frames that were usually 600 to 1200 millimetres high and as wide as the opening into which they were being inserted. The tiles were held together in the frame by a grid of thin metal bars that were either zinc soldered together, or by the later, more complicated and expensive, system of electro-glazing (Neumann, 1995). Typically, the completed Luxfer Prisms frames were installed in one of three ways. The first, termed as a 'Window Plate', was to replace all or some of glazed portions of a typical window. The second, termed a 'Forilux', was to place an independent frame of Luxfer Prisms in front of the opening portions of a window. However, these two methods were not the sole factor in determining the '...character of the installation...' (Crew and Basquin, 1898: 15–6). The character was additionally determined by the arrangement of individual prism and combinations of various available designs. Luxfer proposed a combination of Major and Minor Prisms. Major Prisms were designed to distribute light to almost all the interior portions of a room. Conversely, Minor Prisms were intended to distribute light to the portions of the room that were closer to the Window Plate and Forilux. As such, different levels of brightness could be achieved, depending on where the viewer was positioned in the room. Viewed from the outside, Minor Prisms appeared several shades brighter than Major Prisms. The third method of installing Luxfer Prisms was termed as a 'Canopy'. This involved a Forilux that was fixed above a façade opening and then tilted outward. Canopies were intended for use in instances where the opening to be illuminated was located in dense, high-rise urban environments, such as Chicago. Apart from illumination, Canopies also had further incidental applications; they protected show windows, which thus dispensed with traditional awnings. To achieve '...very beautiful effects', Iridian prisms were further proposed for use in Window Plates, Foriluxs and Canopies. The result was that the '...receiving surface thus shows a rich, substantial texture, sparkeling both inside and outside with an irradiation of crystal lines and forms' (Crew and Basquin, 1898: 17).

By 1898, the Luxfer Prism Company was extremely successful, having created nearly 1,500 installations in nearly 100 cities across the United States of America (Unknown author, 1898). Of these installations, the vast majority were in Chicago, with New York in second place and Philadelphia in third (Neumann, 2010). In an effort to increase their market share, the Luxfer Prism Company further established a number of foreign branches. On 11 May 1898, Luxfer established its first international subsidiary, the London-based British Luxfer Prism Syndicate, Limited (www.luxfercylinders.com). It was established by Basquin, who, in January 1897, became the director of Luxfer's Scientific Department, and, from 1898 to 1899, was the Chief Engineer of Luxfer Prism Companies of Europe (McLean, 1898; www.glass ian.org). In 1899, Basquin also established the German branch, namely the *Deutsche Luxfer Prismen Syndikat GmbH* (German Luxfer Prism Syndicate, Limited) (Neumann, 2010). Other European branches, also established in 1899, included the Paris, Lyon and Brussels-based *Société Luxfer* (Luxfer Society) and the Vienna-based *Luxfer Österreichische Glas und Eisenbau Geschäft, MBH* (Austrian Luxfer Glass and Iron Construction Company Limited). Furthermore, in 1906, the Budapest-based *Osztrák-Magyar Luxfer Prizma Gyár, KFT* (Austro-Hungarian Luxfer Prism Factory, Limited) was established (Neumann, 1995). As a result of these foreign branches, in 1889, the Luxfer Prism Company distinguished the Chicago parent company by renaming it as the American Luxfer Prism Company (www.luxfer cylinders.com).

16 *Bruno Taut's design inspiration for the Glashaus*

The European branches of Luxfer, like their American parent, aggressively pursued the attention of both the public and the architectural profession. In January 1898, the Luxfer Prism Company announced a competition for:

> ...competitive designs setting forth in a definite and comprehensive manner new possibilities in the use of Luxfer prisms as a building material.
> (McLean, 1898: 63)

The competition announcement by *The Inland Architect and News Record* called for solutions that proposed how a product, supposedly as innovative as the elevator, could be both utilised and united with architectural effects. The total prize money offered by the Luxfer Prism Company was $5,000. First, second and third prizes in the Luxfer competition were awarded to Robert C. Spencer, Adamo Boari, and S.S. Beman respectively. The competition judges included the prominent Chicago architects Daniel H. Burnham, William Le Barron Jenny, William Holabird and Frank Lloyd Wright, and Prof. Henry Crew was also present (McLean, 1898). Of note is the fact that while Wright occupied office number 1106 in Steinway Hall during 1899, Adamo Boari was next door in office 1107 with the firm Perkins and Spencer. As such, while each architect designed 'separately', a lively association developed, resulting with each participating in each other's work. Boari later also became a member of Wright's dinner club 'The Eighteen' (Twombly, 1987). Boari is most famous for his later 1904 design for the *Palacio de Bellas Artes* (Palace of Fine Art) in Mexico City.

2.4 Frederick Louis Keppler

In the late 1890s, the Luxfer Prism Company employed Frederick Louis Keppler. Keppler was born on 14 September 1862, in the small town of Schorndorf, just east of Stuttgart, Germany (Keppler, 1896). When Keppler migrated to the United States of America in 1878, he was an unskilled 16 year old (Leist, 1878). However, the *Obituary Records of Yale University* (Unknown author, 1921) listed Keppler as having trained at the *Stuttgart Polytechnikum* (Stuttgart Technical Institute) before he migrated. Additionally, in Keppler's obituary published by the *New York Times* (Unknown author, 1940), Keppler was said to have attended both school and university in Germany. Furthermore, this same article also listed Keppler's father as having been a Court Architect to the Principality of Wuerttemberg. On his arrival in the United States of America, Keppler initially lived in Chicago and Milwaukee, and in 1883, was naturalised as an American citizen in Chicago. In 1896, Keppler's listed occupation was as a Chicago-based builder (Keppler, 1896). Additionally, in both 1895 and 1897, a 'Mr and Mrs Frederick Keppler' were listed as having resided at 5422 Ellis Avenue in Chicago (The Chicago Directory Company, 1894, 1896). Keppler subsequently departed the United States of America, bound for Europe, on 4 January 1898, and was eventually a resident in Berlin from March 1899. Keppler appeared to live in Europe from this point forward. During 1899, his occupation was listed as that of an architect (Keppler, 1899). In 1904, while still in Berlin, Keppler listed his occupation as being associated with the Luxfer Prism Company/Syndicate (Keppler, 1904). An article in the *New York Times* (Unknown author, 1940) stated that, in the late 1890s, Keppler was sent to Germany as a representative of the Luxfer Prism Company.

Exactly how Keppler initially became to be associated with the Luxfer Prism Company is still unclear. In December 1887, a 'Fred Keppler' was mentioned as having been a member of the Chicago Architectural Sketch Club and who was present at its second annual banquet (McLean, 1887). Later, in 1889, Keppler's marriage to Elizabeth Neely was announced, and the article further described him as a prominent member of the Chicago Architectural Sketch Club (McLean, 1889). Keppler's business acumen first became obvious in 1891 when he was described as an architect of considerable local prominence and esteem and who had abandoned the architectural profession in favour of starting the Mackolite Plaster Board Company. Keppler was apparently responsible for introducing Mackolite to the United States of America from Germany (McLean, 1891). Mackolite, invented in Ludwigsburg, Germany, by Messrs. A and O Mack, was ground gypsum that was then mixed with other chemicals and water and moulded into the required shape (Unknown author, 1906). In 1888, the Mackolite Fireproofing Company was the first industry to be established in Chicago Heights (Candeloro and Paul, 2004). On 4 June 1891, Makolite's fire resistance was exhibited in Chicago at the end of Ohio Street; an event deemed of such significance that it was recorded in detail. In these tests, two small structures, one with steel and the other with timber frames, clad in Mackolite and topped with plaster, were set alight. The results indicated that Mackolite would contain a fire within any particular room (McLean, 1891). Interestingly, in 1899, after a Chicago building equipped with Luxfer Prisms survived a fire, Luxfer added fire-proof glazing to its product line (www.luxfer-cylinders.com). As such, in 1900, the Board of Underwriters accepted metallic Luxfer Prism glazing as being fire-proof (McLean, 1900).

As the discussion above indicates, it is highly probable that Keppler joined the Luxfer Prism Company based on his architectural background, business acumen and fireproofing experience. It is also highly probable that Keppler headed the *Deutsche Luxfer Prismen Syndikat* from its very beginning, or very shortly after, in 1899. On 31 December 1899, Basquin departed Hamburg, Germany, bound for New York. He was accompanied by his family; namely, Jersy Basquin, aged 22 and supposedly his wife, together with their son Harold Basquin, aged 6 months (Hamburg-Amerika Linie, 1899). Could the birth of Harold have necessitated the return of the Basquins to the United States of America? If indeed this is correct, then this event would have left the *Deutsche Luxfer Prismen Syndikat* without a Director. Therefore, it is highly likely that in late 1899, Frederick Keppler became the Director of the *Deutsche Luxfer*

18   *Bruno Taut's design inspiration for the Glashaus*

Prismen Syndikat. With Keppler as its director, it soon became one of the most successful of Luxfer's foreign branches. He quickly acknowledged that patented Luxfer Prisms, their methods of construction, and their architectural applications had little practical application value in the European context (Neumann, 1995). Keppler therefore patented a number of innovations, the most notable being a system of structural glazing called *Glaseisenbeton* (Reinforced Concrete and Glass), commonly known as the 'Keppler System'. The 'Keppler System' was initially patented in 1909 and further refined in 1913 (Keppler, 1909, 1910, 1913). At its core, the 'Keppler System' departed from the traditional method of assembling patented Luxfer Prism tiles in two main respects. First, Keppler used reinforced concrete instead of solder or electro-deposition to secure the glass tiles. Second, this use of reinforced concrete resulted in a thicker, heavier glass tile. The resultant 'simplified' glass tiles lacked the precise prismatic ridges of patented Luxfer Prism tiles; had exposed edge ridges that secure the tile into the reinforced concrete; and were also less transparent than patented Luxfer Prism tiles (Neumann, 1995).

2.5 Exhibiting Luxfer products

Since the late-19th century, American and European glass manufacturers had exhibited their products at trade fairs and public exhibitions. According to Neumann (1995), the 'glass pavilions' built for these exhibitions, formed a unique building style that owed much of its effect to the particular details of the products used. Even Taut (1914b) wrote that the *Glashaus* mostly owed much of its magical effect to the products of the *Deutsche Luxfer Prismen Syndikat*. Many of these 'glass pavilions' followed an established programme of glazed domes, staircases, and even the inclusion of a central fountain. According to Neumann (1995), Luxfer's European branches also frequently participated in trade fairs and exhibitions and actively sought the attention of architects. Furthermore, Neumann (1995) stated that Luxfer presented its products in a separate exhibition pavilion at the Brussels International World Fair in 1910. The periodical *Diamant* (1910) made mention of the *Deutsche Luxfer Prismen Syndikat* as having delivered magnificent domes of prism glass for several exhibition pavilions at the Brussels International World Fair. These domes, according to *Diamant* (1910), offered amazing lighting effects. In 1913, the *Deutsche Luxfer Prismen Syndikat* participated in the *Bau-fachausstellung* (Building Trade Exhibition) in Leipzig, where it won a gold medal for a Bruno Möhring–designed domed pavilion that used:

> ...prismatic glass, glass tiles and reinforced concrete.
>
> (Neumann, 1995: 44)

According to *Diamant* (1913), this Leipzig pavilion was located close to the six-sided pavilion of the *Vereins Deutscher Spiegelglasfabriken* (Association of German Plate Glass Factories). This *Kuppelbau* (Domed building) was further described as having had a reinforced concrete structure that was infilled with 'art glass'. The dome was described by *Diamant* (1913) as having been exceptionally beautiful, made from *Elektroglasprismen* (Electro-deposition fixed glass prisms) and that were contained in a dainty copper frame.

While not being examples of exhibition architecture, two further interesting examples of Luxfer installations were the *Brudern Ház* (Brudern House) with its *Párisi Udvar* (Parisian Court) in Budapest, Hungary, and the *Krüger-Passage* in Dortmund, Germany. The *Brudern Ház* was designed by Henrik Schmahl and constructed in 1909 (Heathcote and Collie, 1997). This example is interesting, not because it was like many of the commercial installations to which Luxfer's European branches supplied products, but because the ceiling in its *Párisi Udvar* appears to use prism tiles that are almost identical to Keppler's simplified glass tiles used in the *Glashaus*. While it is not clear who exactly supplied them, it is however interesting to note that Luxfer's Hungarian branch, the *Osztrák-Magyar Luxfer Prizma Gyár, KFT*, supplied the vault lighting. Of further interest is that the *Brudern Ház*'s floor tiling, albeit mostly ceramic, was likewise similar in appearance and layout

Figure 2.2 An ariel view of the 1913 Baufachausstellung in Leipzig. Photo by permission of SLUB Dresden/Deutsche Fotothek.

20 Bruno Taut's design inspiration for the Glashaus

to that of the *Glashaus*. The next interesting example was the Luxfer dome over the *Krüger-Passage*, designed by the architects Hugo Steinbach and Paul Lutter. This dome is of importance because it, like the *Glashaus*, also had a reinforced concrete structure.

Also exhibiting at the 1913 Leipzig Exhibition were the *Deutscher Stahlwerks-Verband* (Association of German Steel Workers) and the *Verband Deutscher Brücken-und Eisenbaufabriken* (Association of German Bridge and Steel Fabricators). These two associations chose Bruno Taut to design their pavilion, the *Monument des Eisens* (Gutschow, 2006). In the *Monument des Eisens*, Taut, much like the architects to the glass manufactures:

> ...used the very material he was hired to advertise and promote in order to create an abstract, geometric, exposed steel-frame construction.
> (Gutschow, 2006: 65)

Neumann (1995) stated that images of the *Deutsche Luxfer Prismen Syndikat's* 1913 Leipzig pavilion are yet to be found. However, if Figure 2.2 is studied in conjunction with the descriptions of the pavilion above, it is probable that one of the circled buildings could well be Luxfer's 1913 pavilion. If this is the case, then it is clear that this existing prototype that was supposedly enforced by the *Deutsche Luxfer Prismen Syndikat* could have both dictated and limited Taut's design choices for the 1914 *Glashaus*. This contention is supported by the fact that while the *Glashaus* had a reinforced concrete structure, Taut initially proposed an iron skeleton for the dome and columns (Thiekotter, 1993). Taut's intended use of structural steel in all probability derived from his experiences with the material in both his *Monument des Eisens*, and his earlier 1910 pavilion for the structural steel manufacturer *Träger Verkafs-Kontor* at the 2nd Ceramic, Cement and Lime Industrial Exhibit in Berlin. Apart from the construction of the *Monument des Eisens*, the Leipzig exhibition could also have been significant for Taut because it could have afforded him an opportunity to make contact with the *Deutsche Luxfer Prismen Syndikat*. Another explanation for the Taut/*Deutsche Luxfer Prismen Syndikat* relationship could be that Luxfer's Berlin offices were located at 204 *Friedrichstra e*, while the offices of Taut and Hoffmann were located a short distance away at 20 *Linkstra e* (Junghanns, 1983; Keppler, 1913).

From the above descriptions of glass pavilions, especially those of the *Deutsche Luxfer Prismen Syndikat*, it is apparent there was a tendency to focus on the areas of these buildings where glazed products were most visible, particular the dome. Other aspects that were frequently mentioned include the geometry, the construction materials, method and technologies. Thus, considering that the products and construction technologies of *the Deutsche Luxfer Prismen Syndikat* were most evident in the upper two-thirds of the *Glashaus*, i.e. the dome and its lower supporting base that contained both the stairs at the periphery and the fountain at its core, these areas will be investigated further.

2.6 The *Deutsche Luxfer Prismen Syndikat* and the *Glashaus*

In keeping with the company's desire to associate with progressive architects, the *Deutsche Luxfer Prismen Syndikat* chose Bruno Taut to design their *Glashaus* pavilion at the Cologne *Werkbund* Exhibition of 1914. *The Deutsche Luxfer Prismen Syndikat* both initiated, majorly funded, donated the building materials, and supplied many of the exhibits to, the *Glashaus* (Neumann, 1995). Nevertheless, Taut, acting much like a modern developer, also sourced other financial contributions and products, and his firm Taut and Hoffmann ultimately contributed 20,000 Marks to the cost of the *Glashaus* (Thiekotter, 1993). In the drawing that Taut and Hoffmann submitted to the Cologne City Council for building approval, the voids between the rhombic structure of the *Glashaus'* dome were drawn as double glazed, with the outer skin labelled as *Spiegelglas* (Plate glass) and the inner layer was labelled as *Luxferprismen* (Luxfer Prisms) (Taut, 1914a). The floor to the Dome Room was labelled as *Boden Luxferprismen mit Betonrippen* (Floor of Luxfer Prisms with concrete beams), while the stairs to the Dome Room were labelled as *Treppe Glassteine auf Eisenkonstru* (Glass-block stairs with steel construction). Furthermore, the glazed, non-structural in-fill that partly surrounded the staircases was simply referred to as *Glassteine* (Glass-blocks), while the flared circular ceiling below the oculus appears to be labelled as *'Uelmfang' Glas*. However, this is in all probability *Umfang Glas* (circumference glass). This contention is partly supported by Taut (1914b) when he stated that the ceiling below the oculus consisted of *Über-fangglas* (conical glass).

It is a common misconception that patented Luxfer Prisms were used in the *Glashaus'* dome. In reality, 'simplified' glass tiles filled the voids between the reinforced concrete structure in the *Glashaus'* dome (Neumann, 1995). When Figures 1.2 and 1.3 are referenced, one can see that these simplified tiles departed from the traditional 100 millimetre-square configuration of patented Luxfer Prism tiles. Supposedly in keeping with the *Deutsche Luxfer Prismen Syndikat*'s desire to diversify its product range, these simplified tiles constituted a variety of square, rectangular, circular and polygonal shapes, and appear to have had a simple pressed-surface design. Furthermore, the simplified glass tiles to the *Glashaus'* dome were held together by copper frames and strips, not according the newer 'Keppler System', but using Winslow's electro-deposition process (Neumann, 1995). This fact is further supported by Taut (1914b). This use of Winslow's electro-deposition process resulted in much lighter triangular-shaped glazed in-fill panels, when compared to the heavier, but newer 'Keppler System'.

Thiekotter (1993) stated that, at some point, the depth of the structural members to the *Glashaus'* dome decreases from an initial 20cm to 12cm. This fact could be indicative of the heavier 'Keppler System' being the initial specification, but later being superseded by electro-deposition. However, Taut (1914b) stated that this reduction in structural size was due to structural optimisation by the reinforced concrete contractor, the *Allegemeinen Beton-*

22 Bruno Taut's design inspiration for the Glashaus

und Eisengesellschaft (General Reinforced Concrete Company) of Berlin. In addition to the in-fill panels of simplified glass tiles, the *Glashaus* also had a second outer layer of simple plate glass; effectively 'double glazing' the *Glashaus*' dome (Taut, 1914b). It has also been proposed that the Glashaus' dome constituted not of two layers of glazing but of three (Thiekotter, 1993). In one particular photograph of the *Glashaus*, there appears to be a 'third' coloured layer, possibly of glass or paint, to the interior of the dome. However, in other photographs, this layer is not visible. This discrepancy could be due to numerous factors. For example, in his later 1913 patent, Keppler stated that the colouring of hollow bricks of blown glass was achieved through either the use of metal deposition or paint (Keppler, 1913). Furthermore, the total unfinished state of the *Werkbund* Exhibition was universally deplored (Thiekotter, 1993). Even five weeks after its opening on 16 May 1914, the *Glashaus* was still not fully operational (Thiekotter, 1993). Additionally, the *Glashaus*' dome was expressly mentioned as multi-coloured, starting at its base in deep blue, then progressing upwards through moss-green, golden yellow and eventually culminating at the apex in brilliant creamy white (Taut, 1919). When all of the above facts are considered, it becomes highly probable that the glazed panels installed in the *Glashaus*' dome were initially clear, with colour only being added later. Once the panels were installed, the most cost- and time-effective way to add colour would have been through painting. As such, the 'third layer of glazing' is in all probability a coating of coloured transparent paint, applied after installation was complete. Keppler (1914), writing in Keppler Glass Constructions, provided surprising insight into this argument. Under a section entitled 'Keppler Crystal Ceilings', Keppler described façade elements that were constructed from a choice of 150 transparent glass units that were relief ornamented. These units were held together in panels by copper electro-glazing, applied at a factory and installed into either the reinforced concrete or steel from-work of the proposed building. Through the use of 'Keppler Crystal Ceilings', a soft and evenly diffused light would be provided that reduced the need for artificial lighting. However, if artificial lighting was provided, then the 'Crystal Ceiling' would increase in its 'value' because of the fine interior reflective surface. Apart from being fire-resistant, the glass units or tiles were only available in either clear or golden amber (Keppler, 1914). It is thus more than likely that the variety of colours to the *Glashaus*' dome could only have come from the application of a third interior skin. Furthermore, given the above arguments and the common confusion around the actual naming of Luxfer's products, it is further evident that even the application of the term *Luxferprismen* might have been incorrect; rather, it should have been named as a 'Keppler Crystal Ceiling'. Additionally, it would have been highly unlikely for the *Glashaus*' dome to have been double-glazed; rather it was triple-glazed.

According to Neumann (1995), the glazed, non-structural in-fill that partly surrounded the staircases was pure 'Keppler System'. The staircases proper, leading from the entrance to the Dome Room and then downward toward the Cascade Room, were constructed using a steel frame that was in-filled with 'prismatic tiles' (Neumann, 1995). However, when the staircases are examined in detail, these 'prismatic tiles' are not the same as those used in the dome, and are fixed according to the 'Keppler System', as evidenced by the presence of thick mortar joints.

The reinforced concrete structure to the floor of the Dome Room comprised 14 beams, which radiated outwards from a small inner ring-beam towards a larger outer ring-beam that was supported by 14 columns. The 14 radiating beams were laterally braced midway by a further third ring-beam. In-filling the gaps between the floor's structural members were circular glass tiles, possibly secured according to the 'Keppler System'. In the drawing submitted to the Cologne City Authorities, this floor was labelled as having comprised *Glassteine und Eisenbeton* (Glass-blocks and reinforced concrete) (Taut, 1914a). The word '*Glassteine*' was also used to describe the walls that surrounded the staircases. According to Neumann, the floor to the *Glashaus*' dome

...was made of concrete with coloured glass lenses embedded in it.
(Neumann, 1995: 43)

Taut (1914b) stated that the floor consisted of yellow- and white-coloured Luxfer Prisms that were round and arranged in a rhombic pattern. However, what is unclear is whether the 'lenses' that both Neumann (1995) and Taut (1914b) referenced allowed the transmission of light to the Cascade Room below. If the floor was a 'Keppler System', then it would seem logical to assume that it did. However, considering the extent of the concrete between the glass tiles, and the load-bearing nature of the surface, if the floor did allow the passage of light, then it could also have been another of the *Deutsche Luxfer Prismen Syndikat's* products – Keppler Floor, Roof and Vault Lighting.

The reality of the construction of the floor below the dome is partly revealed when the ceiling to the Cascade Room below is considered. In the Cascade Room directly below the oculus, Taut constructed a flared circular ceiling. At first glance, the construction of the panels that constituted this ceiling appear to be similar to the dome above in that it is apparently composed of a regular series of framed panels that contained 'glazed' tiles. However, on closer examination, these ceiling panels appear to be similar to the glazed ceramic tiles, or *Glas kacheln*, on the walls of the Cascade Room. The ceiling panels appear to have a thin metal frame to the periphery, which was then immediately lined by one row of square tiles. The rest of the panel was then in in-filled in a regular pattern, also using the same square tiles. However, unlike the panels to the dome above, these ceiling tiles appear to be highly reflective, possibly non-light-transmitting, and strongly coloured, indicating that they could be ceramic glazed tiles rather than 'simplified' glass tiles. Furthermore, if the ceiling panels were constructed using 'simplified' glass tiles, then it would be logical to assume that they would also have been coloured in a similar manner to those in the dome above. While the photographic evidence does not support the use of 'simplified' glass tiles, it does support the notion that the *Glashaus* had a reinforced concrete floor structure that was in-filled with circular glass tiles. These 'glass tiles' and the supporting structure were clearly evident on the upper surface of the Dome Room's floor, but they were not at all evident on the ceiling of the Cascade Room. This can be explained when considering Taut's (1914b) comments that the ceiling consisted of small, bright-red shimmering glass tiles backed with gold leaf, a material commonly known in German as *Goldsmalten* (small, gold-backed glass tiles). Furthermore, the *Goldsmalten* were supported by a leaded frame. Both the ceiling and wall coverings were designed by the Berlin company *J. Schmidt and Gottfried Heinersdorf* (Taut, 1914b).

If all of the above is considered, then it is highly probable that the ceiling was neither constructed with 'simplified' glass tiles or ceramic tiles; rather, it was composed of panels of *Goldsmalten*, which totally restricted or minimised the transmission of light. If the arguments presented in Chapter 2 are considered, then this curiosity becomes less so, in that the 'character' of each of the *Glashaus*' two principal spaces were distinctly different and divergent. The upper Dome Room was intended as a brightly lit, structurally expressive and lively space, while the lower Cascade Room was the opposite in that it was dark, sombre and controlled. Essentially, the Cascade Room was cave-like, while the Dome Room was the opposite.

A further noteworthy element in the *Glashaus* was the cascade. At its highest level, this cascade consisted of a circular pond in the middle of the upper room, directly below the oculus. From the centre of this upper pond, a fountain gushed, with the water then flowing downward over five terraced steps and into a lower basin. The cascade was composed of both mirrored and ornamental glasses that were supported on sheets of plate glass, which were illuminated from the rear and below with Osram branded electric lights. Additionally, the rim of the cascade was lined with black glass tiles, and the floors of the cascade and basins were covered with glazed shards of waste left over from the glass-manufacturing process. The cascade was constructed by the Munich-based company *Zwieseler und Pirnaer*, which specialised in coloured-glass products; this company also supplied the tiles for, and constructed, the wall cladding to the Cascade Room. Once the visitor had descended the blue-and-black-mosaic-clad stairs on either side of the cascade, they would have viewed a steadily paced kaleidoscopic projection, which was composed of artistic creations. The effect of the projection was apparently to remind the visitor of their earliest childhood memories (Taut, 1914b).

In his description of the *Glashaus*, Taut (1914b) further elaborated on the effects of the lighting in the Dome Room. While the effect created was described as a precious and beautiful, highly faceted crystalline diamond, it was amplified through the use of electrical illumination. Seven glass spheres hung from the underside of the dome and each supplied a highly reflective, electric intensity of approximately 1,000-candle power. The light from these seven spheres covered the entire interior of the dome, glittering as it reflected from the prism tiles. At the centre of these seven lights, a large grape-like light hung that contained numerous coloured and white electric light bulbs. All of the electric lighting to the *Glashaus* and the kaleidoscope were fitted with Osram products supplied by the Auer Company (Taut, 1914b).

From the above argument, certain accepted understandings regarding the *Glashaus* become doubtful. First, it seems that patented glass Luxfer Prism tiles were not used in the *Glashaus*. While both the drawing submitted to the Cologne City Council (Taut, 1914a) and Taut (1914b) referred to – *Luxferprismen* as having been applied to both the floor and cladding of the *Glashaus'* dome, in reality, simple pressed-glass tiles of varying shapes were used. The second concerns the origins of 'simplified' glass tiles and the resultant effect that they created. From the argument above, it is highly likely that Keppler's 'simplified' glass tiles were merely a further iteration of the earlier Iridian product of the Luxfer Prism Company. Likewise, the crystalline, sparkling effect of the *Glashaus* dome, rather than being a unique creation of Expressionist architecture, was actually an additional evolution of Crew and Basquin's marketing philosophy. The third, unclear, fact is more important as it concerns the general layout and aesthetics of the *Glashaus*. When the planning of the *Glashaus* is compared to that of the earlier 'glass pavilions', many similarities are evident, such as the use of a glass dome, staircases and a central fountain. Furthermore, the *Glashaus* also owed a significant portion of its sparkling, delicate and jewel-like effect to the particular products used in its construction. It was also similar *to Möhring's* 1913 pavilion, which also used glass tiles and reinforced concrete. Interestingly, this planning arrangement and desire to exhibit the client's materials in the best possible manner also has a connection to the 1913 *Monument des Eisens* because both had similar plans, and both expressed an aesthetic that best portrayed the products of the client. From this, it is clear that the *Glashaus* followed an established prototype, and was not a novel creation of Taut's imagination. It is therefore proposed that examples of these prototypes will be found within the personalities that shaped the Luxfer Prism Company and prior exemplars of exhibition buildings, to which I now turn.

2.7 Exhibition buildings: In search of glazed domes, central features, staircases and structural expression

It has already been proposed, and as one would logically expect, that Taut's *Glashaus* belonged to an existing tradition of exhibition buildings, where the needs of the client and associated products produced distinct building typologies. These exhibition or industrial pavilions were temporary objects that expressed the possibilities of their new and novel materials in an astatically pleasing manner.

In Germany, the exhibition pavilions that industries initially created were simply copies of existing landmarks, and were executed in modern materials that expressed their technical possibilities. It was not until the first decade of the 20th century that the material manufacturers started to demonstrate new formal and aesthetic characteristics of both their materials and their associated technical possibilities. However, these early examples were still largely based on historic typologies, like garden pavilions, mausoleums, and the likes. Additionally, with the emergence of large-scale industrial cartels, enterprises and brand profiles, there was a desire to reinvent sacred central planned buildings (Ciré, 1993). Ciré (1993) further proposed that this situation prevailed until the emergence of highly original exhibition pavilions, like Taut's 1910 pavilion for the *Träger-Verkaufs-Kontor Firma*, where the exhibited material of red and black painted steel profiles became the primary display, while the historical typology, in the form of the small central tempietto, became secondary (Ciré, 1993).

However, while the exemplars that Ciré (1993) exposed alluded to the *Glashaus*, none fully explained it. Consequently, this aspect needs further research to explain how an established prototype evolved and later came to be enforced as the prototype for Luxfer's European exhibition pavilions.

International exhibitions for the display of industrial products had their origins in post-revolutionary France. In 1789, the *L'Exposition publique des produits de l'industrie française* (Public Exposition of French Industrial Products) was held in Paris. On the *Champ de Mars*, a 'Temple of Industry', surrounded by 60 porticos, was erected and filled with a collection of French-produced industrial objects. At this Exposition, a system of awards for excellence in design and workmanship, which were decided by juries of distinguished gentlemen, was initiated. Following the success of this initial exposition, a further exposition was again held in Paris, this time on a much larger scale. This 1801 Exposition was held in a temporary building that was located in the quadrangle of the Louvre. Of the 200 exhibitors, mostly from the cotton- and wool-manufacturing industries, the most notable was Joseph Jacquard and his now famous mechanical textile loom. The success of this exhibition led to the establishment of the *Société d'encouragement pour l'industrie nationale* (Society for the Encouragement of National Industry), thus creating a powerful aid for French industrial sector. In 1802, 1806, 1819, 1823 and 1827, subsequent Parisian expositions were held that evolved in both size and success. At the 10th Industrial Exposition in 1844, 3,960 manufactures exhibited their products in a wooden building designed by Moreau and erected in the *Carre Marigny* on the *Champs Elysées* (Strahan, 1876). Initially, other nations, most notably The Kingdom of Sardinia, quickly acknowledged the French exposition model in promoting industrial development. In 1829, 1832, 1838, 1844, 1850 and 1858, Turin hosted a series of *Esposizione pubblica dei prodotti dell'industria* (Public Exhibition of Industrial Products) (Citta do Torino, 2006). Likewise, Spain, Portugal, Austria, Great Britain, Russia, Sweden, Denmark and the Kingdom of Bavaria also hosted industrial exhibitions, with those from Belgium being noted as the most numerous and important. Nevertheless, each of these exhibitions was strictly nationally based and it was not until 1849 that the possibility of international exhibitions was first discussed in France (Strahan, 1876).

2.8 London's Great Exhibition of the Works of Industry of all Nations, 1851

World Expositions, which started with the 1851 Exposition in London and continued until the 1938 Exposition in Paris (Tjaco, 2004), were explained as having been formulated within an 'era of industrialisation'. The London World's Exposition of 1851, officially named 'The Great Exhibition of the Works of Industry of All Nations', was undoubtedly most famous for Joseph Paxton's Crystal Palace, which, as the canvas, created a scene of industry for 14,000 exhibitors from 94 states, colonies and dependant territories, and attracted over six million visitors. Considering the large number of exhibitors, the organising committee developed a classification system of four sections and 30 classes. The Crystal Palace was subdivided into 1,500 exhibition units and allocated according to countries. Essentially, the plan of the Crystal Palace was based on the traditional religious archetype of the Latin cross. While the main axis of the building was entirely reserved for large sculptures, the cross of the plan was allocated for large palm trees and exotic vegetation. These provided cool and shade for the food and refreshment stalls. Although the 1851 Exposition lacked significant new inventions, the sheer volume of industrial products, from the largest steam engine or locomotive to the smallest precision clock, made the event notable. The primary message of the 1851 Exposition was that Great Britain was the leading industrial and economic nation, a message that served as an example to other nations (Babbage, 1851; Bucher, 1851; Strutt and Tallis, 1852).

Numerous fountains were located inside the Crystal Palace (Clarke, 1852). Among them was the Crystal Fountain, which was located at the very heart of the building – the crossing of the transept and the nave. The Crystal Fountain consisted of a number of glass columns that rose in tapered tiers, with the main tier supporting a basin from which jets of water flowed. As the fountain rose upward, it also tapered inwards, providing the appearance of a firm, well-proportioned and solid structure, despite being made entirely from glass. Crowning the fountain was a delicately lipped central shaft from which a water jet projected. This water jet was described as having been well shaped, and that formed a lily-like flower as it descended. The resultant spray both glittered in the sunlight and sparkled in harmony with the fountain. The Crystal Fountain was manufactured by the Osler Glass Company, weighed a total of four tons, and was 27 feet high. To support this massive weight, the Fountain was placed on a basin of concrete, 21 feet in diameter, that served to catch and collect the falling spray (Clarke, 1852). One period description of the Crystal Fountain described it as having been raised upward like the splinter from an iceberg (Drew, 1852). Visitors to the Exhibition were said to have had a particular regard for the fountain, seeing it both as an

Figure 2.3a The Crystal Palace at Sydenham.

Figure 2.3b The Exhibition Place at the London International Exhibition of 1862. Photo by permission of the Science Museum/Science & Society Picture Library.

object for pilgrimage and a landmark for meeting and orientation (Strutt and Tallis, 1852).

When the Crystal Palace was enlarged and relocated from Hyde Park to Sydenham in 1854, Paxton proposed numerous additional water 'features' for both the building and the landscape on which it stood. In an effort to supply Paxton's ambitious proposals, water tanks were needed to supply adequate water and head pressure (Chadwick, 1961). The most obvious of these 'features' were the two massive water towers located on the nave ends of the Crystal Palace. Designed by Isambard Brunel, each had a 12-sided regular polygon plan, were 284 feet high, and had wrought-iron tanks located at the top, each of which were 47 feet in diameter and could hold 1,200 tons of water (Brunel, 1870). Apart from the Crystal Fountain, which was also relocated to Sydenham, the interior of the Sydenham Crystal Palace contained numerous other fountains and pools (Chadwick, 1961). The most notable of these interior pools were those located at the either end of the nave. The Crystal Fountain was relocated to the centre of the southern pool, or ornamental basin. The ornamental basins were constructed from a product called *granitic-breccia*, which was essentially pre-cast concrete (Routledge, 1854).

As the Sydenham Crystal Palace was placed at the summit of a hill, the associated gardens located below it on the steep slopes were designed with numerous terraces, which allowed Paxton to use water on a grand scale (Chadwick, 1961). As such, the resultant design of the landscape featured an abundance of pools, fountains, and cascades. The Sydenham gardens were planned on a symmetrical arrangement that was centred on an axis, or Grand Central Walk, that originated from the transept of the Crystal Palace. Descending down the hill, the central axis contained a large central pool and had a number of associated water features that were arranged to both the north and south of it. Among these symmetrical water features were:

> ...a cascade on either hand running down from a temple of glass and iron and falling into two great ornamental basins surrounded by terraced walks and with central fountain jets...
>
> (Chadwick, 1961: 150–1)

These 'temples of glass and steel' were Sydenham's Water Temples, and were described by Chadwick (1961) as having been inspired by the almost identical structure at Chatsworth House; the Thomas Archer–designed Cascade House that sat atop the cascade designed by Grillet. The 70-feet-high Water Temples at Sydenham had a structure of cast iron and were topped with a cast-iron and glazed dome. A statue of Mercury, sitting atop a ball, mounted the apex of the dome. A flow of water jetted from the ball and cascaded down the dome into a gutter, which was located on the lip of the dome. As the gutter was perforated, the water then fell in a sheet over each of the arched openings below. A further collection of statues were located at the centre of the Water Temples and the falling water subsequently veiled this statuary in a transparent sheet. In

30 *Bruno Taut's design inspiration for the Glashaus*

addition to statues, the interior of the Water Temples also contained creeping plants. Once the water had fallen to the base of the Temple, it either flowed over the steps of the Temple or was discharged through jets, in the shape of lion's heads, which were located at the projecting angles of the plan. From here, it flowed downward over the sandstone cascade and eventually into the Grand Fountains below (Chadwick, 1961).

2.9 New York's Exhibition of the Industry of All Nations, 1853

Before London held its International Exhibition on Industry and Art in 1862, New York hosted the 'Exhibition of the Industry of All Nations' in 1853. While, strictly speaking, not a World's Exhibition, the New York event was remarkable because it too had a 'Crystal Palace'. In general, the 1853 exhibition building's appearance and materials had a direct correlation to the Crystal Palace of 1851, thus the common naming of the building as the New York Crystal Palace. However, the ground plan, the relative proportions of the materials employed, and the construction technologies were very different, which gave it an architectural character and effect that was entirely of its own making. The general plan of the New York Crystal Palace was a Greek cross that was surmounted with a glazed dome at the intersection of the two axes. The cross was, however, only evident in the upper levels of the building. By in-filling the triangular spaces between the axes, the ground plan was in reality a regular eight-sided polygon; this allowed the provision of adequate exhibition space in the ground plan.

The principal feature of the New York Crystal Palace was a noble and beautiful dome that had a diameter of 100 feet and a height of 123 feet. Intended as an example of beauty and fine architectural effect, the dome was supported by 24 columns that were 62 feet in height. A system of wrought-iron trusses that formed a ring-beam connected the 24 columns at their apexes. This ring-beam, in turn, supported the 32 ribs of the dome proper, all secured with diagonal cross bracing. At their apex, the ribs were held together with a 20-foot-diameter wrought-and-cast-iron ring-beam. This smaller apex ring-beam in turn supported a lantern, which, in conjunction with 32 ornamental stained-glass windows that were located in the sides of the dome, allowed light into the interior. Apart from this glazed lantern, the dome was clad in tin sheeting (Silliman and Goodrich, 1854). A period description of the dome's interior referred to it as an experience that would not have failed to please and surprise the visitor because of its vast sized and extreme airiness; manifest as a:

...balloon expanded and impatient for a flight into the far-off sky.
(Richards, 1853: 9)

A gigantic bronze statue of George Washington on a horse was located under the dome. Additionally, two large Italian candelabra were also located to the north and south of the Washington statue (Richards, 1853). Designed by Monte-Lilla, the interior decoration of the dome, in particular the 32 stained-glass windows, created a rather conspicuous interior effect. The overall decorative scheme of the building was the responsibility of Henry Greenough, who painted the whole of the interior building in white and slightly tinted oil paints. To reach the upper floors of the building, 12 public staircases, two located at each of the four main entrances and four under the dome, were provided. Additionally, eight octagonal turrets that contained spiral staircases for private use were located in the angles of the regular polygonal ground plan (Strahan, 1876).

2.10 London's International Exhibition on Industry and Art, 1862

Following the tremendous success of the 1851 exhibition, London again hosted a World's Exposition, now called 'The London International Exhibition on Industry and Art, in 1862. In an effort to surpass the achievements of the previous exhibition, the organisers built a Captain Francis Fowke–designed Exhibition Palace of enormous proportions that was entered through a highly ornate and elaborately decorated entrance hall. Once the visitor had entered, a central axis or nave spanned the entire building from east to west. Each end of the iron-and-glass nave had an octagonal hall, and these were intended as the main attractions of the Exhibition Palace. Each hall had with a large dome over it as well as transepts that spanned north and south to create the overall 'H' shaped plan. The Exhibition Palace was praised for abandoning glass as the staple cladding material of the building. However, the resultant hall, with its classical façades and two enormous glass-and-steel domes that rose 79 metres with a diameter of 49 metres, was almost exclusively ridiculed. The domes were described as timid and fragile constructions in semi-transparent, gooseberry green. Furthermore, the arrangement of placing dodecagonal domes on an octagonal plan was also condemned.

Condemnation was not solely reserved for the architecture, but also for lack of organisation. Since exhibitors were allowed to organise their allotted space as they saw fit, the French built a wall to separate their exhibit from the main nave and to gain additional display space. The unintended result of this action was that the wall became a powerful symbol of nationalist competition between states for dominance in industrial markets. The 1862 Exhibition Palace was described as having instilled a profoundly serious impression on the visitor. Rather than being a celebratory monument that expressed the idea of the intellectual gifts of British industry, it was described as being akin to a model prison, railway station, or military complex. An earlier proposal by Frederick Sang for colouring the glass domes was rejected by Fowke; however, stained-glass rose windows were installed at the ends of the naves (Beresford Hope, 1862; Laxton, 1862; Mallet, 1862). The interior iron columns of the domes were mostly coloured in dark maroon with lesser

32 *Bruno Taut's design inspiration for the Glashaus*

amounts of light blues and beige or vellum, which was described as extremely opulent, harmonious and majestic (Mallet, 1862).

Given the extremely restricted construction schedule of the 1862 Exhibition Palace and the domes, work was carried out day and night. At night, the ghostly silhouette of the domes' steel skeleton was lit with gas-powered lighting, which captured the attention of journalists (Bell, 1862; Godwin, 1861, 1862; Stewart, 1862). The interior of the building was described as having been preferable to the exterior (Esquiros, 1862). The two large domes likewise also attracted criticism, being described by the British press as a national disgrace and as two colossal soup bowls. To compound matters, even after it opened, the Exposition's construction work was nowhere yet complete; something that would plague almost all subsequent World's Expositions. However, some notable innovations, like the Bessemer process for the production of steel and the Babbage analytical engine, were on display. The 1862 event was also the first World's Exposition to include an art exhibition. By the time the exposition closed, it had recorded some 6.1 million visitors, who had viewed 29,000 exhibitors from Britain and her colonies, along with those of 36 foreign countries (Beresford Hope, 1862; Bucher, 1863; Hollingshead, 1862; McDermott, 1862).

2.11 Paris' *Exposition Universelle*, 1867

Paris, newly revitalised and rebuilt by Georges-Eugène Haussmann, hosted the next World's Exposition, or *Exposition Universelle de Paris*, in 1867. Its organisers chose to express the global radiance of France's Second Empire under Napoleon III through the medium of technological and economic prowess. France expressed this prowess to more than 11 million visitors through two additional innovations. The first was the placement of national pavilions outside of the main exhibition hall. These pavilions were designed by the participating nation and reflected their own individual interests. The second of these innovations was the development and utilisation of a 10-part comprehensive classification system for all of human activity. Under the wider theme of the Exposition, 'The History of Labour', this system encompassed the following: *objects d'art*; material and application in the liberal arts; furniture and domestic appliances; clothing, materials and other objects worn by people (including weapons); industrial products and machines for producing raw materials; instruments and processes in applied arts; foodstuffs; agricultural products; horticultural products; and objects for the improvement of the physical and moral situation of nations (Conway, 1867a, 1867b; Geissler, Grieben and Plessner, 1868; Mainardi, 1989).

To express the French notion of equality, the main Exhibition Palace took the form of a giant oval, which offered each exhibitor a space of equal status. Designed by Pierre Guillaume Frédéric Le Play, the oval was further divided into four quarters and several concentric rings, which, apart from national displays, also contained artistic water spectacles, cafés and foreign restaurants. Among the most notable innovations to be presented by the 52,000 exhibitors from 41 countries was reinforced concrete. The brilliant spectacle, intensity, fraternity and equality of the 1867 Exposition, emphasised through peaceful speeches of the European nobility, however blinded the world to the ancient rivalry between nations (Conway, 1867a, 1867b; Geissler *et al.*, 1868; Mainardi, 1989).

2.12 Vienna's *Weltausstellung*, 1873

A mere three years after the *Exposition Universelle*, France and Germany fought the Franco-Prussian War of 1870, resulting in the total reshaping of the European political and economic landscape. In 1873, Vienna hosted the next World's Exhibition under the general theme of 'Culture and Education'. In offering the first World's Exhibition in a German-speaking country, Austria chose to demonstrate an endeavour that was supported by liberal politicians and Austrian industry and agriculture, and one that demonstrated the economic and cultural revolution of the preceding 20 years. Austria chose to make manifest this phenomenon though enormous construction works in the urban context of cosmopolitan Vienna, the very heart of this social and economic miracle. The objective of the Exposition was to create a harmonious renewal, on Austrian territory, between the peoples of the world. As such, Carl von Hasenauer designed a gigantic Industrial Exposition Palace with a large domed ceremonial hall, or *Rotunde*, at its centre. A Machine Hall, two Agricultural Halls and an Art Hall were also built. Furthermore, numerous smaller pavilions were also erected by 35 foreign countries located in the large open areas between the main halls. In facilitating these smaller pavilions, the 1873 Exposition foreshadowed the later development of products centred in national pavilions, as opposed to large halls. A further precedent of the 1873 Exposition concerned how nations presented themselves; the western nations presented mainly technical and industrial products, while the colonies and non-industrial nations presented their indigenous peoples and associated cultures (Pemsel, 1989; von Lutzow, 1975).

The *Rotunde* was engineered by Scott Russell, who based its design on a dome previously created for the London World's Exposition of 1851. This earlier design was in all probability the 'sheet iron dome' designed by Brunel from the unsuccessful Building Committee design from The Great Exhibition of the Works of Industry of All Nations in 1851. (The Building Committee included Russell, Brunel, C.R. Cockerell, Charles Barry, Robert Stephenson, etc. among others (Chadwick, 1961; Dugan, 1953). The *Rotunde*'s dome itself comprised 32 columns that were each 24 metres high; the columns in turn supported a massive iron ring-beam that had a diameter of 104 metres. This large ring-beam supported a number of 41-metre-long radial girders that converged upward to a further smaller ring-beam that supported two apex lanterns. Zinc roofing plates were attached below the radial structural members, emphasising the structure of the dome. The lower apex lantern

34 Bruno Taut's design inspiration for the Glashaus

Figure 2.4 The entrance to the Vienna Weltausstellung of 1873 with the *Rotunde* in the background.

housed a circular viewing platform that, at 70 metres high, allowed visitors a panoramic view of both the exhibition grounds and Vienna. The diameter of this lower viewing platform was 31 metres. On top of the lower lantern and viewing platform, a further lantern was located that was itself topped with a round dome and a gilded replica of the Imperial Crown set with precious stones. The crown replica was four metres high and five metres in diameter, and formed the highest point of the exhibition at 85½ metres. Access to the viewing platform and crown was via a hydraulic lift. Complementary decorative elements were added to the interior of the *Rotunde*. The supporting iron columns were clad masonry and linked with arches, while the underside of the dome was wrapped in canvas that was decorated with figures. Daylight also played a role, flooding into the interior through both the lanterns and large side windows (Blake and Pettit, 1873). Strahan (1876) described the canvas hanging to the underside of the dome as having been painted with coloured oil paints, and as having had 21-foot-high figures of angels at their centres. Additionally, the interior of the dome was decorated in gold and neutral colours, while the ironwork of the nave was olive green. Located at the centre of the *Rotunde* floor were four large trees from the former *Prater* Park that surrounded a highly ornamental central fountain. The floor of the fountain was lower than the rest of the building (Strahan, 1876).

According to a period description, the *Rotunde* was both the start and finish of any visit to the 1873 Exposition; a place where the visitor could prepare themselves for the impressions to come and where those impressions could be enhanced. Enlivened with a selection of exhibits surrounding a central fountain, the *Rotunde* was described as the finest example of the 1873 Exposition's architecture, with the dome and its high ring gallery that demanded the visitor's attention. The centre of the dome had a large lantern that was decorated with images of rare flowers. As the visitor could experience the dome first-hand by climbing it, the *Rotunde* offered a very different type of sensation that was certainly worth the effort (Buloz, 1873).

World events however overtook the spectacle of the Vienna World's Exposition. One result of the Prussian victory in the Franco-Prussian War was euphoric and unsustainable stock market speculation in both Germany and Austria, but also in the United States of America (Masur, 1974). With the German abandonment of silver as part of its monetary policy, the Vienna stock market experienced it first *Gründerkrach* (Founders' crash) on 9 May 1873. This initial event, which spread to the rest of Europe and the United States of America, ultimately triggered the 'Long Depression' (Angerstein, 1874). Social problems, including massive unemployment and increased cost of living, made the opulence and spectacle of Vienna World's Exposition the inevitable scapegoat, resulting in attendance figures only reaching seven of the expected 20 million visitors (www.expo2000.de).

2.13 Philadelphia's Centennial Exhibition, 1876

Philadelphia's World's Exposition of 1876, or 'Centennial Exhibition: International Exhibition of Arts, Manufactures and Products of the Soil and Mine', opened within the context of the 'Long Depression'. Thus, compared to previous World's Expositions, the architecture of the 1876 Exposition was ordinary and constrained. The planning of the Philadelphia Exposition centred on five main buildings: the Main Exposition Hall, Machinery Hall, Memorial Hall of Art, Horticulture Hall, and the Agricultural Hall. The Exposition also had approximately 200 other smaller buildings, among them buildings for 11 foreign nations; pavilions for 26 of the 37 American states; restaurants; a Conservatory; corporations; and administration buildings. Both the Main Exhibition and Machinery Halls were designed as temporary structures by the architect Henry Pettit and the engineer Joseph Wilson. Constructed from a prefabricated, wrought-iron structure that was in-filled with glazed wooden frames, the Main Exhibition Hall was a conventional 'shed'-like structure that had a main nave that was 1832 feet long by 120 feet wide and 75 feet high. On either side of the central nave, further avenues were constructed that were 100 feet wide and as long as the central nave. A further two aisles were located between the nave and side avenues. In order to relieve the monotony of the plan, three cross avenues or transepts were introduced; the main one was the central transept, which was 416 feet long and 120 feet wide. Four entrances were provided to the Main Exhibition Hall; one at either ends of the nave, with a further two at each end of the central transept. Additionally, four square towers, each measuring 48 feet wide and with a height of 120 feet, were located at the corners of the building. The Main Exhibition Hall was described as having been the most imposing structure of the exhibition. Its interior decoration was described as having been handsomely executed in shades of light blue and cream, while the exterior was painted in light brown with ornamental lines of red and other harmonising hues. A raised band or music stand was located at the very centre of the Main Exhibition Hall (McCabe, 1876). The Main Exhibition Building was described as having been a 'stupendous structure' (Ingram, 1876).

Like the London Exposition of 1851, Philadelphia of 1876 also had a Crystal Fountain. Described as having been '...one of the most beautiful objects in the Main Building...', the Crystal Fountain was constructed by the Washington Glass Company (McCabe, 1876: 283). The fountain was 17 feet high and 48 feet in circumference, and was constructed entirely of cut crystal glass prisms that reflected the changing light, and, in doing so, decomposed it into all the colours of the rainbow. A miniature statue of *Liberty*, 30 inches high, was located at the apex of the fountain. Additionally, the lighting spectacle was continued and amplified at night, when 120 gas lights located inside the Crystal Fountain combined with the water and crystal to create a scene of beauty almost beyond imagination (McCabe, 1876). The Crystal Fountain was located at the crossing of the southern avenue and the easternmost transepts, and executed in a manner so as to create a lasting and positive impression of Washington Glass Company (www.nbmog.org).

Located to the immediate west of the Main Exhibition Hall, the Machinery Hall was designed to showcase machinery in motion, such as the Corliss Engine, which stood at the centre of the Hall. The Machinery Hall was designed in a similar fashion to the Main Exhibition Hall, with a plan of naves, aisles, avenues and transepts. The main portion of the Machinery Hall was 1,402 feet long by 360 feet wide. On the south side of this main portion, a Hydraulic or Pump Annex was located, which was 208 feet by 210 feet in dimension (McCabe, 1876). A hydraulic basin, 60 feet by 146 feet in plan and eight feet deep and that held 30,0000 gallons of water, was located at the centre of the Hydraulic or Pump Annex. Surrounding this basin were numerous pumps, blowers, hydraulic rams, water meters and mining machinery of every kind. The pumps that surrounded the basin drew the water from it, and then discharged it in all possible manners: cascades, jets, nozzles, waterwheels, etc. (Ingram, 1876). A smaller tank, raised 40 feet into the air, was located at the south end of the basin. Into this smaller tank, two steam engines pumped 30,000 gallons of water per minute, which then cascaded down into the main pool below. The weir depth of the cascade was 4 inches and it additionally had a width of 36 feet. The effect of this cascade was said to have been exceptional and formed the principal attraction of the Machinery Hall (McCabe, 1876). Ingram (1876) described the cascade and water basin as the 'miniature Niagara Falls' of the 1876 Exposition.

Constructed primarily from timber and glass, the Agricultural Hall was located on the northern extremity of the Exhibition grounds. The parallelogram plan of the Agricultural Hall was 820 feet long by 540 feet wide, and consisted of a long nave that was crossed by three transepts (Ingram, 1876). At the crossing of the nave and central transept, a glazed cupola rose from the roof. The structure of both the nave and transepts were composed with structurally expressive, exposed-timber Howe trusses constructed in a Gothic manner. Entrances to the building were located at each end of the nave and transepts, and, like the trusses, were executed in a Gothic aesthetic, complete with two turrets and a rose window. The Agricultural Hall was artificially lit with glass lights with reflectors suspended in the trusses. A large bronze fountain was placed at the crossing of the central transept and nave. This fountain jetted water almost as high as the roof and was proposed by James McCabe as having been superior to the fountain in the Main Exhibition Hall (McCabe, 1876).

Both the Horticulture Hall and the Memorial Hall of Art were designed by Herman J. Schwarzmann. Unlike the other main buildings of the 1876 Exposition, these were intended to be permanent structures. The Horticulture Hall was an iron-and-glass structure; 383 feet long by 193 feet wide and had a height of 69 feet when measured at the raised portion of the roof or lantern. A central conservatory, measuring 230 feet long by 80 feet wide, occupied the main central part of the building. A five-feet-wide galley extended out from the central conservatory on all four sides of the building. Rising above the central conservatory was a 170 feet long by 20 feet wide lantern. On both the north and south elevations, the building had curved iron and glass forcing houses, which were 100 feet long by 30 feet wide. Dividing each of these forcing houses were three 30-by-30 feet vestibules. In the interior of the vestibules, ornate stairways led upward to both exterior and interior galleries. Below the main building, a fireproof basement was present that contained the kitchen, heating system, store and coal stores, etc. The aesthetic of the Horticulture Hall was according to the 'Mauresque style', and its exterior was painted in a multitude of colours, giving the building '...a light, fairy-like aspect, in perfect keeping with the graceful design' (McCabe, 1876: 507). Entry to the building was facilitated on the east and west. Each entrance had blue-coloured marble steps, and ornamental tiles were contained in 80-by-20 feet terraces. Open-air kiosks stood at the centre of each entrance. To enter the building, visitors proceeded past internal stairways, through a large archway in black, white and red bricks, and then into the main conservatory. A large marble fountain, designed by Margaret Foley, was located at the very centre of the building; a tall structure, it featured several successive bowls from which water fell downward to a cistern at the base. Two 'superb' chandeliers that vividly illuminated the building at night hung from the lantern. McCabe argued that within the context of the landscaped gardens of Fairmount Park, the Horticulture Hall stood out:

> ...like a central jewel in the midst of a thousand gems of various hues.
> (McCabe, 1876: 515)

38 Bruno Taut's design inspiration for the Glashaus

As far as decoration was concerned, Ingram (1876) concurred and described the building as a 'beautiful gem'.

Abundant examples of glazed domes, central plan features, staircases and structural expression were additionally found in the 1876 Philadelphia Exposition. The Pennsylvania Educational Hall was a separate, regular polygonal structure that had a dome at the centre of its roof. Under the dome, a central hall was located that had an outer hall or corridor running wholly around it. A further building that was planned on a regular polygonal and had a domed roof was the pavilion of the State of Arkansas. This building of approximately 80 feet in diameter was constructed almost entirely of wood. At the centre of the floor plan under the 'double dome', a bronze fountain was located, surrounded by an interior of flags and streamers and exhibits of the agricultural and mineral resources of Arkansas (McCabe, 1876). The Arkansas building was described as a spacious and impressive building that was octagonal in shape with columns being placed to the exterior. As such, the spherical ceiling had an octagonal dome that was 50 feet above the line of the floor. The construction of the building employed a large amount of glass, which made it one of the coolest and most spacious structures of the Exposition. Blue-painted arched Howe trusses supported the ceiling. The interior of the building was painted white, while the exterior was painted in pale tints that had reliefs in dark brown (Ingram, 1876).

Also built on an octagonal plan was the Tunisian Coffee House, which was capped by an eight-sided elongated dome that was decorated red, blue, black, green and gold. The exterior of the building had small, high-set windows on each of it sides, while the roof allowed the continual circulation of air (McCabe, 1876). Ingram (1876) alternatively described the plan of the Tunisian Coffee House as having been decahedral in shape, with four of the ten sides twice as long as the remaining six. Pivoted trefoil-shaped windows supplied light to the interior that was lit in a multitude of colours through the introduction of tinted square glass window panes. The interior of the building was covered with blue and white wallpaper and the underside of the dome was decorated with scarlet coloured shields that were embossed with the Turkish crescent and stars. The interior consisted of a square room that had columns in each corner, ceramic tiles in numerous colours, and a glazed dome overhead (McCabe, 1876).

In addition to a stand-alone Moorish Villa, numerous corporations also delivered numerous 'Moorish Pavilions' inside the main exhibition buildings. In the Main Exhibition Hall, a crescent-shaped Moorish Pavilion was constructed for the jewellery firms of Tiffany and Company, Starr and Marcus, Caldwell and Company, and the Gorham Manufacturing Company. This pavilion was ornamented in rich, warm colours and had a strikingly beautiful design; supposedly, in all respects, it was the most beautiful structure at the Exposition (McCabe, 1876). In the Horticultural Hall, a further example of a Moorish Pavilion was additionally presented by the Glen Cove Company. This pavilion had an imitation stained-glass roof with tile work at it base, and, like the pavilion in the Main Building, was described as one of the most attractive pavilions in the building. In the end, 10 million people experienced the displays of over 30,000 exhibitors at Philadelphia's World's Exposition of 1876 (Strahan, 1876).

2.14 *Paris' Exposition Universelle*, 1878

In 1878, Paris hosted the 3rd *Exposition Universelle*. The site planning was centred on the *Champ Du Mars* on the banks of the River Seine. On the other side of the river, the fair grounds were extended up the slopes of the Chaillot Hill and were terminated in the newly built *Palais du Trocadéro* (Trocadéro Palace), designed by Davioud and Bourdais. Linking the two sites on either side of the river was the *Pont d'Iéna* bridge. The main body of the *Champ Du Mars* was occupied by a huge iron-and-glass Industrial Hall, or *Palais du Champ de Mars,* designed by the engineer Henri de Dion.

At the centre of the *Palais du Trocadéro* was a large circular theatre that could seat 6,000 people. Radiating out on either side of the theatre were two semi-circular 'wings' that enclosed the gardens below. Air was supplied to the theatre through an ingenious system of ventilation, which drew in fresh air from the catacombs below the theatre and circulated it out through a lantern on top of the domed roof. The lantern that also supplied light to the interior of the theatre had a diameter of five metres and was thus larger than the Pantheon in Rome. The main purpose of the *Palais du Trocadéro* was supposedly to serve as the starting point for a system of waterfalls, cascades and ponds that descended down the Chaillot Hill. A 10-metre-high waterfall was located at the base of the *Palais du Trocadéro*, which was supported by an arched opening that led to a subterranean aquarium that was partly decorated in mosaics. From this archway, visitors to the 1878 Exposition could experience a peculiar view of the Exposition gardens and the *Palais du Champ de Mars* through the falling sheet of water. Once over the fall, the water then flowed down a stone cascade and into a 70-metre-wide pool (Delorme, Blanc, de Laberge and Harvard, 1879). Furthermore, the aquarium was approximately 150 by 300 feet in dimension and was excavated from the rock below the *Palais du Trocadéro*. The galleries within the aquarium were lit only from light that first passed through the large fish tanks (Healey, 1877b).

The *Palais du Champ de Mars* was a massive rectangular iron, portalframed structure that had two outer galleries, 35 metres wide by 650 metres long (Brunfaut, 1878). These outer galleries were clad in both masonry and glazing. Occupying the interior of the *Palais du Champ de Mars* were six lower galleries that ran parallel to the main axis of the building and the outer galleries; an axis that extended across the *Pont d'Iéna* bridge and upward to the *Palais du Trocadéro*. At the very centre of the *Palais du Champ de Mars,* the *Pavillonde la ville de Paris* was located in an open air gallery. Completing each of the eight covered galleries and the open air gallery were two grand vestibules that contained the six main entrances or grand galleries/cupolas to

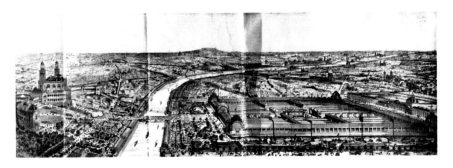

Figure 2.5 A birds-eye-view of Paris' *Exposition Universelle* of 1878.

the *Palais du Champ de Mars*. The vestibules were of great width and height, with the whole of the upper portions being glazed, creating:

> ...the two finest galleries we have yet seen.
> (Healey, 1877a: 345)

In contrast, the whole arrangement of the *Palais du Champ de Mars* was criticised for being too low to allow adequate views. However, in this criticism, the grand galleries/cupolas, in particular those at the four corners of the immense *Palais du Champ de Mars*, were excluded:

> The four especially admirable situations for display are under the domes at the four corners of the building, and these are respectively occupied by the English colonies, the Dutch colonies, a statue of Charlemagne and a trophy of French metallic work – notably, large tubes for telescopes.
> (Knight, 1878: 403)

The grand vestibules were described as having been 1,000 feet long by 80 feet wide, with clerestory windows on both sides, the glazing of which was described as having been executed in geometric patterns with tinted glass, creating a 'fine effect' (Healey, 1878).

Like the Centennial Balloon at Philadelphia's World's Exposition of 1876, a further object of interest at the 1878 Exposition was the *Le Grand Ballon* (Grand Balloon) designed by Henry Giffard. Filled with hydrogen gas, the balloon had a diameter of 56 metres and could lift 25 tons. The huge sphere of the balloon was connected via a rope net to a circular passenger car, which was six metres in diameter and could accommodate 40 to 50 passengers. Two steam engines were connected to a 600-metre length of rope and could raise and lower the balloon high above Paris and the 1878 Exposition (Tissandier, 1878). While not located on the Exhibition grounds, but, rather to the east at the *Palais des Tuileries* (Tuileries Palace), the balloon with its intrepid travellers was the envy of the world with its views of Paris and its grand exhibition (Delorme *et al.*, 1879).

2.15 Paris' *Exposition Universelle*, 1889

In the 1880s, a specific trend toward industry-based exhibitions developed. Some examples include the First International Exhibition of Electricity, hosted in Paris in 1881; The International Cotton Exposition in Atlanta, Georgia, in 1881; the *Exposition Universelle Coloniale et d'Exportation Générale* (Universal Exposition of the Colonies and General Exports), in Amsterdam in 1883; and the World's Industrial and Cotton Centennial Exposition, in New Orleans in 1884. However, large holistic international events were still prevalent, with examples being the *Exposition Internationale d'Anvers* (International Exhibition in Antwerp) in Antwerp in 1885; the *Exposición Universal* (Universal Exposition) in Barcelona in 1888; and the *Exposition Universelle* (Universal Exposition) in Paris in 1889.

Undoubtedly, the 1889 Paris *Exposition Universelle* was best known for the Eiffel Tower and the *Galerie des Machines*. The main location of the Exposition was the *Champ de Mars*, extended across the Seine and upward to the *Palais du Trocadéro*. Additionally, the Exposition's agricultural buildings extended eastward along the *Quai d'Orsay*, and terminated at the *Esplanade des Invalides* with an exhibition of the French colonies. Planning of the *Champ de Mars* consisted of the construction of a series of U-shaped exhibition halls. The arms of the 'U' consisted of the *Palais des Arts libéraux* and the *Galerie Desaix* with the parallel *Palais des Beaux-Arts* and the *Galerie Rapp*, while the base of the 'U' consisted of the *Palais des Expositions diverses* and the *Galerie des Machines*. At the centre of the 'U' plan, the Eiffel Tower served to form a southern gateway to the *Pont d'Iéna* bridge. As with the 1878 Exposition, in the 1889 Exposition, the main central axis extended down from the *Palais du Trocadéro*, across the *Pont d'Iéna*, continued under the Eiffel Tower and through the *Palais des Expositions diverses*, finally terminating in the *Galerie des Machines*. A massive central domed portal was erected to mark the main axis' entrance into the *Palais des Expositions diverses* (Exposition Universelle de Paris, 1889; Monrod, 1889). The dome was considered as the *entrée d'honneur* (grand entrance), as it was the most admired architectural aspect of the Exposition (Blaine, 1890). Two additional, glazed central domes, one each over the *Palais des Beaux-Arts* and the *Palais des Arts libéraux*, were also present at the 1889 Exposition.

Also exhibiting at the 1889 Paris Exposition was the *Compagnie Transatlantique* (Transatlantic Company). Its pavilion was planned on a regular polygon located on the *Quai d'Orsay* to the east of the Eiffel Tower, and in it, the visitor could experience all the luxury and comfort of a transatlantic sea voyage, but without any of the danger. This pavilion featured exhibits of cabins and engine rooms, a bridge and lifeboats together with images of the Company's main destinations (Exposition Universelle de Paris, 1889).

42 Bruno Taut's design inspiration for the Glashaus

A further pavilion of interest was located on the western boundary of the *Champ de Mars*; this modest building housed a 40-metre-diameter globe of the earth. This pavilion was capped with a simple dome and lantern apex configuration. However, the main attraction of this domed pavilion was not the globe itself, but rather the spiral staircase that surrounded it. Of additional interest was an Otis elevator that was installed to mimic the axis of the earth. To access this elevator, visitors would descend via a helical ramp into the entrance of the lift; once in the lift, visitors would ascend upward through the globe from the south to north poles (Exposition Universelle de Paris, 1889).

Les Fontaines Lumineuses (Luminous Fountains) were a further defining feature of the 1889 *Exposition Universelle*. Located in a number of large pools and fountains directly beneath the Eiffel Tower and between the *Palais des Beaux-Arts* and the *Palais des Arts libéraux*, *Les Fontaines Lumineuses* were conceptualised as France illuminating the world and surrounded by Science, Industry, Art and Agriculture. Countan designed the fountains between the *Palais des Beaux-Arts* and the *Palais des Arts* and they consisted of a large central motif, with four large fountains supplying a large flow of water. Immediately adjacent to the central motif were eight smaller motifs, each with 10 fountains, all of which were surrounded by numerous smaller fountains. In total, the whole fountain system could project approximately 500 litres of water per second. The true novelty of *Les Fontaines Lumineuses* however lay in their ability to be lit at night by coloured, electric lighting, creating a sparkling display reflected in the cascades and ponds. Located directly below the Eiffel Tower, the grand fountain was built and sculptured by de Saint-Viadl and was lit by four arc lamps (Monrod, 1889). Paris' illuminated fountain spectacle was however predated by previous examples in Edinburgh and Glasgow (Exposition Universelle de Paris, 1889).

The greatest novelty of the Paris Exposition of 1889 was however that created by electricity, since it was the first international exposition since the practical beginning of the industry (Hering, 1893). Still a relative novelty, the extensive use of electrical lighting transformed the Exhibition grounds into a true 24-hour experience. As the most visible example, the Eiffel Tower was equipped at its apex with both a fixed revolving light and numerous search lights. These lights probed the darkness of night in all directions with coloured light (Monrod, 1889). Furthermore, the largest exhibitor at the Paris Exhibition was the American Edison Company. The exhibit of the Edison Company won the highest award of the Exhibition, namely the 'Grand Prize', which was personally presented to Thomas Edison by the French President Carnot. Among the display of objects as diverse as phonograph recorders and telephones, Edison also presented a mammoth 40-foot-high display of 20,000 incandescent electric light bulbs in various colours. At the apex of this display and standing on a large pedestal was a giant model of a light bulb that contained 13,000 individual 16-candle-power light bulbs. To light this massive model, a 'filament' of 60 'blood red' 150-candle-power electric bulbs were arranged on a two-inch gas pipe (The American Commission, 1889).

If judged solely on exhibitor and visitor numbers, 55,000 and 28.15 million respectively, the 1889 *Exposition Universelle* was undoubtedly a huge success (Johnson, 1897b). However, it was here that the nature of World's Fairs started to transform from showcasing machines and industrial products to emphasising both the effects and characteristics that could be created with new technologies, such as electricity.

2.16 Chicago's World's Colombian Exposition, 1893

At the end of the 19th century, the seminal event that shaped wider American and specifically Chicago's sentiment was the World's Colombian Exposition of 1893. A 2.9 square kilometre area known as Jackson Park on the shores of Lake Michigan was dedicated as its site. The Exposition itself was intended as a celebration of the 400th year anniversary of Christopher Columbus' discovery of America. Frederick Law Olmsted, in conjunction with the architectural form Burnham and Root, developed a site plan that divided the Exhibition grounds through the use of large, artificial water features. At the heart of this plan was a large Central Basin that contained the Columbian Fountains and the Statue of the Republic, at either end. At the western end of the Central Basin, a smaller canal intersected the basin at a right angle. The main buildings of the exhibition were grouped around the Central Basin area, alternatively known as the Court of Honour, and included Machinery, Agriculture, the Railway Station, Mines, Electricity, and Manufacturing and Liberal Arts. These buildings were commonly referred to as the White City because of the overwhelming use of white paint on almost all of their exterior façades. Additionally, the majority of the White City and the other larger structures at the Exposition of 1893 were constructed in the neoclassical Beaux-Art style dictated by the Exposition's management and architects. The South Pond was constructed at the southern end of the canal. Centred on this pond were mostly agricultural exhibits such as Leather, Forestry and Livestock. At the northern end of the canal, a further large Lagoon was constructed, surrounded by the smaller exhibition buildings, which included the following: Transportation, Choral Building, Horticulture, White Star Line Building, Women's Building, Fisheries, and the Government Building of the United States of America. Again at the northern end of the Lagoon, a third and last North Pond was created that formed the centre of a group of buildings for foreign nations, American states and Art Galleries. An amusement area known as the Midway Plaisance protruded outward on the Western extremity of the main exhibition grounds, just behind the Women's Building (Fred Klein Company, 1894; Johnson, 1897b; Truman *et al.*, 1893).

The Midway Plaisance was one of the major innovations introduced at the World's Colombian Exposition. Considering that the attractions of the

Figure 2.6 A view of the Midway Plaisance at the Chicago World's Exposition of 1893, showing the Moorish Palace directly to the left of the Ferris Wheel.

main fair grounds were regarded as a serious endeavour, the Midway was intended from the onset as light entertainment and a necessary distraction. As such, the Midway was designed to incorporate rest, comfort, refreshment, picturesque displays, foreign cultural exhibits, and, above all, amusement. However, this is not to argue that the organising committee was totally at ease with the inclusion of these frivolous, but necessary, distractions. Thus, the chosen location was the narrow allocation of land outside of the main grounds in an intentional effort to prevent:

> ...jarring contrasts between the beautiful buildings and grounds on the one hand, and the amusing, distracting, ludicrous, and sometimes noisy attractions of the Midway.
>
> (Johnson, 1897b: 75)

In an attempt to mirror the success of the Eiffel Tower at the 1889 World's Exposition, a steel tower of similar height was initially proposed for inclusion in the Midway. However, this plan never came to fruition; instead, a design by George W.G. Ferris for a 250-feet-diameter 'Ferris wheel' was built (Johnson, 1897b). Regardless of the Midway's general 'character', it did contain some structures of interest to this study; principal among these were the exhibits displaying interpretations of the Orient.

Located on the eastern end of the Midway near the Ferris wheel, the Moorish Palace contained a garden of palms, a chamber of horrors, a labyrinth, a room of mirrors, a waxwork show, and a theatre of optical illusions (Johnson, 1897a). Additionally, the Moorish Palace was quoted as having contained a *camera obscura*; depictions of trips to the moon and Switzerland; and the exhibit and sale of native goods (Handy, 1893). The chamber of horrors in the Moorish Palace contained the French guillotine 'La Dijonnaise', the very object that ended the life of Marie Antoinette in October of 1793 (Truman *et al.*, 1893). Arguably, the best description of the Moorish Palace came from Flinn (1893): Designed by the German émigré architect August Fiedler, the Moorish Palace had a palm garden surrounded by a continuous labyrinth that was one of the leading attractions of the Midway. Modelled after that in the Alhambra Palace in Granada, Spain, the gardens presented an illusion of boundless space that was created through the clever use of mirrors. The gardens presented a:

> ...fairyland filled with startling surprises. The first thing which impresses the observer within the palace are the elaborate decorations. He [sic] is in a maze of Alabaster-like columns, stretching away in long vistas. The columns are covered with curious hieroglyphics and support a dome and arched ceiling reflecting from its mother of pearl a softly radiant light. Standing on the tiled floor of mosaics, the visitor may cast his eyes upward, and admire the delicate filigree in gold, purple and silver, sweeping in flowing lines, here and there gracefully crossing and forming an intricate net-work of beautiful curves. From the arch depend pretty little stalactites, in gilt, producing a very pleasant effect on the pearly back-ground.
>
> (Flinn, 1893: 34–5)

Once the visitor had exited the 'Magic Maze', the next experience was a 'bottomless well' into which people would satisfyingly gaze. Following this experience, the visitor would then step over a ledge of rock and into a cave. 'The walls of the cave glitter like so many diamonds, and as you turn your eyes upward the sight of a group of devils makes you start. There, in a hole in the rocks above, a lot of red imps are staring at you' (Flinn, 1893: 35). At this point, it should be noted that the palm garden and its labyrinth were in fact an optical illusion contained in a mirror maze; the very same object as the 'Magic Maze'. As Flinn (1893) continued, next was a flight of ascending stairs that led to a 'gigantic kaleidoscope' where the visitor experienced the sensation of being surrounded by a 'thousand people'. From this point, the visitor then progressed upward via a broad staircase to the upper floor of the Moorish Palace. On the upper floor, the visitor could experience fine art obtained from the 'Berlin Panopticon'. Apart from the fine art, other experiences on the upper floor of the Moorish Palace included an exhibition of the guillotine 'La Dijonnaise'; three 'optical illusions', which were skilfully

46 *Bruno Taut's design inspiration for the Glashaus*

executed and afforded the visitor 'food for thought'; and theatres in which respectable presentations were given (Flinn, 1893).

The designer of the palm gardens and associated labyrinth in the Moorish Palace was Gustav Castan (Unknown author, 1893). He and his brother, Louis Castan, were the owners of the Panopticon attraction in Berlin, which first opened in 1873. When the Panopticon moved to its new location at the premises of the Pschorr Brewery at 165 *Friedrichstra e* in 1888, a mirror maze was installed (Saward, 2008). A period description of this installation, or *Castan's Irrgarten* (Castan's Maze), portrayed it in a similar metaphorical language as Flinn (1893), stating that it was complete with an experience of the Cathedral of Cordoba and the Alhambra in Granada (Castan and Castan, 1900).

Gustav Castan was granted a French patent (September 8, 1888, No. 192868) for the mirror maze in 1888, and an American patent in 1895 (Castan, 1895). A comparison of this patent and the progression of the journey as outlined by Flinn (1893), i.e. from 'Magic Maze' to 'bottomless well' then onward to the 'cave' and finally into the 'monster kaleidoscope', are essentially identical. In the patent, a Mirror Maze was to be erected in a building or room. To experience the Mirror Maze, the visitor would enter, pay a cashier and then deposit their cloaks. Having entered the Mirror Maze proper, the first impression the visitor would have is the sensation of being at the end of an immensely long avenue. This impression was in fact created by an image that was placed at the other end of the room and then reflected back to the visitor off numerous mirrors arranged as equilateral triangles. Once the visitor had entered the labyrinth of the Mirror Maze, further experiences became apparent; that of being either in the Lion Courtyard of the Alhambra Palace, or the experience of a lush tropical garden. In reality, these experiences were created by distinct compartments in the Mirror Maze that were accordingly decorated. Once the visitor had found their way through the Mirror Maze, they would then have entered a compartment where the initial image, i.e. that of the immensely long avenue, was located. This compartment, while having some vertical surfaces covered with mirrors, was not entirely covered with mirrors. In this compartment, the visitor became aware that they have exited the Mirror Maze proper. Additionally, in this compartment, the visitor was then exposed to a spiral staircase that led upward to an experience of being in large crowd. In reality, this experience was created by the visitor entering a raised kaleidoscope, a regular tetrahedron arranged in the form of a triangle. Inside the kaleidoscope, the walls and roof were mirrored; the mirrors were connected together in a manner so that joints were not visible. Once the visitor had completed this experience, they would have then exit the raised kaleidoscope via another descending spiral staircase. At the bottom of this spiral staircase, the visitor would then enter a final compartment and then exit the building or room entirely.

A panopticon was however not a new concept. In the early 1850s, the Royal Panopticon of Science and Art was constructed in Leicester Square,

Figure 2.7 The Horticultural Hall at the Chicago World's Exposition of 1893.

London, with the intention of showcasing the best of scientific and artistic endeavours. A 97-feet-high central rotunda was the primary attraction of the Royal Panopticon. Surrounded by three tiers of viewing galleries, the rotunda had an illuminated fountain that was supplied with water from an artesian well. When in operation, the fountain could project a water jet to the underside of the dome that crowned the rotunda. The underside of the dome was decorated in a colourful array of glass, alabaster and enamelled slate, reportedly creating the most splendid room ever constructed for scientific and artistic endeavour (White, 1854).

A building for the Libby Glass Company also occupied a site on the Midway Plaisance at the Exposition of 1893. This building was proposed as the most beautiful of the Midway; based on a rectangular plan with two towers located at each corner of the main street façade, it had a prominent dome with a chimney at its centre. Inside the building, the walls, dome and ceiling all glittered and gleamed in sparkling, prismatic colour that emanated from the myriad of displayed glass products. The main entrance of the building led onto a large semi-circular room that had a large melting furnace located in the middle. This furnace was 100 feet high and adopted the form of a truncated cone that was 25 feet in diameter (Flinn, 1893).

An exact copy of the captive balloon of the 1889 Paris *Exposition Universelle* was also located on the on Midway Plaisance. This balloon could ascend

48 *Bruno Taut's design inspiration for the Glashaus*

1,493 feet into the air, this figure being the same number as the date of Columbus' discovery of America. Views from this balloon allowed the visitor to:

> ...see the great buildings of the Exposition. Domes, towers, spires, winged Victories, bathed in light, waters flashing in the rays of an unclouded sun; so beautiful is the view that it seems hardly real. We are floating over fairy-land.
>
> (Shepp, 1893: 524)

Domes were to be found over many of the main buildings and examples included the Administration Building; the Government Building of the United States of America; the Fisheries Building; and the Fine Arts Building. However, because almost all of the domes had a neoclassical aesthetic, the most modern dome at the Exposition was that over the Horticulture Building. This building was designed by the prominent Chicago architect William Le Baron Jenny. The plan of the Horticulture Building was based on a rectangle that was 1,000 feet long by 287 feet wide. The resulting arrangement creating the grandest and largest building ever erected for a horticultural exhibition (Handy, 1893; Truman *et al.*, 1893). Located at the centre of this plan was an imposing glazed dome that was 114 feet high and 187 feet in diameter. The interior of the dome was both artificially heated and moistened. Beneath the central dome, a 'miniature tropical mountain' was constructed that contained an extensive cave, constructed by Keith and Allabaugh, in its base (Johnson, 1897a). Several cascades, which were described as having sparkling water that leapt from rock to rock beneath the foliage of tree ferns, palms and other tropical vegetation, ran down the sides of the mountain. The entire cave below the mountain was constructed of (real) stalagmites, stalactites and quartz crystals. With the aid of artificial electric lighting, the created effect was both pleasing and dazzling (Handy, 1893). The cave was described as being a reproduction of one of the 1,400 chambers of the Mammoth Crystal Caves of South Dakota. Owing to its exterior, luxurious tropical growths, and interior that displayed:

> ...enchanted chamber glittering with diamond-like stalagmites and other forms of crystal.
>
> (Rand McNally and Company, 1893: 114)

The beauty of the 'miniature tropical mountain' and cave were one of the principal features of the Horticulture Building (Rand McNally and Company, 1893: 114).

Numerous smaller horticultural glasshouses were additionally located on the western end of the Horticulture Building. In addition to these examples, 25,000 square feet of auxiliary glasshouses were also constructed in close proximity to the Horticulture Building. All of these glasshouses were constructed by leading firms, such as Lord and Burnham, Hitchings and Company, and the New York Central Iron Works (Handy, 1893). Also among these glasshouses were two unique pavilions erected by Gustav Falconnier, whose construction employed his patented blown Glass Building Blocks (Rand McNally and Company, 1893). First patented in France in 1886, Falconnier also subsequently patented his design in the United States of America in 1889 (Falconnier, 1889). The larger of these pavilions at the Chicago Exposition of 1893 appeared very similar to an example first published in the journal *La Nature* (Nature); this example was approximately eight meters long by 3.8 meters wide and had a glazed curved span roof, constructed entirely of patented Falconnier Glass Building Blocks (Tissandier, 1893).

Art Glass was also to be found at the Chicago Exhibition; for example, the Midway had a pavilion that housed the Parisian Glassware Company. In this pavilion, glass spinning was demonstrated and finished products were also sold. Furthermore, the Venice-Murano Glass Exhibit occupied a Gothic-styled building that was extensively inlayed with glass mosaics; here too glassware was both made and sold to visitors (Flinn, 1893). The Texas Building had a central assembly hall that had an art glass skylight in the ceiling, with a mosaic of the Texas Star at its centre (Handy, 1893; Truman *et al.*, 1893).

In the Manufactures and Liberal Arts Building, the Tiffany Glass and Decorating Company constructed a pavilion that had a triple-arched entrance, with a 100-foot-high saffron-coloured Doric column that had a globe and golden eagle at it apex. The interior of the Tiffany pavilion was divided into three rooms, the largest of which exhibited a Byzantium-inspired chapel, with a wonderful altar set beneath triple mosaic covered arches. The floor of the chapel was covered with wrought-glass mosaics, as were the steps to the altar and the front of the altar itself. Additionally, the columns were also covered with glittering mosaics. The interior of the chapel was considered as artistically beautiful and exceedingly opulent (Truman *et al.*, 1893). A large ornate lamp, constructed from thick, deep-green glass globes and faceted like emeralds, hung from the ceiling in the chapel. In addition to this light, the Chapel was also lit by coloured glass windows that were constructed from the mosaic system, where light and shade effects were achieved not by paint but by differences in the surface finish of the individual glass pieces or mosaics. So popular was the Tiffany Chapel that, during the exhibition, 1.4 million people visited it (Johnson, 1897a).

Also exhibited at the Chicago Exhibition of 1893 was an Electric Tower, which was the joint pavilion of both the Edison Electric Company and the Phoenix Glass Works. Located at the centre of the Electricity Building, at the crossing of the nave and transept, the Electric Tower represented the crowning achievement of Edison, who had made the incandescent electric bulb his life's work. So important was the Electric Tower to the Electricity Building that the official opening of it was delayed until the tower was complete (Truman *et al.*, 1893). The base of the tower consisted of a colonnade constructed on a circular plan, and a dome was placed above the colonnade that contained the

50 *Bruno Taut's design inspiration for the Glashaus*

tower proper. Contained within the outer extremities of the colonnade was an exhibit of numerous electric fittings manufactured by the Phoenix Glass Works (Arnold and Higinbotham, 1893), while the interior extremities of the tower contained the electrical distribution and control equipment for the tower above. The shaft of the tower was illuminated by thousands of coloured incandescent light bulbs supplied by the Edison Company. The bulbs were mechanically controlled and could be flashed in harmony with accompanying music. Like the Edison pavilion at the Paris Exhibition of 1889, the apex of the tower consisted of a replica of a giant Edison incandescent light bulb. However, unlike the Paris example, this model was constructed from approximately 30,000 prismatic crystals that were illuminated from within. A marvellous effect was created through a:

> '...combination of kaleidoscopic beauties...' by this '...graceful luminous shaft...' which was '...over eighty feet of solid brilliancy.'
>
> (Truman *et al.*, 1893: 358–60)

This electrical brilliance was however not exclusive to the Electric Tower and the Electricity Building, although the Electricity Building was the only building provided with sufficient quantities of electric lighting to allow visitation during the night (Johnson, 1897b). To provide electric lighting to the Manufactures Building, five large electroliers, or coronas, were installed 150 feet above the floor. A corona was essentially a large circular light feature constructed from light angle iron, with light bulbs suspended from it. The largest central corona was 75 feet in diameter and had a total of 102 bulbs, while the remaining four coronas were 60 feet in diameter and had 78 bulbs. The character of the resultant light was pleasing, soft and mellow (Johnson, 1897b). Additionally, according to Johnson (1897b), the most novel application of electric lighting at the Exposition was to the tanks in the Fisheries Building, where the aquariums were illuminated through the use of invisible lamps that shone through the water. However, the most brilliant electric lighting was that of the Gallery of Fine Arts, where bulbs that were only eight inches apart were placed onto nearly two miles of reflecting screens. Thus, the lighting of the Gallery of Fine Arts was said to have been both the most difficult and beautiful of any lighting that had ever been executed. However, the:

> ...most charming electrical effects were produced in the evening as the twilight deepened. All along the margins of the Great Basin lines of incandescent lights flashed out of the shadows, and were answered by other lines along the cornices and pediments of the great white palaces. Long wreaths of light climbed the ribs of the Administration Dome and twined themselves into a brilliant coronet at its summit. Arc lights flamed everywhere like mimic suns and with incandescent bulbs more numerous than the stars were reflected in rippling radiance on the dancing waters

of the lagoons. Then great solid beams from the search-light mirrors smote the air and, as they swung, rested for a moment on the quadriga or the MacMonnies fountain, on the winged figures of Machinery Hall or on the groups on the Agriculture Building, on the 'green sward before the Liberal Arts Building, or on the throngs that swarmed in the plaza, tingeing everything they touched with the prismatic hues of the rainbow arch or the lambent whiteness of an alpine snow. Then at a word the lights vanished, and out of the darkness, with the suddenness of a geyser, the great electric fountains lifted their gushing and gleaming waters. Now a single column, surrounded at its foot by a score of golden sheaves, rose to a height of a hundred feet ; now nearly two thousand jets built up a great cone of limpid light, golden, blue, green, red, or of contrasted or mingled hues. ... When the fountains ceased playing, again the golden lines of electric lights flashed from dome and pediment, cornice and water line, and the giants fenced with search-light broadswords in the upper air.

(Johnson, 1897b: 481)

The above description partly encapsulated the essence of the World's Colombian Exposition for the nearly 26 million people that visited it. However, a more appropriate explanation was offered by Charles Mulford Robinson, when he described the fair as a spectacle, where the visitor would stroll and dream, both in the day and at night (Johnson, 1897b).

2.17 Paris' *Exposition Universelle*, 1900

If the architectural style of the World's Colombian Exposition was overwhelmingly neoclassical, then in 1900, the style of the 5th *Exposition Universelle* in Paris was undoubtedly Art Nouveau. Once again, like the Expositions of 1878 and 1889, the main venue for 1900 Exposition was the *Champ de Mars* and extended across the Seine and upward to the *Palais du Trocadéro*. Additionally, like the 1889 Exposition, the 1900 *Exposition Universelle* stretched eastward along the *Quai d'Orsay*, this portion included *La Rue des Nations* (Avenue of the Nations) and *Section des Armees de Terre et de Mer* (Terrestrial and Marine Forces). The eastward extension of the *Quai d'Orsay* was likewise mirrored on the north or right bank of the River Seine; this portion contained Horticulture, *Palais de la Ville de Paris* (City of Paris) and *Economie Sociale Congress* (Social Economic Congress). Both of these extensions along the banks of the Seine were terminated by the *Esplanade des Invalides,* which itself extended northward across the Seine via the *Pont Alexander III* bridge. Once across the bridge, the Exposition grounds then contained a series of Art buildings, namely the *Petit Palais* (Small Building) and *Grand Palais* (Large Building), which were bounded by the grand entrances of the *Porte Monumentale* (Monumental Entrance) and *Porte Nicolas II*. On the main exhibition ground of the *Champ de Mars*, a

52 Bruno Taut's design inspiration for the Glashaus

large U-shaped exhibition structure was again used. The southern base of the 'U' was formed by the buildings for food and agriculture, centred on the large *Salle des Fêtes* (Hall of Festivities). The electrical building was positioned immediately to the north of the *Salle des Fêtes*. Additionally, the eastern arm of the 'U' comprised the buildings for mines, metallurgy, fabrics, clothing and machines, while the western arm of the 'U' comprised the building for chemicals, civil engineering, transport, sciences and education. Centred on the Eiffel Tower, the area immediately north of the large U-shaped structures was occupied by a number of smaller exhibition pavilions (Picard, 1902c, 1902d).

A large *Chateau d'eau* (Water Palace) was constructed to complete the main north/south axis that ran down the hill from the *Palais du Trocadéro*, across the *Pont d'Iéna* and under the Eiffel Tower. Located on the northern façade of the electricity building, the *Chateau d'eau* was essentially a large fountain that was set back into a large, curved ornate niche, with a grotto positioned below. Water falling from the fountain would cascade into a number of successively lower basins and finally into a large pool at it base. The entire length of the cascade was 125 metres and the total fall was 12½ metres, while the primary materials were masonry and reinforced concrete. The main fountain at the head of the cascade was placed on an upper terrace that led both into the electricity building and downward to the lower terrace of the fountain; a staircase located below the fountain in a grotto joined the lower and upper terraces. Visitors traversing this inner staircase could pause and experience views of the exhibition grounds through a sheet of falling water from the fountain above. The entire cascade was artificially lit with electric lighting. The electrical control equipment for this lighting was located in rooms below the upper terrace (Picard, 1902b). At night, the fountains and water would create a scene of '…polychrome illumination…' (Fullerton and Olsson, 2004: 269).

A further larger façade was constructed and placed behind the main façade of the *Chateau d'eau*. A statue representing the *le Triomphe de l'Electricité* (Triumph of Electricity) in the form of a woman, or Fairy of Electricity, that rode a chariot pulled by *Pegasus* and a dragon and adorned with the date 1900, was placed at the apex of this secondary façade. Placed behind the statue was a 12-metre-diameter star that was lit with hundreds of shining lights. At its highest point, *le Triomphe de l'Electricité* was 71 metres above the ground. The statue of the Fairy of Electricity was constructed of zinc and embossed with opalescent glass mosaics. During the day, the statue glittered like a lacework of glass and steel in the sunlight, while at night it created the fiery impression of changeable lighting effects. Thus, the illumination of the *le Triomphe de l'Electricité*, in conjunction with thousands of additional coloured electric lights and powerful spotlights, created one of the central visual spectacles of the Exhibition (Picard, 1902b). Described as a fairy-land of light and beauty, the spectacle of the *Chateau d'eau* was reportedly '…beautiful beyond expression' (Addison and O'Grady, 1999: 18). It needs to

Figure 2.8 The *Chateau d'eau* at Paris' *Exposition Universelle* of 1900.

be acknowledged that the connection between the *Chateau d'eau* and Bruno Taut's *Glashaus* has already been provisionally exposed by Thiekotter (1993).

Located immediately behind the *Chateau d'eau* was the 410 metre long by 80 metre wide *Palais de l'Électricité* (Palace of Electricity), which was so named not only for being a display area for electrical products, but also because it was the primary electrical generation facility for the entire Exhibition. A visit to the *Palais de l'Électricité* could commence from the *Chateau d'eau*, thus continuing the main axis created by the *Palais du Trocadéro, Pont d'Iéna* and Eiffel Tower. Once in the *Palais de l'Électricité*, this main axis was then further extended southward through the hexagonal-shaped *Salle des Glaces ou Salle des Illusions* (Halls of Mirrors and Illusions) and onward to its final termination in the *Salles des Fêtes*. Additionally, the *Palais de l'Électricité* was constructed with an iron frame that was in-filled with wood, glass and gypsum.

Based on a regular hexagon plan with six arched walls, the *Salle des Glaces ou Salle des Illusions* had a domed roof modelled after the *Sala de las dos Hermanas* (Hall of the Two Sisters) at the Alhambra Palace in Grenada, Spain. At 21 metres high and with a maximum diameter of 26½ metres, the *Salle des Glaces ou Salle des Illusions* was however larger than the original *Sala de las dos Hermanas*. The underside of the dome was highly ornate with numerous copper-clad stalactites, geometric accent lines and star motifs. At the apex of the dome, a hexagonal opening was provided for ventilation.

54 Bruno Taut's design inspiration for the Glashaus

Lighting to the interior was achieved by numerous coloured electric lights. Six large chandeliers provided the main feature of the electric lighting system, which were connected together with strings of white electric lights. The chandeliers themselves were made from stamped zinc forms and had a 12-pointed star suspended from their bases. Approximately 3,000 electric lights, in red, yellow, white and green were placed throughout the interior of the *Salle des Glaces ou Salle des Illusions*, and its six arched walls were decorated with mirrors. The use of these mirrors, in conjunction with the hexagonal shaped plan and the electric lighting, thus created a kaleidoscopic effect. Each element of the electrical design was further converted into an electrical network that could be independently switched on or off, the control of which was facilitated through a control room placed on a mezzanine level, 2½ metres below the *Salle des Glaces ou Salle des Illusions*.

A maximum of 1,000 people could be accommodated in the *Salle des Glaces ou Salle des Illusions* at any one time. Admission was free of charge. Once the required number of visitors had entered the chamber, the access doors were closed and the curtains were drawn. After an electric bell had sounded, a series of bright flashing effects illuminated the chandeliers, stars, arches, and mirrors, reaching a crescendo when all the lights were turned on simultaneously, an event that ultimately led to applause from the astounded audience. Entry and exit to the chamber was via a series of staircases that led to a number of openings positioned in the mirrored archways. In excess of 20,000 people experienced the *Salle des Glaces ou Salle des Illusions* per day. Special visits to the chamber were also facilitated for dignitaries, such as the French President. These were elaborate events with multi-coloured, model butterflies and dragonflies with glittering gossamer wings being displayed in a glittering atmosphere of rain created by fragments of mica. Additional illumination to these special events entailed the opening of a 1.2 metre octagonal hole to the mezzanine below, in which directional lights were installed (Picard, 1902b). Alternatively, the effect of the dome in the *Salle des Glaces ou Salle des Illusions*, with its colour, zinc, and glass, was described as:

> '...metallic lacework...' that created a '...extravagant sumptuous factory rather than an exhibition palace.'
>
> (Wailly, 1900: 51)

Another visitor to the *Salle des Glaces ou Salle des Illusions* described the light show as having resembled a fairy-tale hall from a *Thousand and One Nights*; initially the show started with a bright display of sparkling golden lights and chandeliers, revealing the six-sided kaleidoscopic effect of the mirrors. The lighting then changed to deeper and darker colours, which revealed fluorescing marble columns and a multitude of graceful arabesques from rubies, emeralds, sapphires, gleaming silver pearls. Again and again the picture changed, and the crowd thus cheered loud and roared excitedly (Sauvage, 1900).

Figure 2.9 The *Salle des Glaces* or *Sale des Illusions* at Paris' *Exposition Universelle* of 1900.

Also constructed at *Exposition Universelle* of 1900 was the remarkable *Palais Lumineux* (Luminous Palace). This structure was located on the main exhibition grounds, just to the east of the Eiffel Tower. Described as one of the greatest works of stained glass, glassware and mirrors ever created, the *Palais Lumineux* was designed by Ponsin. The flamboyant Rococo-styled *Palais Lumineux* was built entirely of glass, with a supporting structure made from metal. Located on a 196-square-metre site, the pavilion was constructed on a gigantic granite base, from which a 12-metre-high waterfall emanated. To reach the *Palais Lumineux,* two internally lit, glass staircases were provided, the sides of which were adorned with motifs of marine shells. The main façade to the *Palais Lumineux* took the appearance of a large portico, with high, twisted columns that had golden capitals. The rear façade had the wide portico replaced with a coloured glass rotunda that was constructed from glass blocks. Above the twisted and tormented roof, a statue of an 'Indian' that held a glittering golden globe, was placed. The interior vault was made in a veil of opal yellow, artistically decorated with translucent enamels, while the exterior consisted of a terrace with twisted columns and a roof finished in bright tiles. The interior floor of the pavilion was covered by a transparent shimmering 'carpet', while the curtains that covered the

Figure 2.10 The Palais Lumineux at Paris' Exposition Universelle of 1900. Photo by permission of Agence Photographique de la RMN-Grand Palais.

arched doorways were made from cut beads and adored with sun motifs. Below the pavilion, an underground cave was constructed, adorned with glass stalactites and that housed a number of glassblowers. Thousands of incandescent electric lights were mostly hidden between the glazing of the pavilion's structure and decoration, illuminating the building, giving it a magical appearance. The impression of a mysterious and wonderful spectacle was created for the visitor (Picard, 1902e).

The *Palais Lumineux* was described as having been 110 feet high and 175 feet in circumference and that it was made from glass blocks and sheets cemented together, the stained-glass panels having been made by J.A. Ponsin (Lee, 1901). Ponsin died before the work on the *Palais Lumineux* was complete, and the construction was therefore completed by a collective that comprised the architect M. Latapy, the Saint Gobain Company and Legras and Company of Saint-Denis (Picard, 1902e). Of further importance is the fact that the glass bricks that formed part of the rotunda to the rear of the *Palais Lumineux* were hexagonal in shape and looked remarkably similar to Falconnier blown glass bricks, as illustrated in Tissandier (1893). Falconnier's glass bricks were also mentioned as an award winner at the Paris *Exposition*

Universelle of 1900 (www.glassian.org). Therefore, considering that Falconnier's glass bricks were blown, and that glassblowing was demonstrated in the cave below *Palais Lumineux*, it could be that Falconnier blown glass bricks were used in the *Palais Lumineux*.

At the southern end of the *Champs de Mars*, a large festival hall, or *Salle des Fêtes*, terminated the main axis. The *Salle des Fêtes* had a large monumental glazed dome above its central amphitheatre, which was 42 metres high. The dome itself was supported on 16 pillars and was constructed in three sectional portions: the lower portion of the dome comprised the arched entrances; the second or intermediate portion was partly glazed and mostly intended for the escape of stale hot air, while the upper portion comprised a fully glazed, illuminated canopy that was 40 metres in diameter. While the lower two sections of the dome were decorated in an eclectic mix of neo-classical and baroque styles, the glazed dome was finished in leaded stained glass. Essentially a large solar arrangement, the stained glass had a central 'sun' motif, coloured yellow, purple and red, with numerous radiating rays in orange, green and yellow. Large swathes of dark blue, intermingled with star motifs, surrounded the central 'sun' figure. Eight female figures, throwing stars and comets, completed the composition. Thus, shadow and light mixed with the stained glass and created a nebulous and unpredictable lighting effect (Picard, 1902b).

In addition to the *Palais Lumineux*, *Chateau d'eau* and the *Salle des Glaces ou Salle des Illusions*, numerous other 'traditional' domes were also present at the Paris Exposition of 1900. Designed by the architect A. Gautier, the *Palais de l'Horticulture* (Horticulture Building) was located on the right bank of the Seine, between the *Pont des Invalides* and *Pont de l'Alama* bridges. The *Palais de l'Horticulture* consisted of a pair of identical, arch-shaped, iron-framed glasshouses, measuring 60 metres long by 33 metres wide. Each large glasshouse additionally had seven smaller nave projections on either side. Additionally, the large glasshouse was connected to a smaller elliptical, dome-shaped glasshouse that was 17 metres long when measured parallel to the Seine, and 24 metres wide when measured perpendicular to the Seine (Picard, 1902a). Likewise, large glazed domes, with exposed iron structures were also located above the central portions of the *Grand Palais des Beaux-Arts* and the *Petit Palais du Retrospective D'Art*.

Embodied in structures like Renè Binet's grand entrance portico, or *La Porte Monumentale,* the new artistic plastic yearnings of the Art Nouveau were one of the greatest architectural contributions of the 5th *Exposition Universelle* in Paris. However, within a larger context, possibly the greatest offering of the Exposition of 1900 was a seminal shift away from the serious exhibition of goods towards a more theatrical event that was full spectacle and illusion. But the 1900 *Exposition Universelle* also marked an additional turning point for the 47 million people who visited it, in that the Western world, on the cusp of the 20th century, was:

58 *Bruno Taut's design inspiration for the Glashaus*

'...growing older...'; and the advent of modern technologies like telecommunications and transport '...had the disadvantage of rubbing the novelty off many things.'

(Walton, 1902: 85)

The inevitable result of this disappearance of the feeling of novelty was for the Paris Exposition of 1900 to have provided the visitor with an alternative and mostly emotional experience.

2.18 Conclusion

The *Glashaus* was a round pavilion building with a structurally expressive dome. In section, the building consisted of two distinct portions: a round, upper glazed portion that contained the dome, staircases and the Dome or Cupola Room. And, below this light-filled upper portion, the Cascade Room and kaleidoscope were housed in a darkly lit elongated form that comprised the second portion. In addition to staircases, an oculus positioned in the centre of the Cupola Room's floor connected the upper and lower portions of the *Glashaus*.

A simple comparison between the *Glashaus* and the multitude of exemplars listed above reveals immediate similarities. The *Glashaus'* dome and supporting structure could be argued as having strong precedents in buildings like that of New York's 'Crystal Palace' of 1853, London's Exhibition Palace of 1862, the *Rotunde* of Vienna in 1873, and the numerous examples of the Paris Exhibitions of 1878 and 1889. Likewise, the fountain and cascade present in the *Glashaus* had numerous precedents, such as the water features on the grounds of the Crystal Palace in Sydenham; the Hydraulic Basin at Philadelphia's Centennial Exhibition of 1876; the *Palais du Trocadéro* with its extensive system of waterfalls, cascades and ponds that descended down the Chaillot Hill, which were a defining feature of the Paris Expositions of 1878, 1889 and 1900; and the extensive canal, basin and fountains of Chicago in 1893.

However, it was the World's Expositions of 1893 in Chicago and Paris in 1900 that were the most influential on the design of the *Glashaus*. From Chicago's 1893 World's Colombian Exposition, the Horticulture Hall with its central dome below which sat the miniature tropical mountain with its Crystal Cave, offered an astoundingly similar conceptual arrangement to the *Glashaus*. Likewise, the Moorish Palace with its 'Magic Maze', 'bottomless well' and glittering cave, also offered immediate conceptual similarities with the *Glashaus*. Additionally, the primary building material of the *Glashaus*, i.e. the simple pressed-glass tiles, could also have had their origins at the 1893 Exposition. As Neumann (1995) has mentioned above, it was possible that Crew and Basquin, and not Pennycuick, invented prismatic glass and supposedly exhibited their invention at the 1893 World's Colombian Exposition. In addition to prismatic glass, Falconnier-blown glass bricks were also on display at the Exposition of 1893. The *Glashaus* too had numerous affinities with the new technology of electricity that was to be found in abundance in Chicago, particularly evident in the displays of companies like the Edison Electric Company and the Phoenix Glass Works Electric Tower.

The Paris Exposition of 1900 also had architectural examples that had direct and immediate relevance to the *Glashaus*. The *Chateau d'eau* with its large fountain that was set back into a large curved ornate niche and grotto below can be argued as related to the *Glashaus*. Likewise, the *Salle des Glaces ou Salle des Illusions* – with its regular hexagon plan and arched walls, wondrous' metallic lacework' Moorish domed roof, numerous coloured electrical lighting effects and chandeliers, octagonal oculus, and staircases – could be proposed as an uncannily similar precursor to the *Glashaus*. Nevertheless, the building that best mirrored the later *Glashaus* was the *Palais Lumineux*. Here, all of the principal ingredients of the *Glashaus* were evident: distinct upper and lower portions; glazing in a myriad of forms; staircases; and a fountain. However, just as Neumann (1995) had contended, the *Palais Lumineux* additionally, and more importantly, owed much of its effect to the particular details of the glazed products used.

A further integral constituent of the *Glashaus* was its mechanical kaleidoscope. Supplied by the firm *Eduard Liesegang Fabrik Optischer Apparate* (Eduard Liesegang Factory for Optical Instruments) in Düsseldorf, the kaleidoscope was housed at the base of the cascade, in a 2½-metre-deep room in the basement of the *Glashaus*. Powered by an electric motor, the kaleidoscope projected rotating images onto a frosted glass screen. The images themselves were created by numerous artists, including Franz Mutzenbecher from Berlin and Adolf Holzel from Stuttgart (Ahlstrand, 1993). As seen in the argument above, kaleidoscopic installations and result effects were a feature of Exposition architecture in the 19th century. The first was the 'gigantic kaleidoscope' in the Moorish Palace at the Chicago World's Exposition of 1893, following the earlier development *Castan's Irrgarten* and Gustav Castan's Patent of 1888. Thus, Taut's use of a kaleidoscope, albeit in a different form, can be argued as the continuation of an already existing tradition.

As stated above, the *Glashaus* had two distinct portions; namely an upper structurally expressive round dome and a lower elongated form that contained the fountain and cascade. Considering that in the argument above, most of the domes mentioned were glazed, structurally expressive and were a central defining feature of their parent buildings. Furthermore, the cascades and water features listed were mostly tiered, longer, linear elements. It is therefore clear that both the *Glashaus'* dome and its fountain and cascade were an evolution of well-established precedents, albeit as a smaller example. It is therefore highly likely that the two distinct portions of the *Glashaus*, in particular their form and aesthetics, evolved directly from these earlier precedents. Likewise, the *Glashaus* also had numerous affinities with the Expositions of 1893 and

60   *Bruno Taut's design inspiration for the Glashaus*

1900; in particular, the *Chateau d'eau*, the *Salle des Glaces ou Salle des Illusions* and the *Palais Lumineux*. However, unlike the earlier affinities that were more about aesthetics and form, these later similarities were more importantly about character, effect and spectacle.

Therefore, if we consider the *Glashaus*, it would appear to be a continuation of already existing practices and precedents. This would indicate that the person/s involved were acutely aware of these earlier precedents. Additionally, it would seem that they were actively seeking to amalgamate the best features of grand exhibition architecture in the *Glashaus*. But the question would then be who exactly this was.

Frederick Keppler arrived in Southampton on 10 January 1898, and 13 months later he took up residence in Berlin (Keppler, 1899, 1904). Where was Keppler for these 13 months, between January 1898 and February 1899? To answer this question, some preliminary contextual facts first need to be considered. The first of these facts is that Keppler was first in Britain, and then later made his way to Germany. The second fact is that Keppler was a man of diverse talents: architect, builder, entrepreneur and employee of the Luxfer Prism Company. Third, Keppler, in all probability, departed for Europe to commence his employment with the *Deutsche Luxfer Prismen Syndikat*. Given this, it is thus highly likely that Keppler was fully aware of Luxfer products and the associated work of Henry Crew and his assistant Olin H. Basquin. Therefore, it is also likely that Keppler was aware of Crew and Basquin's 1898 publication, the *Pocket Hand-Book of Use of Electro-Glazed Luxfer Prisms*. Keppler would have known of Crew and Basquin's desire to create new luxurious and crystalline lighting effects though the use of Iridian Luxfer Prisms. Therefore, considering that Keppler was primarily in Europe to both expand the presence and market penetration of Luxfer products, it could well be that his later 'simplified' glass tiles were nothing but a further iteration of Luxfer's Iridian Prisms.

Furthermore, Keppler was in Europe to seek out new business opportunities. It would be logical to assume that he would have wanted to make contact with established European manufacturers, view their product range and establish how they marketed their products. Thus, it would be logical to assume that during the 13 months before he took up residence in Berlin, Keppler was doing just that. However, there is also the possibility that Keppler was doing this well before he even departed for Europe. Considering that Keppler was most likely a resident of Chicago in 1893, can it be assumed that he would have visited Chicago's 1893 World's Colombian Exposition? In all probability he did, and for the sake of this work, it will be accepted that he did. Thus, it would be feasible to assume that while visiting the 1893 Exposition, Keppler had exposure to the Moorish Palace, the Libby Glass Company's pavilion, the captive balloon, the Horticulture Building and its Crystal Cave, the glasshouses that included those of Falconnier, the pavilion of the Tiffany Glass and Decorating Company, and the Edison Electric Company and the Phoenix Glass Works Electric Tower. Similarly, when Keppler is in Britain, would he not have visited seminal glass structures like the Sydenham Crystal Palace? This is clearly feasible considering that the Crystal Palace was destroyed by fire much later in 1936 (Chadwick, 1961). Likewise, the Water Temples were only demolished in 1904 (www.sydenham.org.uk, 2006). Therefore, could Keppler have seen the Crystal Fountain and the Water Temples? After Britain and later while on continental Europe, would Keppler not at the very least have been aware of the wonders of the *Exposition Universelle* of 1900? Thus, would Keppler have been conscious of the *Chateau d'eau*, the *Palais de l'Électricité* with its *Salle des Glaces ou Salle des Illusions, Palais Lumineux*, and all the other electrical and fantastic attractions of the 1900 Exposition?

The fundamental fact remains that Keppler's brief was to introduce the products of the Luxfer Company to European consumers. Furthermore, there was a longstanding tradition of both American and European glass manufacturers exhibiting their products at trade fairs and public exhibitions. Neumann (1995) has also argued that Luxfer's European branches also frequently participated in trade fairs and exhibitions, and actively sought the attention of architects. Moreover, he has indicated that the pavilions they used formed a distinct prototype, with domes, staircases, fountains, and a specific character composed through its use of glass. As evidenced from the descriptions above, domes, staircases, fountains, structural expression and glass 'character' were all prominent elements that had been previously used in Exposition architecture. Additionally, it is clear that the distinct prototype of the Luxfer Company, in all probability, evolved directly from prior exemplars of Exhibition architecture. Considering Keppler's experiences and business aspirations, it is proposed that he was a key figure in formulating the prototype for Luxfer. It is further proposed that Keppler would have briefed Taut on the generic requirements for the *Glashaus* of 1914. Thus, this hypothetical brief could have included the requirement for a 'stand-alone' pavilion building that had a glazed dome; that the pavilion use Luxfer products as the main building product; that the pavilion showcase Luxfer products in the best possible manner; that the building should have two distinct portions, i.e. an upper glazed, brightly lit portion, and lower, darkly lit portion; that the pavilion contain interesting electric lighting; that the electric lighting showcase the building at night; that the structure to the dome should be structurally expressive; and that the building should contain staircases, a fountain and a cascade.

From the above argument, it is clear that the *Glashaus* followed an established prototype. The larger implication is that the *Glashaus* was far from being '...captivating in its individuality and completeness...' (Jensen, 1915: 25); rather, it was forcefully prescribed and controlled. Even Jensen (1915) acknowledged that Taut's *Glashaus* made him think of a prior French glasshouse in Paris during 1900; this 'artistically worthless precedent' was however insignificant when compared to the small jewel that was the *Glashaus*. Could this have been both a direct acknowledgement of a connect-

62   Bruno Taut's design inspiration for the Glashaus

ion to the *Palais Lumineux*, and more importantly, an acknowledgement of the importance of precedent and the continuation of tradition?

The most commonly acknowledged perspective on the *Glashaus* proposes the building as a fanciful, utopian phenomenon; however, this is fabricated, Expressionist propaganda. What the argument above has established is another distinct theory that explains the building from the perspective of the client. When the *Glashaus* is viewed from this perspective, it becomes something very different. Therefore, the *Glashaus* can be proposed as a building whose planning, form and materials closely resemble earlier precedents; and that is the result of an intentional, prescribed formula that best showcased the commercial interests of the client.

Bibliography

Addison, M. (1999). *Diary of a European Tour, 1900*. Jean O'Grady (ed.). Quebec: McGill-Queen's University Press.

Ahlstrand, J. T. (1993). Der 'Künstlerische Erklärer' im Glashaus In A. Thierkotter (ed.). *Kristallisationen, Splitterrungen: Bruno Taut's Glashaus* (pp. 150–155). Basel: Birkhauser Verlag.

Angerstein, W. E. (1874). *Fünfundzwanzig Jahre Oesterreichischer Finanzpolitik: (1848 bis 1873): Ein Historischer Rückblick*. Berlin: Luckhardt'sche Verlagsbuchhandlung.

Arnold, C. D. and Higinbotham, H. D. (1893). *Official Views of the World's Columbian Exposition issued by the Department of Photography*, Chicago, IL: Press Chicago Photo-Gravure Company.

Babbage, C. (1851). *The Exposition of 1851: Or, Views of the Industry, the Science, and the Government of England*. London: John Murray.

Bell, G. (ed.). (1862). *The Journal of the Society of Arts* (Vol. 10). London: The Society of Arts.

Beresford Hope, A. J. (1862). The International Exhibition. *Quarterly Review, 112*, 179-214.

Blaine, J. G. (1890). *Reports of the United States Commissioners to the Universal Exposition of 1889 at Paris*. Washington: Printing Office of the United States.

Blake, W. and Pettit, H. (1873). *Reports on the Vienna Universal Exhibition, 1873*. Philadelphia, PA: United States Centennial Commission.

Brunel, I. K. (1870). *The Life of Isambard Kingdom Brunel, Civil Engineer*. London: Longmans, Green, and Company.

Brunfaut, J. N. (1878). Le Palis de l'Exposition. *L'Exposition universelle de 1878 illustrée, 70*.

Bucher, L. (1851). *Kulturhistorische Skizzen aus der Industrieausstellung aller Völker*. Frankfurt: E B Lizius.

Bucher, L. (1863). *Die Londoner Industrie-ausstellung von 1862*. Berlin: L. Gerschel.

Buloz, F. (ed.). (1873). *Revue des Deux Mondes: Recueil de la Politique, de l'administration et des Moeurs* (Vol. 43). Paris: Revue des deux mondes.

Candeloro, D. and Paul, B. (2004). *Chicago Heights: At the Crossroads of the Nation*. Chicago, IL: Arcadia Publishing.

Castan, G. (1895). *Mirror Maze*, United States of America Patent No. 545678: United States Patent Office.

Castan, G. and Castan, L. (1900). *Fuhrer durch Castan's Panopticum*. Berlin: Castan's Panopticum

Chadwick, G. F. (1961). *The Works of Sir Joseph Paxton 1803–1865*. London: The Architectural Press.

Ciré, A. (1993). Exponat und Monument: Bildbeispiele zur Bautypologie des Glashauses. In A. Thierkotter (ed.). *Kristallisationen, Splitterrungen: Bruno Taut's Glashaus* (pp. 126–128). Basel: Birkhauser Verlag.

Città di Torino. (2006). Le esposizioni torinesi.

Clarke, W. M. (1852). *The Crystal Palace, and Its Contents: Being an Illustrated Cyclopedia of the Great Exhibition of the Industry of All Nations 1851*. London: W. M. Clarke.

Conway, M. D. (1867a). The Great Show at Paris. *Harper's New Monthly Magazine, 35,* 238–253.

Conway, M. D. (1867b). More of the Great Show at Paris. *Harper's New Monthly Magazine 35,* 777–792.

Crew, H. and Basquin, O. H. (eds). (1898). *Pocket Hand-Book of Use of Electro-Glazed Luxfer Prisms*. American Luxfer Prism Company. W. B. Conkey Company Printers.

Delorme, R., Blanc, C., de Laberge, A. and Harvard, H. (1879). *L'art et l'industrie de tous les peuples à l'Exposition Universelle de 1878: description illustrée des merveilles du Champ-de-Mars et du Trocadéro, par les écrivains spéciax les plus autorisés*. Paris: Librairie Illustree.

Drew, W. A. (1852). *Glimpses and Gatherings, During a Voyage and Visit to London and the Great Exhibition, in the Summer of 1851*. Boston, MA: Abel Tompkins.

Dugan, J. (1953). *The Great Iron Ship*. London: Hamish Hamilton Ltd.

Esquiros, A. (1862). L'Angleterre et la vie Anglaise – XVI – L'Exposition Universelle de 1862. *Revue des Deux Mondes: Recueil de la Politique, de l'Administration et des Moeurs, 40,* 50–90.

Exposition Universelle de Paris. (1889). *L'Exposition chez soi 1889* (Vol. 1). Paris: L. Boulanger.

Falconnier, G. (1889). *Glass Building Block,* United States of America Patent No. 402073: U. S. P. Office.

Flinn, J. J. (1893). *Official Guide to the Midway Plaisance – Otherwise known as the Highway through the Nations with an Absolutely Correct Map and Numerous Illustrations*. Chicago, IL: The Columbian Guide Company.

Fred Klein Company. (1894). *Unsere Weltausstellung: Eine Beschreibung der Columbischen Weltausstellung in Chicago, 1893*. Chicago, IL: Fred Klein Company.

Fullerton, J. and Olsson, J. (eds). (2004). *Allegories of Communication: Intermedial Concerns from Cinema to the Digital*. Herts: John Libbey Publishing.

Geissler, R., Grieben, T. and Plessner, J. (1868). *Plaudereien über Paris und die Weltausstellung*. Berlin: Theobald Grieben.

Godwin, G. (1861, 21 September). *The Builder an Illustrated Weekly Magazine for the Architect, Engineer, Archaeologist , Constructor and Artist,* 647.

Godwin, G. (1862). *The Builder an Illustrated Weekly Magazine for the Architect, Engineer, Archaeologist , Constructor and Artist,* 227.

Gutschow, K. K. (2006). From Object to Installation in Bruno Taut's Exhibit Pavilions. *Journal of Architectural Education, 59*(4), 63–69.

Hamburg-Amerika Linie. (1899). Passenger Manifest for the ship Pennsylvania Hamburg: Hamburg-Amerikanische Packetfahrt Actien Gesellschaft.

64 *Bruno Taut's design inspiration for the Glashaus*

Handy, M. P. (1893). *The Official Directory of the World's Columbian Exposition, May 1st to October 30th, 1893*. Chicago, IL: W. B. Conkey Company.

Healey, E. C. (1877a). The Paris Exhibition No 1. *The Engineer*(16 November), 345.

Healey, E. C. (1877b). The Paris Exhibition No 2. *The Engineer*(23 November), 366.

Healey, E. C. (1878). The Paris Exhibition No 7. *The Engineer*(11 January), 20.

Heathcote, E. and Collie, K. (1997). *Budapest: A Guide to Twentieth-century Architecture*. London: Ellipsis London Limited.

Hering, C. (1893). *Electricity at the Paris Exposition of 1889*. New York: The W.J. Johnston Company Limited.

Hollingshead, J. (1862). *A Concise History of the International Exhibition of 1862: Its Rise and Progress, Its Building and Features and a Summary of All Former Exhibitions*. London: Her Majesty's Commissioners.

Ingram, J. S. (1876). *The Centennial Exposition: Described and Illustrated: Being a Concise and Graphic Description of this Grand Enterprise Commemorative of the First Centenary of American independence*. Philadelphia, PA: Hubbard Brothers.

Jessen, P. (1915). Die deutsche Werkbund-Ausstellung Köln 1914 *Jahrbuch des Deutschen Werkbundes 1915*. Munich F. Bruckmann.

Johnson, R. (1897a). *A History of the World's Columbian Exposition held in Chicago in 1893* (Vol. 3 Exhibits). New York: D. Appleton and Company.

Johnson, R. (1897b). *A History of the World's Columbian Exposition held in Chicago in 1893* (Vol. 1 Narrative). New York: D. Appleton and Company.

Junghanns, K. (1983). *Bruno Taut, 1880–1938*. Berlin (West): Elefanten Press.

Keppler, F. L. (1896). Passport Application for Frederick Keppler. Arkansas United States of America, Department of State.

Keppler, F. L. (1899). Passport Application for Frederick Keppler Berlin: Embassy of the United States in Germany.

Keppler, F. L. (1904). Passport Application for Frederick Keppler. Berlin: Embassy of the United States in Germany.

Keppler, F. L. (1909). Great Britain Patent No. 24457: B. P. Office.

Keppler, F. L. (1910). Great Britain Patent No. 21130: B. P. Office.

Keppler, F. L. (1913). Great Britain Patent No. 14999: B. P. Office.

Keppler, F. L. (1914). Keppler Glass Constructions – Pavements, Floors, Roofs, Walls, Partitions, Windows and Crystal Ceilings. Translucent but not Transparent. New York: Friederick F Keppler.

Knight, E. H. (1878). The Paris Exposition of 1878. *Lippincott's Magazine of Popular Literature and Science, 22*, 403–418.

Laxton, W. (1862). *The Civil Engineer and Architect's Journal* (Vol. 25). London: W. Kent and Company.

Lee, W. H. (1901). *Glimpses of the Rainbow City Pan American Exposition, at Buffalo*. Chicago, IL: Laird and Lee Publishers.

Leist, C. (1878). Passenger Manifest of the ship, Elbe. New York: Port of New York.

Mainardi, P. (1989). *Art and the Politics of the Second Empire: The Universal Expositions of 1855 and 1867*. New Haven, CT: Yale University Press.

Mallet, R. (ed.). (1862). London International Exhibition 1862. *The Practical Mechanics' Journal Scientific Record of the International Exhibition of 1862. London: Longman, Green, Longman and Roberts*.

Masur, G. (1974). *Imperial Berlin*. London: Routledge & Kegan Paul Plc.

McCabe, J. D. (1876). *The Illustrated History of the Centennial Exhibition: Held in*

Commemoration of the One Hundredth Anniversary of American Independence Philadelphia, Chicago and St. Louis: The National Publishing Company.

McDermott, E. (1862). *The Popular Guide to the International Exhibition of 1862.* London: W.H. Smith and Son.

McLean, R. C. (1887). The Chicago Architectural Sketch Club. *The Inland Architect and News Record, 10*(7), 85.

McLean, R. C. (1889). Mosaics. *The Inland Architect and News Record, 14*(3), 42.

McLean, R. C. (1891). Fire Test of a New Fireproof Material. *The Inland Architect and News Record, 17*(5), 61.

McLean, R. C. (1898). An Interesting Competition. *The Inland Architect and News Record, 30*(6), 6–64.

McLean, R. C. (1900). Interesting Development of the Building Arts: The Steel Skeleton, or the Modern Skyscrapers – The Engineering Problems. *The Inland Architect and News Record, 34*(6), 8.

Monrod, E. (1889). *L'Exposition Universelle de 1889: Grand Ouvrage Illustré, Historique, Encyclopédique, Descriptif* (Vol. 1). Paris: E. Dentu.

Neumann, D. (1995). 'The Century's Triumph in Lighting': The Luxfer Prism Companies and Their Contribution to Early Modern Architecture. *The Journal of the Society of Architectural Historians, 54*(1), 24–53.

Neumann, D. (2010). Translucent vs Transparent Glassblocks and Prism Glass at the beginning of Modern Architecture. In R. Corraro (ed.), *Glassblock and Architecture Evoluzione del Verromattone e Recenti Applicazione.* Florence: Alinea Editrice

Pemsel, J. (1989). *Die Wiener Weltausstellung von 1873: Das Gründerzeitliche Wien am Wendepunkt.* Wien: Böhlau.

Pennycuick, J. G. (1885). *Window-Glass,* United States of America Patent No. 312290: U. S. P. Office.

Pennycuick, J. G. and Collamore, P. (1881). *Tile for Illuminating Purposes,* United States of America Patent No. 247996: U. S. P. Office.

Picard, M. A. (1902a). *Exposition Universelle Internationale de 1900 à Paris. Rapport Général Administratif et Technique* (Vol. 2). Paris: Imprimerie Nationale.

Picard, M. A. (1902b). *Exposition Universelle Internationale de 1900 à Paris. Rapport Général Administratif et Technique* (Vol. 3). Paris: Imprimerie Nationale.

Picard, M. A. (1902c). *Exposition Universelle Internationale de 1900 à Paris. Rapport Général Administratif et Technique* (Vol. 1). Paris: Imprimerie Nationale.

Picard, M. A. (1902d). *Exposition Universelle Internationale de 1900 à Paris. Rapport Général Administratif et Technique* (Vol. 9). Paris: Imprimerie Nationale.

Picard, M. A. (1902e). *Exposition Universelle Internationale de 1900 à Paris. Rapport Général Administratif et Technique* (Vol. 7). Paris: Imprimerie Nationale.

Rand McNally and Company. (1893). *The Columbian Exposition Album.* Chicago and New York: Rand, McNally and Company.

Richards, W. C. (ed.). (1853). *A Day in the New York Crystal Place and How to Make the Most of it.* New York: G.P. Putnam and Company.

Routledge, G. (ed.). (1854). *Routledge's Guide to the Crystal Palace and Park at Sydenham: With Descriptions of the Principal Works of Science and Art, and of the Terraces, Fountains, Geological Formations, and Restoration of Extinct Animals, Therein Exhibited.* London: George Routledge and Company.

Sauvage, J. (1900). *Eine Reise nach Paris.* Berlin: R. Gaertners Velagsbuchhandlung.

Saward, J. (2008). The Origins of Mirror and Wooden Panel Mazes. *Caerdroia, 37,* 4–12.

66 *Bruno Taut's design inspiration for the Glashaus*

Shepp, J. W. (1893). *Shepp's World's Fair Photographed.* Chicago and Philadelphia: Globe Bible Publishing Company.

Silliman, B. and Goodrich, C. R. (eds). (1854). *The World of Science, Art, and Industry Illustrated from Examples in The New-York Exhibition, 1853–54.* New York: G.P. Putnam and Company.

Stewart, W. J. (1862, 8 February). Progress of the International Exhibition Building. *The Illustrated London News, 40,* 157.

Strahan, E. (1876). *The Masterpieces of the Centennial International Exhibition* illustrated: fine art (Vol. 1). Philadelphia, PA: Gebbie and Barrie.

Strutt, J. G. and Tallis, J. (eds). (1852). *Tallis's History and Description of the Crystal Palace: And the Exhibition of the World's Industry in 1851.* London and New York: London Printing & Publishing Company.

Taut, B. (1914a). *Glashaus Köln.* (19, A12/4, 25). Historical City Archive, Cologne

Taut, B. (1914b). Glashaus: Werkbund-Ausstellung Köln 1914, Führer zur Eröffnung des Glashaus. Cologne: Werkbund

Taut, B. (1919). Beobachtungen über Farbwirkungen aus meiner Praxis. *Die Bauwelt, 10*(38), 12–13.

The American Commission. (1889). Edison's Display at the Paris Exhibition. In The American Commission to the Paris Universal Exhibition (ed.), *The Paris Universal Exhibition Album, 1889: l'Exposition Universelle de Paris; La Exposicion Universal de Paris.* Washington, DC: The American Commission.

The Chicago Directory Company. (1894). *The Chicago Blue Book of Selected Names of Chicago and Suburban Towns* (Vol. 1895). Chicago, IL.

The Chicago Directory Company. (1896). *The Chicago Blue Book of Selected Names of Chicago and Suburban Towns* (Vol. 1897): The Chicago Directory Company.

Thiekotter, A. (1993). *Kristallisationen, Splitterrungen: Bruno Taut's Glashaus.* Basel: Birkhauser Verlag.

Tissandier, G. (1878). *Le Grand Ballon Captif à Vapeur de M. Henry Giffard: Cour des Tuileries, Paris 1878.* Paris: G. Masson.

Tissandier, G. (1893). En Briques de Verre Souffle. *La Nature: Revue des Sciences et de Leurs Applications aux Arts et a l'Industrie, 21,* 43-44.

Tjaco, W. (2004). Three eras of World Expositions: 1851–present. *Cosmopolite: Stardust World Expo & National Branding Newsletter.*

Truman, B. C., Davis, G. R., Palmer, T. W., Plamer, P., Handy, M. P., Burnham, D. H., Thorpe, J. Bryan, T. B. (1893). *History of the World's Fair: Being a Complete Description of the Columbian Exposition from its Inception* Philadelphia, PA: H. W. Kelley.

Twombly, R. (1987). *Frank Lloyd Wright: His Life and His Architecture.* New York: John Wiley & Sons.

Unknown author. (1893). Attractions for the Moorish Place, *Chicago Daily Tribune.*

Unknown author. (1898). American Luxfer Company. *The Economist, 20,* 199.

Unknown author. (1906). *Sweet's Indexed Catalogue of Building Construction.* New York and Chicago: The Architectural Record Company.

Unknown author. (1910). Die Glasindustrie auf der Brüsseler Weltausstellung. *Diamant: Glas-Industrie-Zeitung, 31,* 834–836.

Unknown author. (1913). Die Inter. Baufachausstellung in Leipzig. *Diamant: Glas-Industrie-Zeitung, 35*(August), 439–444.

Unknown author. (1921). *Obituary Record of Yale Graduates: 1920–1921* (Vol. 22). New Haven, CT: Yale University.

Unknown author. (1940, 8 January). F.L Keppler, Leader in Structural Glass, *The New York Times*.

von Lutzow, C. (ed.). (1975). *Kunst und Kunstgewerbe auf der Wiener Weltausstellung 1873*. Leipzig: E.A. Seemann.

Wailly, G. (1900). *A travers l'Exposition de 1900* (Vol. 7). Paris: Fayard.

Walton, W. (1902). *Exposition Universelle, 1900: The chefs-d'uvre* (Vol. 10). Philadelphia: George Barrie and Son.

White, W. (1854). *The Illustrated Handbook of the Royal Panopticon of Science and Art: An Institution for Scientific Exhibitions, and for Promoting Discoveries in Arts and Manufactures*. London: John Hotson.

Winslow, W. H. (1897). *Method of Electrolically Uniting Glass Tiles*, United States of America Patent No. 574843: U.S.P. Office.

www.expo2000.de. Experience Expo2000: The History of the World Expositions. Retrieved 9 May, 2013, from www.site.expo2000.de/expo2000/geschichte/index.php

www.glassian.org. Glassian. Retrieved 24 April, 2013, from http://glassian.org/index.html

www.luxfercylinders.com. Luxfer: A History. Retrieved 1 May, 2013, from www.luxfercylinders.com/about-luxfer

www.nbmog.org. The Centennial Fountain. Retrieved 20 May, 2013, from www.nbmog.org/CentFountainPage.html

www.sydenham.org.uk. (2006). What is the history behind the name 'Jews Walk'. Retrieved 30 September, 2013, from http://sydenham.org.uk/forum/viewtopic.php?t=432&postdays=0&postorder=asc&start=0

3 *Victoria regia's* bequest to the *Glashaus*

3.1 Introduction

Starting with a discussion of horticultural glasshouses, this chapter then exposes the unique glasshouses which evolved for the cultivation of the *Victoria regia* lily. Contrary to popular understanding, it will then be established that Taut was aware of the *Victoria regia*, its botanical habits and the distinctive glasshouses that were constructed for its cultivation. This knowledge was then employed by Taut to serve as design inspiration in the *Glashaus*. Opposing its accepted Expressionist origins, the result is an understanding of the *Glashaus* that is firmly rooted in botanic precedent.

3.2 Taut, the Crystal Palace and the *Victoria regia* lily

In his dissertation *Seeing Through Glass: The Fictive Role of Glass in Shaping Architecture from Joseph Paxton's Crystal Palace to Bruno Taut's Glashaus*, Ufuk Ersoy argued, like Banham (1959) before him, that the history of glazed architecture needs to be reconsidered because it is primarily understood from a 'historicist perspective' (Ersoy, 2008: 8). Stemming from Alan Colquhoun (1983) the 'historicist perspective' argued that simply documenting the history of architecture according to a limited contextual understanding of objects was insufficient. Instead, Colquhoun proposed a method of history aware of preceding cultures and practices as well as how these transform both the context and the object. Instead, Ersoy followed Banham's lead and quoted some 'respectable' literary sources from which the *Glashaus* had either been totally omitted or relegated to obscurity. These sources are Arthur Korn's 1929 *Glas im Bau und als Gebrauchsgegenstand (Glass in Construction and as a Commodity)* and Konrad Werner Schulze's 1929 *Glas in der Architektur der Gegenwart (Glass in Contemporary Architecture)*. Ersoy (2008) thus concurred with Banham's (1959) arguments by investigating what fictive metaphors could be attached to both Joseph Paxton's Crystal Palace and Taut's *Glashaus*. He stated that, for Paxton, it was the fictive metaphor of the table and the tablecloth, while for Taut, it was the surface and the crystal. According to Ersoy (2008), there were numerous similarities between the Crystal Palace and the *Glashaus*: both were exhibition pavilions (Crystal Palace was constructed for the Great Exhibition of 1851 in Hyde Park, London); both served the interests of the glass industries of the day; and both were designed as temporary structures. Yet, there were also differences. The main one was that, while the Crystal Palace rose to unimaginable heights of cultural and architectural recognition, the *Glashaus* remained relatively obscure (Ersoy, 2008: 25).

Ersoy (2008) argued that the Crystal Palace's 'atmospheric effect', which was the result of its glass cladding, was what attracted Taut to it (Taut, 1921: 36). For Taut (1921), glazed cladding was thus to be used as a light filter that effectively dissolved the wall with light. In his 1921 article, 'Das Bauen mit Glas' ('Building with Glass'), Taut argued that the iron and steel train stations, factories, and exhibition-hall structures of the 19th century challenged both the fundamental and traditional definition of rooms (space surrounded by solid walls), which were based on the laws of gravity. For Taut, iron and steel construction reinvigorated the Gothic way of enclosing space. Once again, glass was used as the enclosing element. He noticed that the 19th century structures, while very appealing in their atmospheric effect from a distance, were less appealing at close range. The iron skeleton was thus a massive improvement as a means of enclosing space. However, the main problem was the glass or sheet panels that in-filled the spaces between the iron structural elements. Taut proposed that architects should rather treat the glass cladding as expressive of the materials' '...outstanding conditionality...', thereby expressing more sensitivity to the world outside through its dealing with light and air (Taut, 1921: 37).

Taut may have been introduced to the Crystal Palace via Hermann Muthesius' 1902 work, *Stilarchitektur und Baukunst*. Muthesius was the German cultural attaché to London and spent several years there observing the results of English industrialisation. Muthesius is credited with shaping both the theoretical framework for and being the founding figure of the German *Werkbund*, which he achieved primarily through two seminal works –*Stilarchitektur und Baukunst* (Style-architecture and Building-art, 1902) and his subsequent 1904 three-volume work *Das Englishe Haus (The English House)* (Maciuika, 2005). Taut, through his involvements with the *Werkbund*, must have known of Muthesius and his publications.

In a discussion on the formative origins of the Crystal Palace, Ersoy (2008) discussed Joseph Paxton's earlier horticultural experiences with the cultivation of the *Victoria regia* lily. Furthermore, Ersoy (2008) argued that this lily was the initial impetus for Paxton's subsequent buildings. Interestingly, Taut in his 1920 work 'Die Galoschen des Glucks' ('The Lucky Shoes') specifically mentioned the *Victoria regia*, while his 'Die Grosse Blume' ('The Big Flower') image, which appeared in his 1920 work *Die Auflösung der Städte* also looked remarkably similar to the leaf of the *Victoria regia*. A closer examination of 'Die Galoschen des Glucks' reveals remarkable affinities between Taut's thinking, the *Glashaus* and the *Victoria regia*.

Figure 3.1a A period illustration depicting the flower of the *Victoria regia* lily.

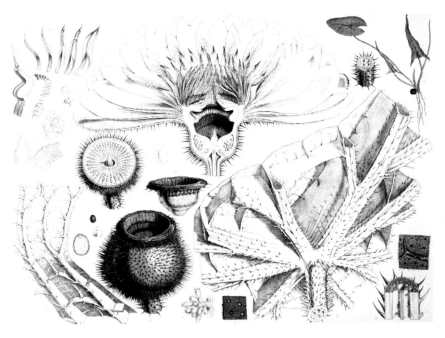

Figure 3.1b A period illustration showing the anatomy of the *Victoria regia* lily.

3.3 Bruno Taut and 'Die Galoschen des Glucks'

Translated into English by Iain Boyd Whyte (1985), 'Die Galoschen des Glucks' formed part of a set of correspondences, called the Crystal Chain Letters, between Taut and a select group of his peers. This correspondence took place in the period during and immediately after World War One, a time when German architects were forced to pursue other interests, such as writing, instead of building, owing to the poor economic situation. Dennis Sharp (1966) referred to the Crystal Chain Letters as having been the most important exchange of theoretical architectural ideas of the 20th century.

Taut began 'Die Galoschen des Glucks' by emphatically stating that its intention was to show, in a tangible manner, the ideas that inspired the group. Taut continued by stating that he had included parts in the script reflective of the particular thinking of other members of the group: 'metamorphosis' for Herman Finsterlin; a 'radiant cathedral' for Carl Kram; and a 'flame building' for Wilhelm Bruckmann (Whyte and Taut, 1985).

The script proper started with the description of a desolate unemployed youth accompanied by a 'hollow-cheeked girl' in the context of a blighted urban industrial landscape. In an attempt to escape this environment, the youth decided to relocate to the countryside. On his arduous journey out of the city, along an endless desolate highway, the youth encountered the 'Shoes of Fortune', which had been left on the road-side by the 'Child of Fortune'. After the youth tried these shoes on, everything changed; his current clothes, which were mere rags, became splendid garments, and the road once desolate and blighted was lined with trees that were bathed in bright sunshine and fresh air. Reinvigorated, the youth continued along the transformed highway and entered a wooded area, in which he discovered a clearing. Located at the edge of this clearing, surrounded by glittering, sparkling trees, was a gleaming building. This building appeared to be both man-made and the product of nature – like trees, springs, and all creation that grew. Standing in front of the building, the youth clapped his hands in amazement. The house opened and a man stepped out to greet him. The man was described as bearded, handsome and dressed in a similar manner as the youth. The man then invited the youth into the building that was occupied by family, hospitality and purity, and decorated with flowering growths of stone and glass. The man then led the youth upward into a room of glass, where he pointed outward to the glittering woods. When the man's wife entered the room, her features reminded the youth of a previous association, and the youth then started to cry. In an attempt to console the youth, the man then led him into a wondrous chamber that contained '...many strange growths, great floating leaves (like *Victoria regia*) and many others' (Whyte and Taut, 1985: 120). The man then took a peculiar rod and stimulated the growths with its point,

> ...and out of the leaves grew houses... as sparkling and dreamlike as his own, like opalescent domes, butterfly-wing buildings – oh, inexpressible

72 Bruno Taut's design inspiration for the Glashaus

– a fairy-tale city reflected in the water, ravishingly beautiful.

(Whyte and Taut, 1985: 120)

Overpowered, the youth then lost consciousness and later awoke, once again on the initial bleak, desolate highway.

Before continuing further with this script, it would be appropriate to offer some interpretation and contextualisation. The youth could represent Taut. In an attempt to mediate or mitigate the worst effects of industrialisation, Taut, through his actual interests in urban planning issues and particularly his involvement with the German Garden City Movement, sought the reintroduction of 'nature' into cities. The journey out of the city could be argued as synonymous with this quest. The script started in an industrial, rapidly urbanising city, which is undoubtedly German and possibly Berlin. The script makes particular mention of a blighted urban environment and that it contained *Mietskasernen,* which were the dreary and crowded tenement houses common to German cities of the time. The *Mietskasernen* can thus be proposed as the metaphor for the polluted, overcrowded industrial city. The 'Shoes of Fortune' and the 'Child of Fortune' thus envisage a better future for mankind in the industrial German city. Alternatively, they could be representative of the knowledge or ideas being proposed by Taut and his peers to achieve the transformation of the German industrial city. The discovery of the growing house in the woods could be indicative of many things but is undoubtedly connected to Taut's conception of his new glass architecture, as embodied in his earlier *Glashaus.* For Taut, in conjunction with Garden City ideas, the architectural elements that represented the reintroduction of 'nature' into the industrial city could be botanical glasshouses, or even the glazed public Winter Gardens and *Floras.* This last aspect will become more apparent as this chapter progresses.

In *Glasarchitektur* (1914), Scheerbart made particular mention of the glasshouses at the Royal Botanical Gardens in the Berlin suburb of Dahlem. Scheerbart was also apparently instrumental in introducing Taut to horticultural glasshouses. As such, the man in the story who greeted the youth could be proposed as representing Scheerbart. By guiding the youth through the growing house, Scheerbart thus 'introduces' Taut to glasshouses. The sparkling and flashing woods that surrounded the growing house are likely connected with Taut's earlier exposures of opinions concerning the 'atmospheric effect'. The argument that the growing house is Taut's own new glass architecture, as personified in his *Glashaus,* is further reinforced by the description of the growing house that the youth enters. It referred to the youth and man that entered a 'room of glass'; this is distinctly similar to the *Glashaus* where the visitor entered and then proceeded upward, via the semi-circular staircases to the Cupola Room. Once in the room, the man pointed outward to the 'glittering treetops' – this is once again distinctly similar to the 'atmospheric effect' created for the visitor by the Cupola Room's glazed skin of coloured glass and Luxfer prism tiles. Alternatively, it could also be the experience of the route of the upward staircase, lined with clear glass bricks, once again creating the desired 'atmospheric effect'. It could thus be argued that the sparkling, glittering or gleaming trees, bushes, and nature in general were metaphors for Taut's desired 'atmospheric effect'.

The building or 'apartment' that they then entered, with its hospitality, family and 'blossoming growths of stone and glass', could be presented as a Gothic Cathedral. On 28 January 1920, Taut wrote a short note to the Crystal Chain group:

> Tonight I went up the tower of the Strasbourg Minster, through all kinds of scenery, cried with delight, and came to a wood, where houses grew on the trees instead of leaves.
>
> (Whyte and Taut, 1985: 46)

However, in the German version of the same book, the event is translated very differently. Taut did not climb the tower, rather he is said to have travelled towards the tower of Strasbourg Cathedral:

> Diese Nacht fuhr ich auf dem Turm vom Strassburger Muenster…
>
> (Whyte and Schneider, 1986: 47)

This later translation i.e. Taut having travelled towards the cathedral tower is, according to Manfred Speidel, correct. (Personal e-mail communication with Speidel, 2015).

Strasbourg Cathedral has an 'openwork' spire above its north-western corner. 'Openwork' is a technical term that refers to the spire structure having no infill or cladding material. Both Taut's (1985) letter and the openwork spire of Strasbourg Cathedral sound distinctly similar to both the growing house in the clearing in the forest and also the *Glashaus'* rhomboid reinforced concrete dome structure.

Based on Taut's (1920b) reference to the *Victoria regia* lily, the second room into which the man led the youth, in an attempt to console him, is in all probability a metaphor for a type of glasshouse intended for aquatic plants. Interestingly, after Paxton cultivated the *Victoria regia* in Britain for the first time in 1849, he built the lily a dedicated glasshouse the following year. Paxton's *Victoria regia* house was basically a regular cube of glazing that was raised above a low stone plinth. Its interior had a large circular pool that was located at the centre of the plan for the lily (Chadwick, 1961). With the subsequent spread of *Victoria regia* cultivation to continental Europe, further unique glasshouses were developed that differed from Paxton's prototype by having a circular or regular polygonal plan with a flattish glazed dome (Kohlmaier and von Sartory, 1986). These European examples of *Victoria regia* glasshouses were, however, similar to Paxton's prototype in that they had a central pool and low stone or masonry plinth. A comparison between these continental European *Victoria regia*

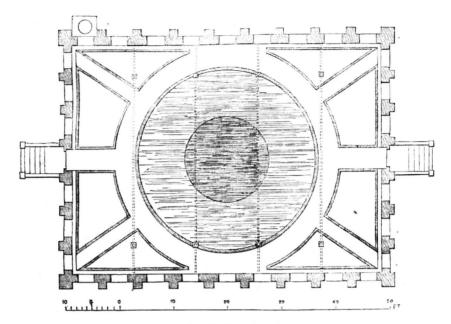

Figure 1.—Ground Plan.

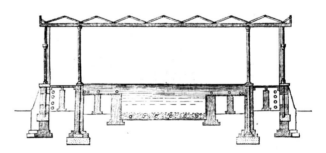

Figure 2.—Transverse Section.

Figure 3 —End Elevation.

Figure 3.2 Joseph Paxton's 1850 *Victoria regia* glasshouse at Chatsworth House, Derbyshire, England.

glasshouses and Taut's *Glashaus* reveals immediate similarities in both planning and appearance.

The connection between 'Die Galoschen des Glucks' and the *Glashaus* is further strengthened by what Taut (1920b) wrote in the script regarding the man agitating leaves with a peculiar rod. The rod in the script could be directly synonymous with the central light feature that was present in the *Glashaus'* Cupola Room. Furthermore, the agitated leaves could be the central *oculus*, or pool, that connected the lower Cascade Room to the Copula Room above. However, this sequence could also have been a direct reference to the inspiration that Paxton derived from the *Victoria regia's* leaf for the design of his 1850 glasshouse. In an article published in the *Illustrated London News*, Paxton (1850) admitted that the origin of the Crystal Palace derived from his gardening experiences, particularly from the glasshouse that he built for the *Victoria regia*. He even went so far as to concede:

> ...to this plant and to this circumstance that the Crystal Palace owes its direct origin.
>
> (Fay, 1951: 11)

Taut's statements in the script directly referring to the *Victoria regia* suggest it may have been an important source of inspiration for the *Glashaus*:

> ... and out of the leaves grow houses ... as sparkling and dreamlike as his own, like opalescent domes, butterfly-wing buildings – oh, inexpressible – a fairy-tale city reflected in the water, ravishingly beautiful.
>
> (Whyte and Taut, 1985: 120)

The 'fairy-tale city reflected in the water' could well be Taut's 'Die Grosse Blume' illustration as it appeared in *Die Auflösung der Städte*. The script abruptly concluded this portion by leaving the youth once again on the bleak, desolate highway. This passage seems to suggest the period in Taut's life after both the *Glashaus* and the outbreak of World War One.

Taut's 'Die Galoschen des Glucks' script continued with the youth once again waking up on the desolate highway. Running after the youth was the 'hollow-cheeked girl', who is approached by the 'Child of Fortune' and offered various 'Shoes of Fortune'. The girl tried on a pair of shoes that were different from the youth's, and once again the desolate highway and the girl were transformed; the context changed to a summer night with blossoming bushes next to the road. The sky was likewise filled with meteors and twinkling stars, with the girl, in light clothing, barefoot and with loose flowing hair, running happily along the road. The girl was then joined by numerous other 'happy people' and they proceeded toward a 'city of flames'. In the 'city of flames', all the buildings appeared to be glowing, with some being incandescent, and it was impossible to tell if the buildings were actually built from flames. The group of 'happy people' then entered an incandescent

76   Bruno Taut's design inspiration for the Glashaus

house, and a lively display of sparks and fire, a cascade of water and a 'fire-bathing party' ensued. Gradually, the bright fiery display diminished until there was only a faint sparkle left. The girl then finally sank to the floor, but she could not sleep. The girl then looked at the faint sparkle playing high up in the room, and saw the face of her 'loved one'. Distraught and emotional, the girl then started to weep and was comforted back to sleep by the 'Child of Fortune', who then left a pair of luck shoes that were the same as the youth's. When the girl awoke in the morning, she was amazed to find herself in a 'sparkling, dew-fresh' garden in front of the house that the youth initially entered. The house opened and a woman and child emerged, followed later by the youth and the bearded man. The youth and girl were in a state of bliss, staring at the house in amazement before continuing their journey.

It would appear as if this portion of the script was included for Wilhelm Bruckmann, but was also overlaid with some thoughts of Taut's *Glashaus*, in the form of the 'incandescent house', 'cascade of water', and the 'fiery sparkle high up in the room'. Furthermore, the perspective is not that of Taut in the character of the youth, but from another unidentified personality in the form of the 'hollow-cheeked girl'.

The script continued with the youth and girl approaching a high plateau, with buildings being seen in the distance. These shining 'crystalline' buildings, seen from a distance, were scattered enchantingly, and sparkled delightfully, in the landscape. The youth and girl were drawn towards the buildings and, suddenly, a landing airship appeared. The youth and girl boarded the airship and they soared above the earth. While on the airship, the couple experienced a 'radiant vision' that comprised a view of all of the crystalline buildings from a perspective that was below the clouds, both near and far. These experiences of crystalline buildings in the landscape are apparently illustrated in *Die Auflösung der Städte*.

The couple then landed and joined a ceremonial procession, which then turned off a road and led toward a 'radiant cathedral'. Stopping at the doorway of the cathedral, the couple were overpowered by a 'display of ecstasy'. An older gentleman, apparently a priest, approached the couple and led them into the cathedral's library. Inside, the youth took down a book that detailed men not waging war, but 'building in the Alps'; the girl also took a book, but hers detailed nothing but misery, which included the trenches of World War One and the *Mietskasernen*. Finally, the couple saw their own families in a wretched slum, with appalling living conditions, and they started to cry inconsolably. Departing from the 'radiant cathedral', the couple then saw a distorted disturbing image of the cathedral being overpowered by a vision of the *Mietskasernen*. Fleeing these disturbing and 'exotic' surroundings, the couple then ran through a wood and arrived, exhausted, at a 'deeply set spring under a dark roof of trees'. Here they drank, and fell asleep on moss as evening faded to night.

It would appear that this portion of 'Die Galoschen des Glucks' was written for Carl Kram (and Taut himself stated that the 'radiant cathedral' was intended for Kram). It could also be proposed that some of Taut's ideas are clearly evident. The images of men 'rebuilding the Alps' and those from the airship are likely to be the same images found in Taut's *Alpine Architektur* of 1919. The idea of the cathedral being the central nodal focus of European medieval cities, which was then 'overpowered' by the sprawling *Mietskasernen* of the modern industrial city, is distinctly reminiscent of Taut's *Die Stadtkrone* also of 1919, in which Taut argued that this lack of a central focal feature in the industrial city was like a 'torso without a head'. Furthermore, it is also highly likely that this section of the script was a reiteration of the first section: in both instances, the youth and the girl fled the worst excesses of the German industrial city, as personified in the *Mietskasernen*. Likewise, in both cases, they fled through a forest and ultimately arrived at a location that was the *Glashaus*. In the first instance, they arrived in the glazed upper portions of the *Glashaus*, while in this instance, they arrived in the Cascade Room with its kaleidoscope. As stated above, the kaleidoscope room or passage of the *Glashaus* was also clad in violet-coloured velvet. This velvet could be comparable to the moss upon which the couple fell asleep. The spring that they drank from could be the waterfall that was located in the Cascade Room. The 'dark roof of trees' that covered both the sleeping couple and the spring, could have been the Cascade Room that was mostly clad with glazed tiles. However, the argument that best supports the contention that this portion of the script relates to a description of the *Glashaus'* Cascade Room is given by Taut himself in his publication *Die Weltbaumeister* (*The Global Master Builder*, or, *Global Architect*). On Plate 17 of Die *Weltbaumeister*, Taut wrote: 'The empty space is purple – green leaf shapes and flowers float from the top and down the sides' (Taut, 1920a: 17). Thiekotter (1993), in turn, linked this sentence to the *Glashaus'* Cascade Room, specifically to a Jan Mutzenbecher glass panel that was located in the glazed, semi-circular wall at the top of the Cascade Room.

The script of 'Die Galoschen des Glucks' continues: darkness then enveloped the sleeping youth and girl. All of a sudden, glow-worms appeared and when viewed from above, these were '…illuminated glass domes. One unfolds and turns into an architectural flower, with a moving light at its base. We seem to fly inside. At the bottom of the flower, the shoe library of the Child of Fortune' (Whyte and Taut, 1985: 122). The Child of Fortune was surrounded by compartments that were box-like, with each containing a specific pair of shoes of fortune. Located on a glass table in the middle of this shoe room were the shoes that the couple had worn. These shoes were then placed in a container. The Child of Fortune took from a container two pairs of wooden clogs, which were apparently from a bygone age. With these clogs in hand, the Child of Fortune flew out of his 'blossoming house' and placed the clogs beside the sleeping couple in the 'grotto'. When the couple awoke, they were overjoyed to see the clogs. Having tried the clogs on, the couple were then transformed into 'young country-folk', 'returning from the fields.' The couple then returned to a farmhouse that was bright

78 Bruno Taut's design inspiration for the Glashaus

and new, quite unlike the boorish, stuffy farm of the past. Parents and children greeted each other and the setting sun shone through the farmstead window, reminding the couple of the many strange things that they had experienced. A 'happy meal' then ensued in a garden under the leaf cloak of a tree.

3.4 Bruno Taut and the *Victoria regia* lily

In the last portion of 'Die Galoschen des Glucks' there is another uncanny connection to the *Victoria regia* lily. Along with certain other members of the families *Nymphaeaceae* and *Araceae*, *Victoria regia* (today called *Victoria amazonica)* is pollinated by a specific genus of *Cyclocephala* scarab beetle. Both the *Cyclocephala* beetles and Neotropical *Nymphaeaceae* have thus co-evolved. Currently, there are four known species of *Cyclocephala* involved in the pollination of Neotropical *Nymphaeaceae* (Prance, 1980). While this fact in isolation might be nothing more than interesting, the term glow-worm as referenced by Taut '...is used in connection with the flightless females of *lampyrid* fireflies...' (Meyer-Rochow, 2007: 251). Considering that Taut in all probability wrote his script in a European context, it could be that he is referencing a European species of glow-worm. The common European glow-worm, or *Lampyris noctiluca*, has an extensive distribution, ranging from Portugal to China (Tyler, 1986), and, according to Day (2005) this distribution probably makes it the most studied of all the *Lampyridae*. Thus, could Taut have been referencing the *Lampyris noctiluca*, which belong to the order *Coleoptera*, and are actually classified as beetles and not 'worms'? This confusion with 'worm' might arise since certain adult female *Lampyridae* resemble worms in appearance but are in fact flightless adult laviform females, which have the same appearance as larvae but with compound eyes. According to Sala-Newby *et al.* (1996), the colours emitted from luminous beetles range through green, yellow, orange and red. However, *Lampyris noctiluca* emits a light that is apparently green during all stages of its life. As previously mentioned the colours of the *Glashaus'* dome began at the base in deep blue and progressed upward through moss-green, then golden yellow and eventually culminated at the apex in brilliant creamy white. Apart from the blue, these colours are not that dissimilar to those emitted by the so-called 'luminous' beetles. This poses the question: did Taut's choice of colours for the *Glashaus'* dome derive from the colours emitted by these beetles? Taut (1920b) stated that his glow-worms seen from above are 'glass domes', which, when unfurled, became an 'architectural flower'. Thiekotter (1993) argued that in bad weather, the reflecting glazed facets of the *Glashaus'* dome assumed a greenish-yellow colour, which resulted in the visiting public naming the building 'Asparagus-head'. Alternatively, when approached from a distance, the *Glashaus* supposedly looked like a sprouting seed or a flower bud that was about to bloom. Thus, the association of the *Glashaus* with botanical metaphors is not an entirely unique concept. However, this does not answer the question as to why Taut would refer to an 'architectural flower' as opposed to just mentioning it as a 'flower'.

In 1849, the English botanist Robert Spruce described the underside of the leaf of *Victoria regia* as suggestive of some

> ...strange fabric of cast iron, just taken from the furnace, – its ruddy colour, and the enormous ribs with which it is strengthened increasing the similarity.
>
> (Allen, 1854: 6)

According to another description, when a new leaf of the *Victoria regia* first broke the surface of the water, it was initially an inverted red-brown mass covered in spines that slowly unfurled to reveal an upper smooth green surface, with a prominent upturned rim. The red-brown or deep purple underside of the leaf consisted of a prominent lattice or structure of air-filled members. Eight primary members radiated from a central stem point, which then subdivided into numerous smaller radial members. Perpendicular to these main radial members were concentrically arranged struts that divided the lower surface of the leaf into quadrangular chambers. Covering all these structural members were prominent spines (Moore and Ayres, 1850). Taking this description into account, as well as Taut's (1921) views on the iron skeletal structures of 19th century Europe, and Joseph Paxton's connection to the *Victoria regia*, it becomes probable that Taut's 'architectural flower' had a direct link with *Victoria regia*. The contrast between the highly textured red-brown or deep purple undersides of the leaf with the smooth green upper surface is also highly indicative of the *Glashaus*' purple-velvet-lined kaleidoscope enclosure and glazed Dome Room, which included moss green.

What is remarkable about *Victoria regia* is the species' sheer size, rapid growth patterns and intriguing pollination habits. The first European to discover *Victoria regia*, Thaddäus Haeneke, is said to have fallen to his knees in admiration at the first sight of *Victoria regia* in flower. French naturalist Alcide d'Orbigny described the *Victoria regia* as having been, without a shadow of doubt, the most exquisite plant ever known to Europeans because of its overall composition of leaves, flowers, size, colour and elegant location in the water. This sentiment was later also shared by Robert Schomburgk, when he, in 1842, encountered the *Victoria regia* in South America. Schomburgk described *Victoria regia* as having been one of the grandest productions of the botanic kingdom, owing to the superior magnificence of it leaves and the splendour of its flowers with their associated fragrance (Allen, 1854). Another description stated that when the flower of *Victoria regia* first broke the surface of the water, it was initially as a pear-shaped bud furnished with a dark brown, protective cover. This bud, like the underside of the leaf, was also covered by protective spines. When the bud bloomed, it was initially a brilliant white colour. Since the flowering of *Victoria regia* is nocturnal, the flowers were described as having first opened at about five

80 Bruno Taut's design inspiration for the Glashaus

o'clock in the evening, and having been approximately 25 to 38 centimetres in diameter when fully unfurled (Moore and Ayres, 1850). Furthermore, the flower was described as having been strongly pineapple scented, and, as the *Victoria regia* bloomed, the flower raised its internal temperature through a thermo-chemical reaction (Schrader, 2008). This pineapple scent then attracted the scarab beetles that pollinated the flower. The flower was recorded as having closed on the morning of the second day. By closing, the flower is said to have captured numerous beetles that were still actively pollinating it. On the second evening, the flower once again opened and subsequently released the captive beetles. The flower was transformed from its initial brilliant white into a pinkish, rose colour. At about 11 o'clock on the second night, the flower then closed permanently and sank below the surface of the water to develop its seeds (Moore and Ayres, 1850).

What is most interesting when comparing the flower of the *Victoria regia* and 'Die Galoschen des Glucks' are the references to 'flying inside' and then 'the bottom of the 'architectural flower'. A comparison between a cross-section of the *Glashaus* and the *Victoria regia* flower reveals numerous similarities: they both have distinct brighter upper and darker lower portions; the upper portion, or Cupola/Dome Room, of the *Glashaus* can be compared to the petals of the *Victoria regia* flower, while the lower Cascade Room of the *Glashaus* can be compared to the lower ovary area of the *Victoria regia*.

From the discussion presented above it would be reasonable to deduce that the *Victoria regia* specifically and horticultural glasshouses generally, were a significant source of inspiration for the *Glashaus*. These therefore warrant further investigation.

3.5 Horticultural glasshouses: An overview

As an artefact of the 19th century, the glasshouse personified and embellished humanity's desire to dominate and control nature. Contained within an iron frame and glazed skin, these artificial environments made possible the cultivation, study and exploitation of exotic and fascinating flora – sometimes even fauna – from all over the globe. Within them, people could exercise scientific control over natural processes. Put alternatively, the historical evolution of glasshouse was driven by a desire to nurture and protect exotic plants in a controlled environment (Hix, 2005).

Glasshouses always carried complex connotations. Many feared that rapid industrialisation and the colonial practices of European nations were leading to the destruction of nature. Glasshouses were thus seen as sanctuaries for preserving nature, and fulfilled a role not unlike the museum. This was particularly evident in rapidly developing urban centres. Furthermore, because of the enormous expense required in their operation and maintenance, glasshouses were also seen as objects of social prestige. The possession of a glasshouse, like the ownership of a fine art collection, embodied gentlemanly refinement, sophistication, desire, culture and wealth. As such, the glasshouse and its contents could also be regarded as a work of art because of its skilful execution. Initially the enjoyment of nature-as-a-form-of-art was the sole preserve of the aristocracy and the upper middle classes. With the progression of the industrial revolution and the eventual separation of work and leisure, the urban enjoyment of nature soon became a reality for the working classes. Nothing could have contrasted more with the quiet contemplation and study of the tranquil private glasshouse than the public winter gardens, in which masses of paying patrons flitted through the vegetation in search of amusement.

As a distinct building type, the glasshouse as it is known today, did not come into existence until the second half of the 19th century (Hix, 2005; Kohlmaier and von Sartory, 1986; Koppelkamm, 1981). Much confusion exists around the actual names applied to 'glasshouses'. Koppelkamm (1981) explained the function of the 'glasshouse' comprised either an orangery, greenhouse, conservatory or a winter garden.

Inspired by similar structures from 200 years previous, the first horticultural building, the orangery, was a plant house of the 18th century that housed citrus, pomegranates, myrtles, etc. during the cold winter months. The most important function of the orangery was to keep the interior temperature of the room above freezing. Generally, the orangery was constructed of brick or stone, had a solid roof and large, south-facing windows. Orangeries were often located within the precinct of castles and had an architectural style that was similar to the surrounding structures. Koppelkamm (1981) also distinguishes other structures that formed a transitional typology between the initial orangery and the later large plant house of glass and iron. These were described as having a similar outward appearance and plan as the orangery, but had glazed roofs, with a central dome rather than a flat roof, over the central portion of the building. These plant houses of iron and glass first appeared in the first half of the 19th century.

According to Koppelkamm (1981), a 'greenhouse' is apparently also known as a plant or forcing house. The function of the greenhouse was to cultivate both decorative and useful plants. These simple structures were generally purpose built and had a back wall that faced north with an attached sloping glass roof, which faced south. In cross-section, these structures were relatively narrow, while they were additionally elongated in plan. In greenhouses, plants were grown in pots, arranged on pedestals that rose like steps, and that sloped rearward towards the wall. By contrast, Koppelkamm (1981) argued, in the glasshouse or conservatory, plants did not grow in pots, but were rather placed in the ground in beds.

The name 'glasshouse' or 'conservatory' was generally applicable to structures that were used for scientific purposes and/or for the collecting of plants. These buildings were generally tall in cross-section due to the fact that they contained exotic botanic species that reached generous heights, such as bamboo, tree ferns and palms. Plants of a particular species were usually grouped together, with the higher central portion generally being used for tall species, mostly palms. Most glasshouses had a rectangular plan, similar to that of the orangery, and were constructed out of glass and iron. Unsurprisingly, in glasshouses, the glazing comprised the majority cladding material on all of the elevations (Koppelkamm, 1981).

Koppelkamm (1981) referred to 'winter gardens' or conservatories as having been not so much a type, but rather a function. This type of structure encompassed orangeries, transitional structures, glasshouses and conservatories. These buildings could be both private and public. Described as having been 'ornamental and show buildings', they were proposed as mainly having been used to add to the living spaces of residences. Possibly the most significant aspect of the winter garden was the climate; it was maintained not for the welfare of the plants, but rather for the comfort of humans (Koppelkamm, 1981).

3.6 The orangery

The orangery evolved because of the fondness the European nobility and wealthy bourgeoisie had for cultivating citrus and, much later, palms. Limes, lemons, and particularly oranges, with their beautifully fragrant fruit and flowers, fascinated the aristocracy (Hix, 2005). Koppelkamm (1981) argued that the Italian nobility were the first to be fascinated with oranges, and from there, the vogue spread to the rest of Europe. Initially, individual citrus trees were planted in the ground and covered, during cooler periods of the year, with movable sheds that were made from timber boards. Kohlmaier (1986) stated that this method had been used in Germany since the middle of the 16th century, while in Italy, north of Naples, it had been in use since the renaissance (Hix, 2005). As a logical progression, whole groves of citrus trees were soon being covered by a larger, portable wooden orangery. It was at the courts of Stuttgart, Munich and Heidelberg that temporary buildings were first erected (Koppelkamm, 1981). In 1609, a portable fig house was constructed at Stuttgart, while a mobile orange house on rollers was later also constructed in 1626 (Koppelkamm, 1981). An example of such a building was the 280-foot-long structure for the Elector Palatine at Heidelberg, Germany (Hix, 2005). Owing to the success of this wooden structure, the designer Salomon de Caus soon afterwards suggested that a better orangery would include permanent stone walls and only needed a roof and closed windows during winter (Hix, 2005). Hix (2005) argued that this was an early example of the European orangeries-cum-banqueting halls that were enjoyed by the aristocracy during the 17th to 19th centuries. As Kohlmaier (1986) has argued, the cost and time expenditure were significant with the portable wooden system. Koppelkamm (1981), likewise, argued that the disadvantage of these buildings was bad insulation and the need to seal all of the joints every time the structure was reassembled. This meant that citrus trees were soon surrounded by three permanent walls and only the south wall and roof were removable. However, these structures proved unsatisfactory, mainly due to the inability to sufficiently control heating during the cooler periods of the year.

Hix (2005) stated that in parallel with the temporary shed arrangement, a further method of placing citrus trees in pots and moving them into caves or stone buildings during winter was also developed. Koppelkamm (1981) proposed that initially existing structures like garden rooms, grottos or open verandas were used – a method said to have been in use as early as 1555 in France (Hix, 2005). By the 17th century, two methods of preserving plants during the colder months of the year developed; namely, moving potted trees indoors, or surrounding those planted in the ground with temporary sheds. Owing to the technical difficulties of the movable shed enclosure, the 'permanent orangery' soon developed. Technical difficulties were not the only aspect leading to the development of permanent orangeries; aesthetic factors were also of concern (Koppelkamm, 1981). If the unpretentious and purely functional temporary orangeries were to be integrated into the overall aesthetic of a castle, only a building of stone or masonry would suffice. Kohlmaier (1986) described the permanent orangery as elongated masonry buildings, with the south elevation being made of glass panes. The interiors of these buildings were fitted with iron stoves for heating, and care was taken in the construction of the walls and roofs to insulate against heat loss. The permanent orangery reached its peak of development during the period 1700 to 1730. Importantly, the permanent orangery was a versatile ornamental building, adaptable for other uses and functions, such as holding receptions and banquets (Koppelkamm, 1981).

3.7 The glasshouse

Around 1700, in parallel with the masonry walled, permanent orangery, the glasshouse or glazed greenhouse came into prominence (Hix, 2005; Kohlmaier and von Sartory, 1986; Koppelkamm, 1981). What differentiated a glasshouse from an orangery was the fact that, from the start, the glasshouse was purpose built for horticultural endeavour. It was not subject to the demands of any prevailing architectural style (Hix, 2005; Kohlmaier and von Sartory, 1986). Hix (2005) stated that early examples of glasshouses were the European 'forcing frame' or 'Dutch-stove' constructions that were most prevalent in Holland. He further argued that if Holland was the general location of early glasshouse development, its epicentre was located at Leiden University.

Under the directorship of Herman Boerhaave during 1709 to 1730, Leiden became one of the finest horticultural locations in the world, and was termed '... an environmental machine for nurturing and producing plants' (Hix, 2005: 20). By 1720, with improvements in glass availability and manufacturing, the most innovative glasshouses had glazing on the entire south-facing elevation and the roof (Hix, 2005). Kohlmaier (1986) stated that while these glasshouses had solid walls to the sides and rear, both the south wall and the

84 *Bruno Taut's design inspiration for the Glashaus*

lean-to, or ridged roofs, were glazed. Hix (2005) describes the early sloped-fronted, forcing frames as having been optimised to the often unpredictable, wet and cold weather of Holland. Hix (2005) further described these structures as having had massive masonry back walls and floors that provided a large store of thermal mass. Heated by sunlight during the day, this thermal mass then subsequently released warmth during the night. A continuous heat and smoke flue was additionally located in the back wall. The south-facing elevation contained a series of hinged panels that allowed plants to be moved in and out of the structure. In summer, the windows were opened to maximise sun penetration and ventilation. In winter, they were sealed to prevent draughts and only opened on warmer days. In some cases, these windows were opened by a top-hung frame that was operated through a system of pulleys and ropes. Additionally, these windows also had an early form of double-glazing, through the application of a film of oiled paper to the inside pane, with further canvas curtains that supplied additional insulation. The provision of adjustable wooden planks, parallel to the side walls, allowed for protection from prevailing winds (Hix, 2005). After 1750, once the technical basics were established, glasshouses spread to the rest of Europe, but it was not until efficient heating was achieved, that the complete glazing of the glasshouse could be realized (Kohlmaier and von Sartory, 1986).

The onset of the industrial revolution heralded numerous significant changes for glasshouses. Technical innovations, most notably in metallurgy, steam heating and glass, enabled the scale of the glasshouse and its associated glazing to be expanded. Additionally, the focus of horticulture changed from a predominantly European focus to a wider global perspective. Expeditions to the new lands of the East and West Indies, Africa and South America returned to Europe with a bounty of palms and ferns. The palm thus became the '...love of a society weary of Europe' (Tschira, 1939: 97). In the 19th century, palms were the so called 'prince of plants', named because of its 'noble and impressive shape', fecundity and usefulness, botanical novelty and Christian religious connotations (Kohlmaier and von Sartory, 1986). In his book *The Greenhouse, Hothouse and Stove*, Charles MacIntosh (1838), quoted the Bavarian Dr. von Martius as describing palms as the inhabitants of the 'happy countries' of the tropics. Koppelkamm (1981) stated that the palm became a symbol of the longing for these 'happy countries'. The increasingly influential middle classes, empowered by the industrial revolution, expressed their newfound wealth and culture through the acquisition and care of a palm collection (Kohlmaier and von Sartory, 1986). As a result, Kohlmaier (1986) contested, the low and narrow glasshouse then transformed into the spacious conservatory. From this point, the winter garden became an enchanting landscape '...and indeed a tropical one full of secrets.' (Tschira, 1939: 98).

The 19th century interior image of the glasshouse comprised the grouping of shrubs and trees with the inclusion of grottos, springs, fountains and water features (Kohlmaier and von Sartory, 1986). An increase in botanical studies and communication between European learned societies further assisted the rapid development of the glasshouse (Hix, 2005; Kohlmaier and von Sartory, 1986). This allowed the glasshouse to transform into a 'scientific art', constructed with ever-increasing glazing and better heating systems, which enabled the glasshouse to become popular throughout Europe and the Americas (Hix, 2005). The form and volume of the resultant 19th century glasshouses were thus generally determined by the cultivation and display of plants from the warm or tropical regions, which usually included tall trees, but with a particular focus on palms (Kohlmaier and von Sartory, 1986). Hix (2005) surmises these developments perfectly:

> ...larger glasshouses, containing an ever-increasing number of species and sizes of plants, were the result of a new logical and empirical approach derived from a new European tradition of scientific endeavour. Because of the vast improvements in artificial environmental control, these newer, larger glasshouses could let in even greater amounts of natural light. While the colonial legacy of the 18th century had brought about new wealth, patrons and plants, the emergent industrial revolution had facilitated new materials and technologies.
>
> (Hix, 2005)

Therefore, by the dawn of the 19th century, glasshouses/conservatories had evolved into three distinct typologies (which I will discuss in detail in subsequent sections): first, the private winter gardens of the nobility and wealthy industrialists; second, the winter gardens intended for the public; third, those structures associated with botanical gardens (Kohlmaier and von Sartory, 1986). Additionally, the first half of the 19th century witnessed two distinct phases of glasshouse development (Koppelkamm, 1981). The first phase began around 1815, with the curvilinear, façade glasshouses of J.C. Loudon and G.S. Mackenzie, and ended with Paxton's Great Conservatory at Chatsworth. Most of the examples of this phase had simple rectangular, elliptical or circular plans and were of modest scale. The second phase began in the 1840s, and comprised large-scale public buildings that had more complicated plans and were composed of several interconnected structures of varying scale. This phase is important because of the abandonment of any traditional architectural ideals; in these structures, the materials, structure and function became the architectural language (Koppelkamm, 1981).

3.8 Private winter gardens

Early private winter gardens were direct additions to residences; they were joined through the 'open rooms', such as the billiards room, salon or library. Examples of these early private winter gardens were the 1823 conservatory additions to the Grange Manor House in Hampshire, England, and the winter garden that was built at the Berlin Palace for crown Prince Albrecht

86 Bruno Taut's design inspiration for the Glashaus

(Kohlmaier and von Sartory, 1986). However, these early private winter gardens had an outward appearance not unlike the orangery; i.e. they followed the stylistic dictates of the prevailing architectural style. Kohlmaier (1986) contended that these early winter gardens only became a major constituent of the main residential building when they were built at the nobility's summer residences. Examples of these were the 1806 Indian Villa adjoining Sezincote House, Gloucestershire, England; and the 1845 Villa Berg Conservatory, Stuttgart, Germany. Combined with the technical innovations mentioned earlier and the tremendous wealth generated through the colonial endeavour, the nobility, in particular that of Britain, constructed ever larger and lavish winter gardens. The increase in size and space available on the grounds of the summer residence soon resulted in the winter garden becoming a completely detached building (Kohlmaier and von Sartory, 1986). With this development, the winter garden can be considered a separate typology in its own right. The most apparent example of this type was the Great Conservatory of 1836, at the Chatsworth Estate of the Duke of Devonshire. However, it was not at Chatsworth that the private winter gardens of the nobility reached their peak development. Rather, it was in the structures that were constructed at the Royal Glasshouses at Laeken, Belgium, that the crowning achievement of the private winter garden was reached. Starting in 1875, at Laeken, the Belgium King Leopold II constructed a vast complex of 36 interconnected glasshouses, covering an area in excess of 20,000 square metres (Kohlmaier and von Sartory, 1986). At the heart of this vast complex was an enormous, bell-shaped winter garden designed by Alphonse Balat and Henri Maquet (Kohlmaier and von Sartory, 1986). Despite being the most exquisite private winter garden, Laeken also heralded the end of the private winter gardens being associated with the nobility. Within the rising political rights of the middle class, the huge financial cost associated with Laeken could not be sustained or justified. Besides the cost of its construction, the annual 600,000 franc cost of maintaining Laeken resulted in tensions between the king and parliament. Soon, Leopold had to relinquish exclusive use of Laeken to the people of Belgium, and it thus became a 'Palace of the nation' (Kohlmaier and von Sartory, 1986). In 1909, Leopold died, in a small palm pavilion in his beloved glasshouse complex at Laeken. His death ironically also heralded the end to the glasshouse fantasies of the nobility (Hix, 2005).

Kohlmaier (1986) has also discussed the winter gardens of wealthy industrialists. Empowered by newfound wealth, these industrialists soon also sought an opulent lifestyle that could be comparable with that of the nobility. As such, they constructed palatial residences, with large landscaped gardens and with even larger winter gardens. Since their wealth was derived directly from the factory and industry, they built their large estates close to the factories that generated the wealth in a celebratory manner. The close proximity of the factory also allowed the energy of the factory, steam power, to be deployed in the heating of the winter gardens (Kohlmaier and von Sartory, 1986).

Kohlmaier (1986) identified the German industrialists Johann Friedrich August Borsig (who will be discussed in detail later in this chapter) and Louis Fredric Ravené, along with the Danish brewer J. Carl Jacobsen, as having had prominent examples of such winter gardens. Both Borsig and Ravené built extravagant villas, with large palatial gardens, in the industrial Berlin suburb of Moabit. Borsig apparently prided himself on having one the best plant collections in Europe (Kohlmaier and von Sartory, 1986). At the Borsig Villa (1850), both a winter garden, which comprised a colonnaded hall that had a masonry structure with large windows and skylights, and a cast-iron framed forcing house were constructed. Both structures were connected directly to the Borsig Villa; likewise, both were highly regarded and were built from cast-iron components that were cast in the nearby Borsig iron works (Kohlmaier and von Sartory, 1986). Ravené's large villa (1867) was built in *Werftstraße* (Fontane, 1990). So important was Ravené's contribution to the botanical sciences that in 1879, C.D. Bouché, the then director of the Royal Botanical Gardens in Berlin, named the palm genus *Ravenea* after him. In Copenhagen, the classically styled winter garden at the Villa Jacobson (1876) formed an integral component of the Villa and was located directly adjacent to the mansion (Kohlmaier and von Sartory, 1986).

Both the '...peculiar shape and – corresponding to it – the private reception rooms' defined the winter gardens of the aristocracy and the wealthy middle class: 'The patron's contemplation of the natural objects he had obtained was intimate, and he shared it only with friends.' (Kohlmaier and von Sartory, 1986: 37). Alternatively, Hix (2005) stated that the grand winter gardens that were being built worldwide in the 19th century were the result of the sole endeavour and influence of a select few. Much like the winter gardens at Laeken, the death of the private winter garden can be illustrated in the fate of the Grand Conservatory at Chatsworth. With the introduction of coal rationing and labour scarcity during World War One, many of the exotic plants subsequently died from both a lack of artificial heat and care. In 1920, instead of being rebuilt and restocked, the Conservatory was demolished after five attempts at dynamiting the building. The private winter garden had thus lost it elite connotations, due to a changed world of increased travel, knowledge, communication and the ready availability of materials – especially glass (Hix, 2005). With a change in taste, no longer was there much desire to mature exotic fruit during the middle of winter, or to view the botanic wonders of the tropics. Rather, the wider public preferred to have a beautiful 'flower garden' (Hix, 2005).

3.9 Public winter gardens

Winter gardens intended for the public encompassed a large variety of typologies and were generally located in larger urban areas. The appearance of these public winter gardens was closely associated with the large-scale availability of prefabricated building elements and modular coordination

(Koppelkamm, 1981). As such, public winter gardens in *Floras*, hotels, spas, aviaries, aquariums, conservatories and peoples' or winter palaces soon made their appearance on a global scale (Kohlmaier and von Sartory, 1986), and I will describe these manifestations in more detail below. The urban citizenry of Europe felt a need to find a place where they could freely gather without the interference of unpleasant weather. Additionally, the vegetation that the nobility and upper middle classes had become accustomed to also held tremendous attraction to the city-dweller. The very first public winter gardens were generally places of assembly and entertainment, such as dance halls, restaurants and cafés. It soon became evident that the provision of indoor vegetation and glass protection from the weather dramatically increased the attractiveness, i.e. profitability, of such a business (Kohlmaier and von Sartory, 1986). According to Kohlmaier (1986), the very first large-scale public garden was constructed for the Royal Botanical Society (1842–46), and was located in London's Regent's Park. A further early example was the *Jardin d'Hiver*, which opened in 1848 on Paris' *Champs-Elysées*. While Regent's Park was only open on select days and only to the educated public, the *Jardin d'Hiver* was an entertainment venue that was open to all (Hix, 2005; Kohlmaier and von Sartory, 1986). The *Jardin d'Hiver* also differed from Regent's Park in its financing arrangement; the *Jardin d'Hiver* was financed through a joint stock company, while Regent's Park relied on both donations and royal patronage.

In Germany, a curious winter garden typology developed in the form of the *Flora*. These buildings, first constructed in Cologne, then later in Frankfurt and finally Berlin, were mass entertainment venues for the general public's family excursions. Funded by share capital, the *Floras* were multi-storey structures that comprised a large central glazed plant hall, with numerous associated assembly halls leading off from it (Hix, 2005; Kohlmaier and von Sartory, 1986; Koppelkamm, 1981).

Around the middle of the 19th century, the foyer spaces to luxury hotels also appropriated the concept of the winter garden. Much like the *Floras*, these winter gardens formed the central space of the hotel, with restaurants and function rooms leading off from it. Examples of this type included the 1880 Berlin Central Hotel and the 1868 Leeds General Hotel (Hix, 2005; Kohlmaier and von Sartory, 1986). Further examples of similar *Flora*-type public winter gardens were found in buildings for art, aviaries and aquariums. The intention of these buildings was to combine the beauty of natural fauna and flora with that of manmade *objects d'art*. The privately funded, flat-domed, Kibble Palace in Glasgow (1872) was a prominent, late-period example of this type. It contained depictions of ancient myths, embodied in white marble statues all set within a tropical landscape (Hix, 2005; Kohlmaier and von Sartory, 1986). Containing the art collection of J.C. Jacobsen, the Ny Carlsberg Glyptotek (1897) had a central dome that contained a palm garden, fountains, and marble statues and benches. In the Glyptotek, the art collections were housed in isolated exhibition halls that generally surrounded the palm garden; all overlooked by a library at a higher level. Because of the humidity, all other functions were shielded from the palm garden and, as such, the effect of combining art and nature was not as immediate as in the Kibble Palace (Hix, 2005; Kohlmaier and von Sartory, 1986).

A further privately funded precursor of the modern zoological gardens was to be found in Henry Phillips' Glass Menagerie (1830) in London. Also known as the Zoological Conservatory, the building was a large, flat-domed structure that contained birds and caged beasts. The cages were arranged in a central circle that was surrounded by a colonnade that supported the roof; in turn, an open paved area for the public surrounded the colonnade (Hix, 2005; Kohlmaier and von Sartory, 1986). Kohlmaier (1986) also identified the Berlin aquarium (1869) on *Unter den Linden Stra e*, a two-storey building that was constructed behind a conventional façade, as being somewhat similar to the Glass Menagerie. The Berlin aquarium contained a glazed well that was lit from above. The upper floors housed creatures that lived above the earth's surface, and the lower floor, which contained stone grottos, housed those creatures that lived below the earth's surface (Kohlmaier and von Sartory, 1986). The best-known and last group of public winter gardens were 'people's palaces'. With the advent of Paxton's Crystal Palace in 1851, the history of the winter garden reached a defining moment – that being between an earlier period of experimentation and a later one of self-assured purpose and engineering (Hix, 2005). If 1800 to 1830 was a period of early fantasies in iron and glass, and 1830 to 1850 an era of experimentation, then 1850 onwards was a period of triumphal expression that led to the heyday of iron-and-glass construction at the turn of the 19th century (Kohlmaier and von Sartory, 1986). The 'assured purpose' of the 1851 exhibition was something different to the earlier public winter gardens. The Exhibition of the Works of Industry of all Nations, or simply The Great Exhibition, was intended to unify both industry and the arts. Prince Albert, the husband of Queen Victoria, considered the Exhibition as contributing to world peace, in that it might have led to a reduction in trade barriers and increased global industrialisation (Hix, 2005). The grand glazed architecture and the bizarre contents of the 1851 Exhibition were intended as a centre of diversion containing useless merchandise and transient experiences. The visual experience of the Exhibition involved the display of machines as works of art, which were set in and alongside gardens, fountains and statues. As such, the great Exhibitions of the 19th century were the origin of the modern-day pleasure industry and mass advertising (Hix, 2005). The winter garden, originally intended as a pleasure spot, had become a social utopia where the working class could discover its educational and leisured nirvana (Kohlmaier and von Sartory, 1986). However, if the somewhat sinister 'assured purpose' of the 1851 Exhibition is ignored, the 'engineering' triumph of the Crystal Palace did set a glass-and-iron precedent for Worlds' Exhibitions that followed, all of which vied to surpass the previous instalment.

90 Bruno Taut's design inspiration for the Glashaus

In 1854, the *Glas Palast* was constructed in Munich. Located in the Old Botanical Gardens near the city centre and train station, the building was 240 metres long by 84 metres wide, and 25 metres at its highest point. Until it was destroyed by fire in 1931, it served as a multi-functional location for festivals, plays, performances and exhibitions (Hix, 2005; Kohlmaier and von Sartory, 1986). From an 'engineering' perspective, the most important exhibition building was the *Galerie des Machines* (Machine Gallery) at the *Exposition Universelle* (Universal Exposition) of 1889 in Paris (Hix, 2005). Designed by Ferdinand Dutert, the *Galerie des Machines* had a main hall measuring 240 by 115 metres. The ingenuity of the *Galerie des Machines* lay not only in its gargantuan 3-pinned space frame structure that supported a delicate cladding of white and blue glass, but mainly in the effect that it created. Numerous visitors found this arrangement disconcerting (Hix, 2005). Being taller than the highest Gothic nave, the interior of the gallery was said to be superb. With the provision of electric Edison lamps, it became expansive and infinite during the night. The illuminating effect of moonlight, combined with the light emitted by a centrally located lighthouse, created a wondrous interior of red, blue, lilac, orange and green. Under this illumination, the cladding was described as a web of water (Huysmans, 1889). The grand entrance to the *Galerie des Machines* was via a domed structure called the Grand Vestibule. Its domed ceiling was glazed in sixteen segments of coloured leaded glass. At night, the interior of the dome was lit with electric lighting, an arrangement that was apparently without precedent (Durant, 1999). While the international exhibition buildings of the 19th century often had stylised masonry components, they were essentially independent from the constraints of a prevailing architectural style. Innovative structures like the *Galerie des Machines* prepared the way for the modern movement, where style was a matter of novelty, rather than a dictate (Hix, 2005).

3.10 Winter gardens associated with botanical gardens

Technically, the structures associated with botanical gardens were glasshouses or conservatories (Koppelkamm, 1981). The very first European 'botanical' gardens were herb, medicinal, kitchen or physics gardens, like those that were maintained by Aristotle and his pupil Theophrastus (Thanos, 2000). During the European Dark Ages, the kitchen gardens of monasteries became important stores of both edible and medicinal plants (Hill, 1915). However, it was not until the 14th century that 'botanical' or 'physics gardens' were significantly revived, and became widespread in Italy. Botanical gardens like that at Salerno's *Schola Medica Salernitana* (1310) arose as a result of the establishment of early medical faculties. During this period, the interests of 'botanical' gardens were generally devoted to the plants of Asia Minor, the Mediterranean rim and Western Europe (Hill, 1915). In the 16th century, 'botanical' gardens became more prevalent with the founding of the universities of Padua (1533), Pisa (1544), and Bologna (1568) (Kohlmaier and von

Sartory, 1986). These university-associated gardens were arranged to provide for the cultivation of medicinal herbs, or 'simples' (Hill, 1915). At Padua, Francesco Bonafede founded the first European chair of 'simples' (*Lectura Simplicium*) (Hill, 1915). Thereafter, botanical gardens were soon established at Zurich (1560), Leiden (1577), Leipzig (1579), Montpellier (1593), Paris (1597), Heidelberg (1593), Giessen (1605), Strasbourg (1620), Oxford (1621), Jena (1629), Uppsala (1657), Chelsea (1673), Berlin (1679), Edinburgh (1680), and Amsterdam (1682) (Hill, 1915).

From approximately 1550 onward, a tendency to grow plants not only for practical medicinal purposes but also for aesthetic reasons also developed. From this point onward, a healthy competition developed between botanic establishments to grow as many species as possible (Hill, 1915). With an increase in maritime trade and discovery, a plethora of new exotic species subsequently became available. As such, artificial environments were constructed, where the vigour of the plants, rather than the human visitor, was of primary importance. Thus, the forms of glasshouses that were associated with botanical gardens were generally dictated by the form and specific needs of the plant being contained (Kohlmaier and von Sartory, 1986). Considering that no plant can thrive without sufficient quantities of light, the form of glasshouses had to be optimised for maximum sunlight penetration. Herman Boerhaave, Carl Linnaeus, Michel Adanson and Nicholas Facio de Douillier were early pioneers in the scientific study of light penetration and resultant glasshouse design (Loudon, 1817).

The countries of northern Europe initially dominated the glasshouse endeavour (Koppelkamm, 1981). The horticultural improvements of the 'Flemings' were held in high regard in all the 'Low Countries' during the 17th century (Loudon, 1817). However, in the early-19th century, Britain became dominant because of its position as the leading industrialised nation of the period, its extensive empire and a traditional passion for gardening (Koppelkamm, 1981). Gentlemen, such as Sir George Mackenzie, Sir Joseph Banks, Charles Macintosh and T.A. Knight, and associations like the Horticultural Society of London dominated; however, it was John Claudius Loudon who became preeminent in the field of horticulture.

3.11 John Claudius Loudon

Loudon was best known for both his preoccupation for the design of spherically formed glasshouses and his pioneering work on the ridge-and-furrow system that Joseph Paxton later perfected (Koppelkamm, 1981). Loudon's fascination with spherically formed glasshouses was initiated through an 1815 article that Sir George Mackenzie wrote to the Horticultural Society of London (Koppelkamm, 1981). In this article, Mackenzie (1815) argued that the most suitable form for glasshouses was one-quarter of the segment of a globe, i.e. a semi-dome. Mackenzie (1815) concluded that this arrangement, applied in section, elevation and plan, would receive the greatest possible

92 Bruno Taut's design inspiration for the Glashaus

quantity of sunlight, and provided both a neat and elegant solution; supposedly when compared to the ridge-and-furrow system. While Loudon (1817) agreed that Mackenzie's form was an elegant addition to horticultural architecture, he disagreed that it was the most suitable form. For Loudon, the best form was not a semi-dome but a '...flattened semi-dome, or segment of an oblate spheroid...' and whose base should not exceed two-thirds of its height (Loudon, 1817: 20). Loudon added that the form of a '...segment of a circle...' was better, and the '...portion of an ellipse...' was thus best when ompared to Mackenzie's pure semi-dome (Loudon, 1817: 20–1). Loudon's flattened semi-dome, which was praised for its most elegant appearance and satisfactory combination of structural strength and efficiency, was proposed as an important addition to greenhouse, conservatory and botanical hothouse architecture (Loudon, 1817). An accumulated apex to efficiently remove rainwater and a flaring of the base for the planting of small plants were further refinements of the flattened semi-dome. Additionally, Loudon (1817) proposed that a freestanding flattened semi-dome, admitting light through glazing on all sides, was preferable for both aesthetic reasons and the welfare of the plants. Loudon (1817) also discussed the large impact that his freestanding flattened semi-dome would have had on the then accepted practices of glasshouse heating, glazing, ventilation, structure and workmanship. While Loudon might have considered using ridge-and-furrow cladding on a polygonal plan for economic reasons, the glasshouses that he designed after 1818 only ever used smooth curved skins (Koppelkamm, 1981).

In 1816, Loudon design a patented iron sash bar for use in his curved buildings; however, the commercial rights to this invention were transferred to the firm W. & D. Bailey. Two examples of Bailey designs using Loudon's sash bar were a glasshouse for the nursery of Conrad Loddiges in Hackney, and an 1824 design for a semi-circular glasshouse that stood against a north-facing masonry wall for Lord St. Vincent. In 1827, Bailey produced a design for an imposing glass dome at Bretton Hall in Yorkshire, while in 1831, Loudon submitted a 'doughnut'-shaped proposal for a glasshouse at the Birmingham botanical gardens (Koppelkamm, 1981). Kohlmaier (1986) argued that Loudon's design for Birmingham geometrically resembled Karl Schinkel's design for the truncated cone-shaped 1821 palm house at the Royal Botanical Gardens at Berlin-Schoenberg (Kohlmaier and von Sartory, 1986). Koppelkamm (1981) contended that a palm house at Bicton Gardens, whose designer is unknown, was in all probability designed by Loudon and built by Bailey; alternatively, Hix (2005) emphatically stated that it was constructed by Bailey. As well as reiterating his thoughts on the freestanding flattened semi-dome, or as he later termed it, the 'Accumulated Semi-Globe', Loudon published his concept for an aquarium or water-plant glasshouse in 1822 (which I will detail more fully later in this chapter).

The tendency towards a freestanding glasshouse that contained a specific species or vegetation group from a particular geographic location was not, however, new. As outlined above, the orangery and palm house had

Victoria regia's *bequest to the* Glashaus 93

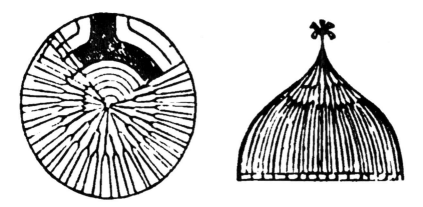

Figure 3.3a John Claudius Louden's proposal for an Accumulated Semi-Globe glasshouse.

Figure 3.3b John Claudius Louden's proposal for an Aquatic glasshouse.

developed in response to a desire to cultivate these exotic specimens in northern Europe; further common types were dry houses for succulents, orchid houses, and houses for the plants of New Holland (Australia). During the 18th century, the cultivation of pineapples was also in vogue, while in the 19th century, it was fashionable to cultivate, among other things, the Camellia (Koppelkamm, 1981). As such, Loudon designed a curvilinear pineapple and vine glasshouse in 1817, which was constructed for a Mr Stuckey at Langport in Somerset (Hix, 2005).

As both the technology of iron construction and the industrial revolution progressed, so too did the size and audience of the horticultural glasshouse. By the second half of the 19th century, particularly the 1870s and 1880s,

94 Bruno Taut's design inspiration for the Glashaus

prefabricated and mass-produced greenhouses became the norm (Koppelkamm, 1981). With the construction of Paxton's Great Conservatory at Chatsworth, an important era in glasshouse development came to an end. The Conservatory not only demonstrated the large-scale possibilities of an iron structure, but it was also the first large glasshouse to allow daylight in from all sides. From this point onward, it was Loudon's and Paxton's buildings that firmly established the precedent for any successive development (Koppelkamm, 1981). These subsequent developments of size and iron were best illustrated by the public winter gardens mentioned above, but also by large-scale palm houses, to which I will now turn.

3.12 Palm houses

Early examples of palm houses were those at Syon House (1820–27), the glasshouses (*Le Botanique*) at the Brussels Botanical Gardens (1826), and The Great Conservatory (1822) (*Gro e Gewächshaus*) in the Mountain Park (*Bergpark*) in Wilhelmshöhe, Kassel (Koppelkamm, 1981). These early palm houses were much like their orangery predecessors in that they were dictated by prevailing architectural style and their owners' aristocratic tastes. Koppelkamm (1981) argued that once again it was the Britons, this time Richard Turner and Decimus Burton, that led developments. The palm house at the Belfast Botanical Gardens (1839–40), designed by Charles Lanyon, was one of the first structures to be associated with Turner. In the mid-19th century, as palm houses increased in both size and prestige, architects inevitably became involved because of the desire for aesthetics. However, because of the complexity of these large glasshouses, architects needed to work with engineers and fabricators in completing the final building (Hix, 2005). Turner was therefore ideally positioned, as he was both the owner of the Hammersmith Iron Works in Dublin, and an engineer and designer.

In 1843, Turner designed and constructed the palm house for the Royal Dublin Society, at Glasnevin, Dublin. Turner and Burton were best known for the palm house (1845–49) built for the Royal Botanic Society of London at Kew Gardens (Hix, 2005). By this stage, horticultural glasshouses generally started to appear in the centre of grouped complexes. This central glasshouse contained taller tropical species but mainly palms. It was loosely referred to as the palm house. Adjacent to this large, central structure were a number of lower, less prominent wings for smaller species, either grouped by similarities or by geographic location. These wings generally had different climates from the central, tropical palm house.

This typology developed because of two factors. The first was the prevailing prototype developed for the nobility, such as the orangery or the winter garden, attached to the stately mansion. The second was economic. As the number of species and resultant geographically dispersed specialised glasshouses proliferated, so too would the cost of maintaining the artificial climate and associated equipment. It would seem logical to group these dispersed glasshouses in one location and 'power' them using centrally located equipment. While Britain might have led the initial development of public palm houses, enthusiasm for glasshouses was just as intense on continental Europe (Hix, 2005). Earlier British glasshouses, or palm houses, tended to be curvilinear. This contrasted with later German examples, which tended to be rectilinear and classical in style (Hix, 2005; Koppelkamm, 1981). It has even been proposed that the curved roof never became popular in Germany (Koppelkamm, 1981). While German designers were very familiar with British developments, iron was regarded as simply too expensive even as late as the mid-19th century, which led to the preference for traditional building materials like timber, which resulted in a straight surfaces, regular plans and span-roofs (Koppelkamm, 1981).

However, in the rest of continental Europe, curved roofs did appear. Charles Rohault de Fleury designed a large glasshouse complex (1833–34) for the *Jardin des Plantes* at the Museum of Natural History, Paris. De Fleury's glasshouses were described by Gideon (1976) as having been both the prototype for all large iron-framed conservatories, and the first large structure to consist entirely of iron and glass. However, this is inaccurate, as the first was a glasshouse constructed at Stuttgart-Hohenheim in 1789. According to Hix (2005), this building was, in all probability, the first iron-framed glasshouse in Germany. The Copenhagen palm house (1872), designed by Tyge Rothe, was a further example. Built in the same form as the Brussels Botanical Gardens and occupying a site similar to that of *Jardin des Plantes,* the Copenhagen palm house was commissioned by the previously mentioned brewer Jacobsen. While both the glasshouses at Brussels Botanical Gardens and Copenhagen were not exactly curved, their truncated, coned centres created a pleasing and rational building (Hix, 2005).

In Germany, most large palm houses were only built after 1860 (Koppelkamm, 1981). While many, similar to that at Strasbourg (1877–82) and Munich Botanical Gardens (1860–5), were 'regular' (as described above), the one at Vienna, Schönbrunn (1884), was closer to the British curved type. While it was not as elegant as the Kew example, because of protruding skylights that were arranged along the ridge line, the Schönbrunn example was innovative because of its placement of the structure to the outside of the glazing (Koppelkamm, 1981). Hix (2005) referred to the Schönbrunn glasshouse as being having been a prominent example of expressed structural ironwork. The new glasshouse complex (1905–7) in the Berlin suburb of Dahlem, for the German Royal Botanical Gardens was undoubtedly inspired by Schönbrunn. This complex was designed by the Royal Building Inspector, Alfred Koerner, and contained several interconnected climatic chambers, centred on a large palm house. Like the *Galerie des Machines*, this large palm house had a three-pinned portal structure (Hix, 2005). However, unlike the *Galerie des Machines*, the structure was placed outside of the glazing. Similarly, like both the *Jardin des Plantes, Le Botanique* and the palm house at the Copenhagen Botanical Gardens, the building occupied a sloping site.

96 Bruno Taut's design inspiration for the Glashaus

Two remarkable examples of large-glazed palm house complexes also existed in the United States of America. In San Francisco, a group of wealthy citizens donated a British prefabricated complex to the city park administration. Opened in 1879, the timber-structured complex followed the accepted typology of a prominent central pavilion with two radiating wings (Koppelkamm, 1981). In New York (1900–2), another glasshouse complex was constructed that was representative of those in many major cities of the period (Hix, 2005). This glasshouse, designed by William Cobb, was modelled after the British curved prototype (Koppelkamm, 1981).

The heyday of the glasshouse was undoubtedly the second half of the 19th century. However, by the beginning of the 20th century, and as later amplified in a post–World War One world, the building material of reinforced concrete, competing ideologies, and modernism appeared to displace existing conditions. Apart from the few examples listed above, the infatuation for large glass-and-iron structures rapidly dissipated and they were subsequently rendered redundant.

3.13 *Victoria regia* glasshouses

As discussed, Loudon's curved, smooth-skinned botanical glasshouses first appeared in Britain, and were initially uncommon in continental Europe, especially in Germany. This situation is reversed with the wide range of botanical glasshouses developed for species with specialist climatic requirements, such as camellias and orchids; i.e. curved-form glasshouses for these species first developed in continental Europe. Initially, only species like citrus were collected and propagated. As European colonialism and industrialisation aggressively spread, the desire to collect even larger plant specimens as part of ever-increasing collections likewise dramatically increased. This in turn resulted in more numerous, larger and increasingly complex glasshouses. Along with the palm houses, which contained the largest or tallest of species, a proliferation of equally specific and functionally optimised glasshouses, such as the camellia, lily, aquatic and orchid glasshouses also resulted.

Following the first European cultivation of the *Victoria regia* lily in 1849, a specific glasshouse, the *Victoria regia* glasshouse, was developed (Hix, 2005). Glasshouses generally acquired their names according to a rational, scientific classification – either botanically, according to their wider *family* (e.g. palm houses), or sub-family, or *genus* (hence, camellia and lily glasshouses). Alternatively, glasshouses were also named geographically, according to their original climatic regions (e.g. sub-tropical glasshouses). The naming of a glasshouse according to a specific *species* – namely, the *Victoria regia* glasshouse – was consequently extremely uncommon. This would indicate that there was something extraordinary about *Victoria regia* lily.

3.14 The initial European cultivation of the *Victoria regia*

In the 19th century, Joseph Paxton, the Head Gardener for the Duke of Devonshire at his Chatsworth Estate, was considered an eminent cultivator of exotic plants. In 1836, Paxton tested a curvilinear pleated (ridge-and-furrow) roof on a 60-by-26 feet forcing-house, which became the initial home for *Victoria regia* lily until the construction of a subsequent, even more specific glasshouse (Jones-Loyd, 1851). Owing to his status, Paxton had received a *Victoria regia* seedling from the Kew Royal Botanical Gardens on 3 August 1849 (Cavendish, 1999). Initially, he placed the seedling in a 12-square-foot, heated tank that was protected by the curvilinear roofed glasshouse (Flanders-Darby, 2002).

The *Victoria regia* did phenomenally well in this initial artificial environment; within a mere six weeks after its initial planting, the leaves measured 3 feet 6 inches in diameter. On 1 October, the leaves had increased to 4 feet in diameter, and, by 15 October, to 4 feet 5½ inches (Lindley, 1849). At this stage, *Victoria regia* outgrew its initial pool and had to be relocated to a larger tank, which was twice the size of the first (Flanders-Darby, 2002). Continuing its phenomenal growth, *Victoria regia* then outgrew its pond on a further two occasions (Markham, 1935).

The *Victoria regia* lily flowered for the first time in Britain between 8 and 10 November 1849. On 15 November 1849, Paxton personally presented one of its initial flowers and a large leaf to Queen Victoria (Harley and Harley, 1992). Having discovered *Victoria regia*'s cultivation requirements in the experimental forcing-house, Paxton then began to construct a purpose-built glasshouse that was completed in the spring of 1850 (Chadwick, 1961). Paxton described this structure as having measured 61 feet 6 inches long by 46 feet 9 inches wide. At the centre of this rectangular plan was a circular pond for *Victoria regia*, which measured 33 feet in diameter. This pond had a deeper central portion measuring 16 feet in diameter, and contained the soil for the *Victoria regia*. Eight smaller ponds were additionally located in the corners of the house (Lindley, 1850). These eight smaller tanks contained other exotic aquatic species, such as *Nymphaea*, *Nelumbium* and *Pontederia*. Sitting on almost square foundations, the building consisted of a masonry base that rose 37 inches from the ground. Contained within this base were the raised ponds, their heating pipes and low-level ventilation openings. Four-inch iron heating pipes were embedded in the deep central soil of the pond, while 2-inch lead pipes were additionally placed in the shallower portion of the pond. The house was heated by 2-inch iron pipes that ran between the piers of the basement wall. Air flowed over the heating pipes and into the house through 30 low-level openings in the basement walls. Stale, heated air was expelled through roof openings operated by simple machinery.

Within the central pond, four small waterwheels added a gentle motion to the water, and, above each, a supply of cold water was provided to 'normalise' the temperature of the pond as required (Chadwick, 1961). Above the masonry base, Paxton's *Victoria regia* glasshouse extended upwards in glass,

98 Bruno Taut's design inspiration for the Glashaus

wood and steel. The main vertical structural façade consisted of cast-iron columns at 6-foot intervals, which were topped with rounded arches. Behind this façade, a secondary structure of vertical glazing was constructed; specifically, it consisted of wooden sash bars that contained 5-by-10-inch glass panes. The horizontal glazed roof of the building was a ridge-and-furrow system, with a parallel Paxton Gutter housed in the valleys or furrows. Before this *Victoria regia* glasshouse, Paxton had used his gutter as the main structural support to the ridge-and-furrow roof. Paxton then developed an independent structural support system that ran perpendicular to both the gutter and the ridge-and-furrow. This comprised four 54-inch wrought-iron master joists that were 5 inches deep, with the addition of 1-inch-diameter steel tie-rods below. Supporting each of the master joists were two hollow 3½-inch cast-iron columns (Chadwick, 1961).

With the development of distinct structural and cladding systems, Paxton's *Victoria regia* glasshouse gradually emphasized the horizontal space-frame. One could rightly enquire as to why he did this. On previous occasions, Paxton noted that he was impressed by the massive carrying capacity of the *Victoria regia*'s leaves. In 1849, after the *Victoria regia* had initially bloomed, Paxton placed his seven-year-old daughter Annie on one of its leaves, a weight it carried with ease. In early May 1850, Paxton conducted the same experiment with a leaf of 5 feet in diameter in a small stream near the Kitchen Gardens at Chatsworth. For this later experiment, Paxton constructed a lightweight circular trellis that was placed on the leaf surface so as to distribute the applied weight evenly. Paxton placed 112 pounds of weights onto this trellis before water started to flow over the upturned edges of the leaf. After the weights were removed, two men of approximately 10 to 11 stone were individually carried by the leaf for a period of between two and three minutes (Allen, 1854). On 13 November 1850, Paxton presented a series of drawings of his Crystal Palace building to the Royal Society of Arts. Along with the drawings, Paxton also presented a leaf from his *Victoria regia* lily, and noted that its underside represented an excellent example of natural engineering:

> ...in that the cantilever that radiate from the centre, where they are nearly two inches deep, with large bottom flanges and very thin middle rib, and with cross girders between each pair to keep the middle ribs from buckling...
>
> (Jones-Loyd, 1851: 6)

Paxton admitted that the origin of the Crystal Palace derived from his gardening experiences, particularly from the glasshouse that he built for *Victoria regia* (Paxton, 1850). As Fay quotes:

> [it is] ...to this plant and to this circumstance that the Crystal Palace owes its direct origin.
>
> (Fay, 1951: 11)

While history generally acknowledges Paxton as having been responsible for the first European blooming of *Victoria regia*, this could be argued as only partially, or even totally, incorrect.

In May 1849, the German horticulturalist Karl Eduard Ortgies was hired to work at Chatsworth, where he was later entrusted by Paxton with the daily care of *Victoria regia* (Wittmack, 1894). It was Ortgies who reported to Paxton that the first bud was about to open on 8 November 1849 (Wittmack, 1894). As mentioned above, this first blooming did not occur in Paxton's celebrated *Victoria regia* house; rather, it took place in the experimental ridge-and-furrow forcing house he had designed in 1836 (Jones-Loyd, 1851). As such, Paxton's design of the later *Victoria regia* house raises the question as to what interested him the most – the botanical habits of lily itself, or the building of a glasshouse that best framed the achievement of bringing the lily to bloom?

These two factors were undoubtedly of concern to Paxton. However, it was the design of a further and larger iteration of his ridge-and-furrow structural glazing system that interested him the most. In the wake of his 1836 building, and the Great Conservatory, Paxton had already been refining this system, and in 1840, he first employed it horizontally in a conservatory at Darley Dale (Jones-Loyd, 1851). A full nine years later, Paxton had the opportunity to deploy the 'final solution' in relation to a horizontal ridge-and-furrow roof (Chadwick, 1961), the use of which dictated the resultant cuboid form of Paxton's *Victoria regia* glasshouse. For Paxton, the *Victoria regia* glasshouse was intended as the final prototype before the full-scale deployment of the ridge-and-furrow system on even larger buildings, such as the Crystal Palace of the Great Exhibition of 1851. According to Kohlmaier (1986), Paxton intended that his ridge-and-furrow system both be optimised for mass production and widely applied to a variety of buildings, including dwelling houses, railway stations and assembly halls.

3.15 Further British examples of *Victoria regia* glasshouses

The *Victoria regia* seedling for Syon House arrived during the '…second week of September, 1849', and was initially nurtured in a number of increasingly larger pots that crucially allowed for the continual movement of water (Moore and Ayres, 1850: 229). On 5 January 1850, the lily was moved to '…a low-roofed lean-to house, in which a Mr Beck had been ordered to prepare a slate tank for its reception, twenty-two feet long by twelve feet wide' (Moore and Ayres, 1850: 230). In this tank, water movement was facilitated by a small water wheel that was placed under the main water-supply pipe. This *Victoria regia* flowered in the lean-to glasshouse on 10 April 1850 (Moore and Ayres, 1850). After this blooming, the *Victoria regia* at Syon was apparently moved again. In 1851, its location was described as having a '…span-roof erection, with a porch and second door … It contains a slate tank 21 ft. square, which is occupied principally by the Victoria. …

100 *Bruno Taut's design inspiration for the Glashaus*

Several other aquatics ...are grown at the sides and towards the corners of the tank' (Weale, 1851: 509–10). Thus, this later structure is clearly not the same as the glasshouse in which the *Victoria regia* first flowered. Additionally, in this later glasshouse, the *Victoria regia* was described as having been planted in the centre of the tank, surrounded at the edges, chiefly, by *Nelumbium*. The hot-water supply to the tank ran over a small water wheel, providing motion to the water in the tank (Weale, 1851). Both Paxton's *Victoria regia* glasshouse at Chatsworth and the 1851 *Victoria regia* glasshouse at Syon were located in kitchen gardens (Flanders-Darby, 2002; Weale, 1851).

The cultivation of the *Victoria regia* lily at Kew followed a similar pattern as Syon and Chatsworth; i.e., in all cases, the lily first bloomed in back office–type environments before a glasshouse was either purpose built or converted for it. As the initial cultivator of the Chatsworth and Syon lilies, The Royal Botanical Gardens, Kew produced its first *Victoria regia* flowers in June of 1850 (Desmond, 1995). Kew appears to have first propagated the *Victoria regia* sometime after June 1846. Of the 25 seeds bought, only two germinated and formed rudimentary leaves, and then promptly died (Desmond, 1995).

Undoubtedly inspired by this event, in 1847, William Hooker, as Director of The Royal Botanical Gardens, published details of the *Victoria regia* in both *Curtis's Botanical Magazine* and a special edition book (Hooker, 1847a, 1847b). Subsequently, in February 1849, Kew received seeds of the *Victoria regia* in small phials of purified water. From these seeds, in March of the same year, Kew subsequently germinated half a dozen vigorous plants, and, by midsummer, had raised 50 in a former tropical propagation glasshouse (Desmond, 1995). Both the Chatsworth and Syon lilies originated from these 50 plants (Desmond, 1995). In 1849, a combination of poor lighting and impurities in the water supplied from the River Thames resulted in the Kew lilies dying without producing flowers. In 1850, the *Victoria regia* was finally bought to flower '...in a large tank in the former tropical propagation house...' (Desmond, 1995: 185). Having discovered the initial cultivation requirements of the lily, Kew also constructed a dedicated glasshouse for the lily.

The design of the Kew Gardens' *Victoria regia* glasshouse, or Water Lily House, which still exists, was initially attributed to Richard Turner; however, the actual designer is unknown (Desmond, 1995). Before the construction of this glasshouse, the *Victoria regia* was on display at Kew Gardens in 'House No. 6', which was apparently '...one of the very few places where it can be seen by the public...' (Weale, 1851: 474–5). When it was time to build a dedicated glasshouse, Hooker initially proposed a '...house, 100 feet long, with two tanks – one for the *Victoria regia* and the other for aquatics'. However, this plan was vetoed by the then Commissioner of Works in favour of the current Water Lily House (Desmond, 1995: 186). The new span-roofed 1852 *Victoria regia* glasshouse, whose construction was supervised by the Commissioner's district manager, was finished in December 1852. According to Desmond (1995), this glasshouse did not suit the *Victoria regia* as it was poorly designed and ventilated. As such, in 1858, the *Victoria regia* was moved to a '...square slate tank in one of the smaller houses, while much of its former abode was transformed into a tropical habitat of white, blue and red water lilies, ferns, papyrus and hanging gourds' (Desmond, 1995: 186).

Other early examples of regular *Victoria regia* glasshouses were found at The Exotic Nursery in Kings Road, Chelsea; the Herrenhausen Gardens in Hanover; and the old Berlin Botanical Gardens in the suburb of Schöneberg. A brief discussion of each follows. The *Victoria regia* glasshouse at The Exotic Nursery was described as having had a plan of 37-by-30 feet and covered by a glazed two-span roof supported by iron columns. This glasshouse was correctly referred to as an aquarium (Weale, 1851), which was a generic 19th century term used to describe a glasshouse for aquatic plants. Hix (2005) identified two earlier glasshouses that used the term aquarium; one belonged to the Marques of Blandford, and was housed in Whiteknights Park, Reading, and the other was Loudon's prototype of 1822. At the centre of The Exotic Nursery glasshouse's plan was a slate tank, 30 feet by 22 feet 9 inches, in which the *Victoria regia* was located. A path on three sides surrounded this central tank, while the fourth (and eastern) side of the tank abutted the edge of the building, which allowed the cultivation of tall aquatics, such as papyrus. In addition to the *Victoria regia*, the tanks also contained *Nymphcea, stellata, rubra, coerulea,* and *sanguine*. Small vases, at 7-feet intervals, that contained *Nymphoea pygmoea* were placed on the lip of the tank. Additionally, the underside of the glazed roof had suspended pendant vases for orchids and other species. Water movement in the tank was achieved, not through the use of a water wheel, but by an 'off axis' copper vessel that was fixed under the main water supply. When the level of the water in the copper vessel reached a certain level, it would then tip into the tank, agitating the water surface (Weale, 1851). While this means of water movement was considered novel, it was felt that the appearance of the '...little device may be clothed in a more elegant form' (Weale, 1851: 536).

3.16 Continental European examples of *Victoria regia* glasshouses

The Herrenhausen Gardens had long been associated with the royal families of Saxony. In 1841, the eminent botanist and Director of the Gardens, Heinrich Ludolph Wendland, laid out an orchids and cuttings glasshouse in the Mountain Garden (*Berggarten*) portion of the Herrenhausen Gardens. In the spring of 1851, the architect Georg Heinrich Schuster provided the plan for the conversion of this glasshouse, so as to cultivate *Victoria regia*, which flowered for the first time on 29 June 1851. This *Victoria regia* glasshouse was low span-roofed structure of approximately 43-by-23 feet, which contained a large tank at one end that measured approximately 32-by-21 feet. Unlike the *Victoria regia* glasshouses at Chatsworth, Kew, Syon and Chelsea, the Herrenhausen glasshouse did not have an interior circulation route for visitors; the tank was immediately surrounded by a low masonry wall, 1 foot wide and 3 feet high, which served as the perimeter wall to the glasshouse (Meyer and Schultze, 1916). Therefore, it would appear as though visitors to the Herrenhausen *Victoria regia* would have viewed the lily from the outside, rather than the inside. Interestingly, the seeds for the Herrenhausen *Victoria regia* were procured from Syon House and the Royal Botanical Gardens, Kew (Meyer and Schultze, 1916).

In May 1852, the Director of the Berlin Botanical Gardens, Schöneberg, Professor Alexander Braun built a heated glasshouse for tropical aquatic plants. Earlier Braun demanded that the honour of the Gardens be protected by bringing *Victoria regia* to its highest perfection. Carl Freidrich Bouche, as the Berlin Botanical Gardens' Technical and Horticultural Director, obtained seeds for *Victoria regia* apparently on a trip to Hamburg in 1851. Built according to Bouche's plans, the *Victoria regia* glasshouse was described as a simple square commercial building with oil-painted wooden walls, which contained a cistern made from concrete or cement. The gabled roof to the glasshouse was framed in timber and in-filled with glazing (Lack, 2004). The heating of this glasshouse was rather crude because the hot water flowed directly into the cistern, which resulted in large water temperature differences within different parts of the cistern. Additionally, this continual movement of water through the boiler, which had been in contact with outside organisms, caused the growth of algae, which in turn hindered the vitality of the *Victoria regia*. When the glasshouse was demolished nearly three decades later, a fountain was built in its place (Schultze, 1883).

At the Berlin Botanical Gardens, the *Victoria regia* was the central attraction, drawing large numbers of both scientific research scholars and casual visitors. As a result, Braun had to hastily extend the opening hours of the Gardens to accommodate approximately 5,000 visitors per day. However, entrance to the glasshouse was strictly controlled. Visitors could only enter under supervision, during set times, and had to leave their bags and coats at the entrance (Lack, 2004). While the achievements of Herrenhausen and Schöneberg were undoubtedly remarkable, they were not the first sites to bloom *Victoria regia* in Continental Europe. This honour belonged to the van Houtte Nursery, owned by Belgian Louis Benoit van Houtte, which bloomed *Victoria regia* on 5 September 1850 (van Houtte, 1850–1).

Van Houtte was best known as being the part proprietor of the van Houtte Nursery located in Gentbrugge, near Ghent in Belgium, and as the editor of the journal *Flore des Serres et des Jardins de l'Europe (Flowers of the Greenhouses and Gardens of Europe)*. Reportedly, van Houtte, in the mid-19th century, '...was burning with desire to be the first on the continent to cultivate *Victoria regia*' (Wittmack, 1894: 226). Exactly why is somewhat unclear. However, it was likely due to his passion for botany and the commercial aspects of his nursery business. It could also be likely that he might have encountered *Victoria regia* or *Victoria cruziana*, or heard rumours of it, during his travels to South America during 1834–6. Reportedly, van

Houtte asked his head of plant cultures, Benedikt Roezl, to write to Ortgies and ask him to request a seedling of the *Victoria regia* from Paxton; Roezl had met Ortgies in London in 1848 (Wittmack, 1894). Van Houtte also proposed (if Paxton consented) to employ Ortgies and make him the Head of the Culture of Aquatics and Orchids (Wittmack, 1894).

Even though Paxton was inundated with requests for seedlings of the *Victoria regia* and only four seeds had subsequently germinated, he agreed to van Houtte's request at once. On 26 May 1850, the *Victoria regia* arrived in Gentbrugge (van Houtte, 1850–1). While on 1 April 1850, Ortgies started his new position under van Houtte, and a *Victoria regia* house was built according to Ortgies' plans (Wittmack, 1894). In addition to being the first to bloom the *Victoria regia* lily in Continental Europe, the van Houtte Nursery was also the first to construct a spherically formed *Victoria regia* glasshouse (van Houtte, 1850–1).

Ortgies' *Victoria regia* glasshouse had a diameter of 11.03 metres, and a circumference of 35.3 metres. The exterior walls were 1.05 metres high and supported an iron structure of curved, wrought iron for the glazed elliptical dome, which, in turn, was crowned with an octagonal lantern. The glasshouse's tank for the *Victoria regia* was 8.2 metres in diameter, with a deeper central portion that was 1.8 metres deep. The tank held 40 cubic metres of water and was surrounded by a passage that was 0.9 metres wide. The glasshouse was heated through a series of iron tubes placed below the walkway and the bottom of the tank. Furthermore, water movement was achieved by a small waterwheel placed below a cascade that was created by the hot water supply to the tank (van Houtte, 1850–1).

Considering Ortgies' earlier employment with Paxton at Chatsworth, and his undoubted familiarity with the developments at both Syon and Kew, it would be logical to assume that Ortgies' *Victoria regia* glasshouse would have adopted a similar regular, cuboid form. This was clearly not the case. The spherical form of Ortgies' *Victoria regia* glasshouse is explained by an investigation into the above-mentioned 1822 aquarium of J.C. Loudon. Recall that Loudon proposed that the '...Accumulated Semi-globe...' was indisputably the most perfect form for a glasshouse because plants would have almost equal access to sunlight in the glasshouse as those placed outside (Loudon, 1822: 357). With specific reference to the cuboid-formed aquarium at Whiteknights, Loudon further proposed that while this span-roofed form was well suited to aquatic plants that 'grow to some height above the water; it was not so for those plants whose leaves floated on its surface' (Loudon, 1822). As such, Loudon then proposed a circular glasshouse, with glass on all sides, as the '...most elegant plan...' for an aquarium (Loudon, 1822: 927).

Loudon argued that his aquarium should contain a cistern at the centre for river plants, surrounded by a pathway. Surrounding the pathway would be a further outer circular cistern for those plants that grew in '...stagnant water...' (Loudon, 1822: 927). Loudon's plan was 'elegant' because of numerous factors first explained in his earlier concept of the 'Accumulated Semi-globe';

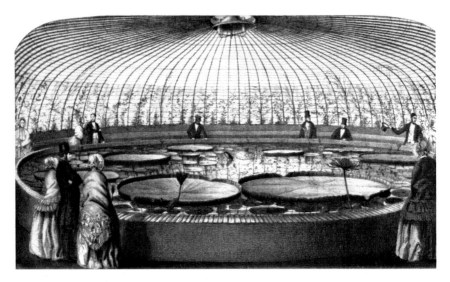

Figure 3.4 Interior of *Victoria regia* glasshouse designed by Eduard Ortgies for Louis van Houtte at his Gentbrugge nursery.

the spherical dome over Loudon's aquarium first sloped low over the cisterns at approximately 15° and was then gathered at the centre in a 'accumulated apex'. This form allowed both the 'floating leaves' in the outer cistern, and those plants that grew 'to some height above the water' in the central cistern, equal exposure to the same amount of sunlight. According to Loudon, the 'accumulated apex' is necessary to allow for the exclusion of rain (Loudon, 1822). Additionally, Loudon's aquarium was notable for the presence of a large basement containing machinery that was positioned below the central cistern. This machinery agitated the water of the central cistern to '…imitate the effect of the motion of water…' (Loudon, 1822: 927).

Considering that Ortgies was responsible for the day-to-day care of the Chatsworth *Victoria regia*, he must have also been intimately aware of the lighting benefits Paxton's ridge-and-furrow system supplied to the lily. Additionally, Ortgies could have known of Paxton's intention to file a patent for the ridge-and-furrow system, and appeared to leave Paxton's employ on very amicable grounds. These reasons could thus have negated the use of a ridge-and-furrow roof in the *Victoria regia* glasshouse designed by Ortgies. It is also highly likely that Ortgies was aware of Loudon and W. & D. Bailey's commissions that were described above. Furthermore, it is proposed that Ortgies must have known of Loudon's writings about the 'Accumulated Semi-globe' and aquarium, including the proposed lighting benefits for the *Victoria regia*. These factors could have influenced Ortgies' choice for a spherically formed *Victoria regia* glasshouse. As such, it seems that Ortgies adapted the better-suited Loudon aquarium to the specific requirements of the *Victoria regia*. In Ortgies' glasshouse, the floating leaves of the *Victoria regia* were contained in the central pond. As such, the need for a higher central dome to accommodate plants that grew 'to some height above the water' was negated. This in turn also negated the need for a steep 'accumulated apex'. Ortgies' design also departed from the Loudon prototype in the functioning of the 'accumulated apex'. No longer was it only for the exclusion of water; now it was primarily intended for ventilation. As already stated, poor ventilation was one of the primary reasons for the failure of the 1852 Kew *Victoria regia* glasshouse. Therefore, it could be assumed that poor ventilation was common to the cuboid form. The Ortgies glasshouse also replaced Loudon's machinery basement with a deeper central portion to the central cistern; a concept already established by all prior *Victoria regia* glasshouses.

An alternative explanation could also hold true. The leaves of the first Chatsworth *Victoria regia* started at approximately 0.15 metres and after only three-and-a-half months, on 13 November, had reached a maximum size of 1.49 metres (Lindley, 1849). By comparison, after three-and-a-half months, the largest leaf of the van Houtte *Victoria regia*, which also started at 0.15 metres (on 1 May 1850), measured only 1.25 metres (van Houtte, 1850–1). Interestingly, on 1 October 1849, Paxton wrote to the Duke of Devonshire saying that the weather had 'set in' and turned wet and cloudy; on this date, the largest leaf diameter was recorded as having reached 1.22 metres (Flanders-Darby, 2002). Despite the inclement weather, the leaves of the Chatsworth lily continued to grow. If assessed on leaf growth and size alone, then clearly the Chatsworth was the healthier of the two lilies, that is, it received more sunlight and was more vigorous. Could this have meant that the ridge-and-furrow system was better at sunlight collection than the spherically formed glasshouse? If this is indeed correct, then, from a botanical cultivation perspective, the use of a spherical *Victoria regia* glasshouse would make less sense. What ultimately emerges from the above discussion is that, while Ortgies and van Houtte were both very interested in *Victoria regia*, their motives were somewhat different. To illustrate this, it is worth exploring their histories in a bit more detail.

In 1876, when van Houtte died, he was described as a workaholic, having spent most of his time in his nursery office; he had apparently not been through his nursery grounds for almost three years (Johnson and Hogg, 1876). Cultivating the *Victoria regia* was not listed as among his main achievements, but rather his work for *Flore des Serres et des Jardins de l'Europe* and his endeavours in cultivating gloxinias and camellias. Furthermore, the successful economic aspects of the nursery were praised: 'Mr Van Houtte has left behind him a rare example of industry' (Johnson and Hogg, 1876: 389–90). After van Houtte's return to Ghent in 1839, he was formative in founding one of Belgium's two gardening schools (*Tuinbouwscholen*) in 1849. The other school was located at Vilvorde, and was under the directorship of Laurent de Bavay (*Ecole D'horticulture Pratique a Vilvorde*). van Houtte's school was located at Gentbrugge (Parent, 1850). In addition to

Flore des Serres et des Jardins de l'Europe, van Houtte, in collaboration with Charles Francois Antoine Morren, also founded the publication *L'Horticulture Belge* (*Belgium Horticulture*) (Morren, 1833–8). Furthermore, van Houtte was elected as the Mayor of Gentbrugge because of his business acumen, flair for languages and botanical knowledge (Johnson and Hogg, 1876). van Houtte was said to have prided himself on retaining and rewarding 'good' men (Johnson and Hogg, 1876). Ortgies was undoubtedly one of these men.

Before joining Paxton at Chatsworth, Ortgies had started a gardening apprenticeship with H. Böckmannn in Hamburg on 1 May 1844. After three years in Hamburg, Ortgies visited certain renowned nurseries in Berlin, Dresden, Leipzig, Magdeburg and Potsdam. On 1 March 1848, he became employed at the A. Henderson and Co. Pineapple Place Nursery in London. In the spring of 1851, Ortgies was placed in charge of German and English correspondence and the preparation of catalogues, and was then transferred to the offices of the van Houtte Nursery. But, refusing to become totally office bound, Ortgies remained as the Head of the Culture of Aquatics and Orchids. In this new role, Ortgies successfully cultivated from seed and later bloomed *Nymphaea gigantean*, while additionally creating the hybrid *Nymphaea Ortgiesiano-rubra*. In 1855, Ortgies reluctantly left the employ of the van Houtte Nursery (Wittmack, 1894) when he was appointed as the Chief Gardener of the Zurich Botanical Gardens. The above represents a narrative of an enthusiastic man, who, while undoubtedly talented at administration, management and leadership, was additionally first and foremost a 'hands-on' gardener.

Having described the two men, it seems clear that their motives for cultivating the *Victoria regia* were different; while Ortgies was interested in literally cultivating it, van Houtte was more interested in financially cultivating it. Indeed, the van Houtte nursery was unquestionably interested in the cultivation of *Victoria regia* for its commercial potential. In the best traditions of marketing, a highly desirable product is nothing without adverting and display. The economic potential of the *Victoria regia* could well have resulted in van Houtte packaging the lily in a glasshouse that used those most modern materials of glass and iron, along with a very contemporary spherical aesthetic. The referencing of another spherically formed *Victoria regia* glasshouse will develop this argument further.

After van Houtte's Nursery, the next to bloom *Victoria regia* in Continental Europe was the Botanical Gardens at Herrenhausen, on 29 June 1851. This was followed by the Botanical Gardens of Hamburg in 1851 (Hochstetter, 1852), and Berlin (Schöneberg) on 22 July 1852 (Lack, 2004). Three days prior to the latter (i.e., 19 July 1852), the previously mentioned industrialist Johann Borsig bloomed his *Victoria regia* at his Moabit Villa in Berlin (Hinckeldeyn and Sarrazin, 1883). In 1851, Borsig instructed the engineers who worked at his famous *Borsig Werke* (Borsig Works) to design and construct a glasshouse for the *Victoria regia*. This glasshouse was described as a detached iron-and-glass structure that had a glazed dome that was heated with water from the nearby Borsig Works (Lack, 2004). Alternatively, the glasshouse was described as an elegant glass temple construction of dainty iron rods (www.bgbm.org, 2010). Planted on 9 May 1852 and flowering two months later, the *Victoria regia*, in its new *Glaspalast* (Glass palace), transformed the formerly tranquil Borsig Gardens. From this point onward, the Borsig Gardens became a major Berlin attraction (Wittmack, 1894). By the end of 1852, the lily was additionally found at Tübingen, Leipzig, Dresden, Bonn, Stuttgart, Karlsruhe, Konstanz, and at The Botanical Gardens at Schönbrunn in Vienna (Hochstetter, 1852).

In many ways, Borsig was very similar to van Houtte. Prussia, in the first half of the 19th century, set itself on a course of industrialisation. Through prominent personalities, such as Peter Beuth, Karl Schinkel and Peter Lenné, Prussia sought to mirror the very best of British industrialisation – its material wealth, freedoms and national power – without its faults; i.e. pollution and disease. Prussia would rather have an aestheticized version of industrial society (Thompson and Galison, 1999). As such, in 1821, a new institution, the *Preu ische Gewerbeförderung* (Trade Promotion Institute of Prussia) was established (Baumol, Mokyr and Landes, 2010). In the early part of the 19th century, Prussia was almost totally dependent on, mostly British, imported precision tools and machinery – importantly, steam engines (Wise, 1995). Thus, along with the *Gewerbeförderung*, numerous *Gewerbeschule* (Trade Schools) were established, including Beuth's in Berlin. At the Berlin *Gewerbeschule*, British machinery was illegally imported and carefully studied, with the ultimate aim of copying the machinery and manufacturing clones in Prussia (Kitchen, 1978). Borsig was one of the Berlin *Gewerbeschule*'s prominent pupils (Wise, 1995). Initially, Borsig was trained as a carpenter, but, having attended the *Gewerbeschule*, he quickly established his reputation as a master mechanic (Sheehan, 1989). With the aid of Prussian government subsidies, in 1837, Borsig established a steam-engine manufacturing business in Berlin. Initially, the Borsig factory supplied steam engines for sugar beet refining, but in 1841 produced its first locomotive based on an American design. By 1848, Borsig was in a position to supply the entire demand of the Prussian railways, and, by 1854, had produced some 500 locomotives (Biesinger, 2006).

The neoclassical Borsig Villa was built in the new industrial Berlin suburb of Moabit. Separating the Villa from the adjacent Borsig Works was a park design by Lenné. As stated above, adjoining the Villa, in a manner typical of private winter gardens, was a cast-iron glazed glasshouse in the form of a masonry colonnaded hall, with skylights and large window openings. This winter garden was directly accessible from the Villa via the salon and living room. Adjoining this winter garden was a long, lean-to, cast-iron-framed forcing house, which opened out onto the garden. The roof of the forcing house was constructed according to the ridge-and-furrow principle and the front elevation comprised a series of thin cast-iron columns that had a highly ornate cast-iron frieze. Both of these glasshouses were constructed from

108 *Bruno Taut's design inspiration for the Glashaus*

components made in the Borsig Works. A separate, large cubic-shaped palm house was additionally located in the garden. This structure had lean-to ends and was apparently similar to the Great Palm House at the Berlin Botanical Gardens (1857–79) at Schöneberg (Kohlmaier and von Sartory, 1986). The glasshouses were heated by waste hot water from the Borsig factories. This hot water was also drained into open-air ponds in the garden, which contained numerous gold fish and the hybrid *Nymphaea*, developed by Carl Bouche in 1852–53. The sight of these open air ponds, with their exotic inhabitants, was unique to Europe and England; it created a surreal impression of being on the banks of the Rivers Nile or Ganges (Koch, 1857). The *Victoria regia* glasshouse was built in close proximity to these ponds, at the end of the garden, near the banks of the River Spree. The possession, cultivation and public display of rare botanical specimens in technologically advanced glasshouses meant that the Borsig Gardens became part of what would today be termed 'public relations' (Kohlmaier and von Sartory, 1986). Admission fees to the Borsig Gardens formed the basis of a disability fund for the Borsig Works employees. This fee also allowed the visitor to enter the *Victoria regia* glasshouse.

Borsig's intentions in constructing his *Victoria regia* glasshouse were not purely intellectual curiosity; he too was interested in profit and advertising. Moreover, Borsig was not only motivated by horticultural ambition; this new glasshouse was additionally intended as a technical prototype. Indeed, if the glasshouse was a success, it could have been used to expose the public to current or intended products of the Borsig Works, i.e. glasshouses, fountains and irrigation equipment (Lack, 2004). Considering this statement, Borsig's *Victoria regia* glasshouse could also have been an extremely powerful commercial symbol for the product that Borsig was most famous for during the 1840s: steam locomotives – in particular, the *Beuth*. One of the prominent features of the *Beuth* locomotive was the large steam-dome located above the firebox. The purpose of the steam-dome is twofold: it collected dry or superheated steam and then directed the steam into a Steam-funnel/pipe and then onward into the driving mechanism. In turn, the steam-funnel/pipe was projected into the interior of the steam-dome. This kept the top of the steam-funnel well above the water level of the boiler, and prevented the water from entering the driving mechanism. Analogies are immediately apparent: the spherical *Beuth*'s steam-dome could be equated with the hot and humid glazed spherical dome of the *Victoria regia* glasshouse; the steam-funnel could be the central cistern containing the *Victoria regia*, raising the lily above the water level. This analogy is even more pertinent considering the fact that Borsig instructed his engineers – who were first and foremost locomotive engineers – to design the *Victoria regia* glasshouse.

Both the van Houtte and Borsig *Victoria regia* glasshouses established a prototype that was distinct from earlier, mainly British, examples that were regular in plan and cuboid in form. While both borrowed the planning and central location of the cistern from the earlier British examples, they established an overall spherical form that supposedly derived from Loudon's pioneering work. Additionally, these two glasshouses used the then advanced technology of a self-supporting iron frame. The use of curved glazing, in comparison to regular flat planes, was also more expensive to manufacture (Koppelkamm, 1981). Therefore, the spherical glasshouse had an added aura of opulence. It is further proposed that the smooth spherical form of their glasshouses not only suited the botanic needs of the *Victoria regia*, but also satisfied the very important need for promotion and publicity. In turn, the procession and cultivation of the *Victoria regia*, displayed in a technologically, aesthetically advanced and opulent glasshouse, became an item to aid consumerism. From about 1860, most subsequent *Victoria regia* glasshouses were executed according to the circular or polygonal plan, which were covered by flattish curved glazed domes (Kohlmaier and von Sartory, 1986). The setting of the dome low over the central basin was intended to facilitate the economical heating of the interior (Koppelkamm, 1981).

3.17 Further examples of Continental European *Victoria regia* glasshouses

The polygonal plan was apparently first used in Europe by Alphonse Balat in 1853 (Goedleven, 1997). Balat's *Victoria regia* glasshouse was initially located at the Old Brussels Zoo, the present site of the Leopold Park. From the corners of an elegant octagonal plan that measured 46 feet in diameter, curved iron trusses mounted on low stone walls extended upwards and culminated in a decorative crown (Hix, 2005). Supposedly, because of this crown the glasshouse was known as *Kroonserre* (Crown Glasshouse). The structural trusses were placed on the outside of the glazed skin; supposedly solving the problem of cold condensation droplets that could have fallen onto and harmed the interior foliage (Koppelkamm, 1981). An additional aesthetic intention was also implied through the use of ornamental braced trusses and the wrought-iron ribs (Kohlmaier and von Sartory, 1986). The exposed truss structure of Balat's glasshouse was the largest glazed structure of its type in Europe in 1853 (Lack, 2004). As such, Balat's exterior use of structure predated the large structures of Laeken by 20 years, Schönbrunn by 30 years, and Dahlem by 50 years.

A further example of a spherically formed *Victoria regia* glasshouse was constructed at the Botanical Gardens of the University of Leiden in 1870 (Hix, 2005). Here, the *Victoria regia* bloomed for the first time on 8 July 1872, an event to which nearly 30,000 people came to marvel (Hix, 2005).

In 1883, the old wooden *Victoria regia* glasshouse at the Berlin Botanical Gardens, Schöneberg, was replaced. This was because of its dilapidated condition, but also because it did not confirm to the aesthetic standards for current *Victoria regia* glasshouses, which were by then established in Dutch, Belgian and English botanical gardens (Lack, 2004). In the planning of the replacement *Victoria regia* glasshouse, Prof. A.W. Eichler, as the then Director of the

Figure 3.5a The *Victoria regia* glasshouse at the Botanical Gardens at the University of Leiden. Photo by permission of Leiden University Library Collections.

Figure 3.5b The *Victoria regia* glasshouse at the Berlin Botanical Gardens in Schöneberg. Photo by permission of Landesdenkmalamt Berlin.

Gardens, emphasised the need for a prestigious and magnificent building. The result was a building planned on a decagon containing a central cistern for the lily. Rising above the masonry decagon base was a flat iron and glazed dome, which terminated at the apex in a ventilation lantern (Lack, 2004).

The use of *Tausende von Glasschuppen* (thousands of glass flakes/plates) created an extraordinary interior effect in the new Schöneberg *Victoria regia* glasshouse, or *Glaspalastes* (Glass Palace) (Lack, 2004). This 1883 *Victoria regia* glasshouse was intended to have a distinct analogy with the lily: the structure of the dome, with its radiating purlins that were in-filled with thousands of small glass plates, was clearly a comparison to the underside of the *Victoria regia*'s leaf structure (Lack, 2004). In a description of his new glasshouse, the designer F. Schultze made no such comparison (Schultze, 1883). However, Schultze (1883) did mention that the *Victoria regia* formed the central attraction of the botanical gardens. He (1883) also contended that ever since its initial blooming in 1852, large crowds continually flocked to the Schöneberg gardens to see the annual blooming of the lily. As such, he argued, the time was right to construct a new *Victoria regia* glasshouse that would correspond in both size and shape to those that had been built in major European cities during the previous 10 years (Schultze, 1883). The new Schöneberg *Victoria regia* glasshouse's regular decagon had an outside diameter of 16.25 metres. A large central tank of 8½ metres in diameter was centrally located that had a 1-metre-deep central portion for the lily, while the outer extremities of the tank were only 0.3 metres deep. Surrounding the central tank was a circular shaped pathway that was 1½ metres wide. Likewise, a further circular tank, intended for other aquatics and also 1½ metres wide, surrounded the pathway. Furthermore, the external masonry walls were 0.51 metres thick and supported the glazed dome. Crowning the glazed dome was an ornate ventilation lantern that was in-filled with venetian-vent panels and capped with an elaborate iron crown. The glasshouse was heated through a system of closed copper pipes. Schultze was also at pains to claim that if the Berlin Botanical Gardens was to rise in rank and prestige through the construction of facilities such as the new *Victoria regia* glasshouse, then continued financial support would be required from donors so that the Gardens could be comparable to the very best in Europe (Schultze, 1883).

The aims of the Berlin Botanical Gardens were apparently not unique. On 17 March 1887, the Lyon City Council decried the fact that, while most European cities had a glasshouse dedicated to *Victoria regia*, their city did not. Thus, in 1888, a *Victoria regia* glasshouse was constructed according to the plans of M. Oddos, who was the city's Chief Engineer of Roads and Water. This relatively small spherically formed building had a central cistern for the lily that was 7.9 metres in diameter, and surrounded by a 1-metre-wide pathway. This glasshouse, like that at Leiden, had a prominent double-door entrance 'airlock'. Additionally, it also had a simple ventilation lantern at the apex of the glazed dome. *Victoria regia* flowered for the first time on 14 June 1894 in this newly constructed glasshouse. In 1929, the glasshouse was renovated, and a circular basin was added to the outside of the walkway, and the dome structure and cladding were totally remodelled. Even though this design conformed to the already established prototypes, like that at the Berlin Botanical Gardens of 1883, it was unique in France even as late as 1929 (www.jardin-botanique-lyon.com).

A further example of a *Victoria regia* glasshouse was located at the Strasbourg Botanical Gardens. It was inaugurated in 1884, and designed by

112 Bruno Taut's design inspiration for the Glashaus

Georg Peter Hermann Eggert. The plan consisted of a 12-sided regular polygon that measured 12 metres in diameter. A circular cistern, which measured 7 metres in diameter and 0.5 metres deep, was located at the centre of this plan for the *Victoria regia*. A further deeper portion of 0.5 metres was provided at the centre of the cistern. The central cistern was, in turn, surrounded by a circular pathway that was 0.96 metres wide. Surrounding the pathway was a further outer cistern that was 0.71 metres wide. The entrance to the glasshouse consisted of a prominent double-door 'airlock' structure clad in stone, with the boiler room and flue located directly opposite. The glasshouse additionally had a regular iron structure, which rose from low walls (Eggert, 1888). Likewise, in 1888, a *Victoria regia* glasshouse was added to the Copenhagen Botanical Gardens. Located to the east of the 1872 palm house, this glasshouse consisted of a plan that was a regular 24-sided polygon. The Copenhagen *Victoria regia* glasshouse had relatively steep sloping glazing, which was undoubtedly necessitated by the need to shed snow during the Scandinavian winter.

3.18 The Berlin Botanical Gardens relocated to Dahlem

By 1888, the spread of tenements (*Mietskasernen*) had rapidly surrounded the Berlin Botanical Gardens, Schöneberg, and was literally choking the air from the Gardens. By this time, many of the existing glasshouses were in poor condition, and the Gardens were without a Director (Lack, 2004). Within this context, the Assistant Director of the Berlin Botanical Gardens, Ignatz Urban, proposed that the Gardens should be relocated to a new 40-hectare site in the Berlin suburb of Dahlem. Initially, the new Director, Prof. Adolf Engler, appointed in 1889, was sceptical of these proposed relocation plans. Apart from the potential loss of valuable botanic specimens, Engler also feared that the proposed move would additionally create a physical dislocation between the Gardens and the Berlin city centre. Despite these reservations, on 26 June 1897, a new law formally relocated the Berlin Botanical Gardens to Dahlem, and 4 million German marks were provided for the new gardens and structures (Lack, 2004). The architect Alfred Korner, together with the landscape architect Axel Fintelmann, began the design of the new gardens.

On 24 May 1910, Engler, along with botanists from around the world, celebrated the official opening of the Berlin Botanical Garden at Dahlem. Engler, who had previously visited a number of other botanical gardens, initially proposed an axial-designed glasshouse complex that followed the design of the glasshouses he had encountered – a large central palm house with a smaller spherical glasshouse (*kugelförmigen Eckbau*) located on either side of it (Lack, 2004). This description of Engler's design proposal is undoubtedly reminiscent of examples such as the palm houses of Kew and Belfast. In contrast, Korner, who was commissioned by the Ministry of Public Works, in his first sketch designs that were first published in 1895, proposed a much larger rectangular or 'C' shaped glasshouse complex. Interestingly, in this 1895 plan, the *Victoria regia* glasshouse was not yet part of the central glasshouse complex; Korner, instead, proposed that the relatively new 1883 Schöneberg *Victoria regia* glasshouse be relocated to Dahlem. In the spring of 1899, Engler decided to integrate the *Victoria regia* glasshouse into the centre of the 'C' shaped glasshouse complex. This development followed the advice given by Director Siebert of the Frankfurt *Flora*. In 1905, the *Victoria regia* glasshouse was formally incorporated into the main glasshouse complex that was considered a masterpiece of engineering and was equipped with the very latest in technology, like electric lighting, water humidifiers, and electrically operated vents. The heating of the new glasshouse complex was accomplished by four boilers that circulated steam in iron pipes to the individual glasshouses. Consequently, in the summer of 1910, the first Dahlem *Victoria regia* was brought to bloom in the newly constructed glasshouse (Lack, 2004). The design of the Dahlem glasshouse complex was almost certainly influenced by the wider tendency towards such large, centrally located installations.

In 1905, the Frankfurt Botanical Gardens constructed a new glasshouse complex. Unlike Dahlem's 'C' planning, Frankfurt was designed as a 'solid' rectangular planned complex of glasshouses that were centred around a large central palm house with two smaller wings to the left and right. Contained within this complex was a span roofed glasshouse for the *Victoria regia* (Sarrazin and Schultze, 1907). At approximately the same time as Frankfurt, similar 'solid' rectangular planned complexes of glasshouses were additionally constructed in the Munich suburb of Nymphenburg.

Apart from these German examples, the American glasshouse complexes at New York and San Francisco can be considered as examples of the tendency toward large, centrally planned glasshouse complexes. The glasshouse, complex or Phipps Conservatory, at the Philadelphia Botanical Gardens is also of interest. In the later decades of the 19th century, the eastern Pittsburgh suburb Oakland was considered the richest neighbourhood in the world. Oakland, alternatively known as the East End, was home to prominent industrialists and armature botanists like Henry Frick, Henry Heinz and Henry Phipps. As a result of these and other individuals' immense wealth, the East End predictably contained many large gardens and glasshouses. In these settings, Frick cultivated outstanding roses and orchids and was an acknowledged expert on growing mushrooms. Heinz, in turn, nurtured pansies and chrysanthemums in a garden that rivalled Versailles. As the East End's glasshouses contained many exotic flowers and trees, they were open to the public during the weekends. As a result of this public interest, in 1893, Phipps financed the construction of the Phipps Conservatory (Skrabec, 2010). Phipps was a business partner and childhood friend of Andrew Carnegie. Both of them were deeply involved in steel production (Skrabec, 2010), but Phipps' fortune additionally came from speculation in real estate (Squirrel Hill Historical Society, 2005). The Phipps Conservatory was constructed by

114 *Bruno Taut's design inspiration for the Glashaus*

the firm Lord and Burnham and consisted of nine display glasshouses that had 'silvered' glazed vaults (Squirrel Hill Historical Society, 2005). As the prominent glasshouse contractor of its time, Lord and Burnham were also responsible for the glasshouse complex in New York. Both the glasshouse complexes at New York and Philadelphia had similar Victorian aesthetics. Interestingly, Lord and Burnham pioneered curvilinear iron framed glasshouses in the United States of America, with the 1881 construction of the glasshouse complex for the railroad magnate Jay Gould at his Lyndhurst Estate (Kohlmaier and von Sartory, 1986). In its day, this glasshouse complex was the largest in the United States of America (Renehan, 2008). On opening, the Phipps Conservatory featured a large collection of tropical plants from the 1893 World's Colombian Exposition in Chicago (Squirrel Hill Historical Society, 2005). Interestingly, the *Victoria regia* was displayed in numerous locations at the World's Colombian Exposition. The first display was located in an open air pond between the glazed dome of the Horticulture Building and the artificial lagoon (Hays, Chandler and Crane, 1892; Igleheart and White, 1893). The second was located inside the Horticulture Building, in the south court which contained a wine cellar from the Rhine area in Germany. Here the *Victoria regia* was located in several artificially heated basins with other aquatic plants (Handy, 1893). Likewise, as early as 1895, the *Victoria regia* was also on display at the Phipps Conservatory (Skrabec, 2010).

3.19 Conclusion

This detailed analysis of glasshouses seeks to propose alternative explanations for the origins of Bruno Taut's *Glashaus*. It has been shown that these can be found within the affinities that the *Glashaus* shared with the glasshouses constructed for the *Victoria regia* lily. Likewise, it has been shown that the *Victoria regia* glasshouses did not themselves evolve in isolation – they too had distinct similarities with earlier glasshouse precedents.

Hix (2005) has argued that glazed modern architecture was the result of almost 250 years of experimentation with horticultural glasshouses. A similar view is expressed by Kohlmaier and von Sartory (1986) when they stated that horticultural glasshouses prepared the way for modernist architecture. What is most significant about this last statement is that while the relationship between horticultural glasshouses and modernist architecture has been alluded to by numerous authors, such as Gideon (Giedion, 1928, 1976), Gloag and Bridgewater (1948), Hitchcock (1958), Henning-Schefeld and Schmidt-Thomsen (1972), Roisecco (1972), Pevsner (1976) and Benevolo (1978), it had yet to be '...systematically investigated and described' (Kohlmaier and von Sartory, 1986: 5).

Two facts are immediately apparent if the *Glashaus* is considered in light of Kohlmaier and von Sartory's (1986) call for further investigation. First, the aesthetics of the *Glashaus* closely resembles that of certain horticultural glasshouses. Second, the *Glashaus* occupied an important junction between modernist architecture and preceding periods. The initial conclusion is that horticultural glasshouses were 'inspiration' for the *Glashaus*' design. However, two links are still required: the initial explicit linking of the horticultural glasshouse 'inspiration' to both the 'design' of the *Glashaus* and Taut's writings, and the deciphering of the 'poetics' inherent in Taut's writings.

The explicit linking of the horticultural glasshouse 'inspiration' to the 'design' of the *Glashaus* is possible. Accepting the argument that Scheerbart's role has been overstated does not however totally dismiss his contribution. Scheerbart, apart from having an uncanny technical knowledge of modern materials and botanical glasshouse construction, also named specific glasshouses at the Berlin Botanical Gardens, Dahlem, in his 1914 publication *Glasarchitektur*.

As mentioned, the construction of the main glasshouse complex at the Berlin Botanical Gardens, Dahlem, began in 1907, and later officially opened in May 1910 (Lack, 2004). Taut returned to Berlin in 1908 to pursue further studies at the *Technische Hochschule* in Berlin-Charlottenburg, and subsequently opened his own Berlin office in 1909 (Hartmann, Nerdinger, Schirren and Speidel, 2001; Junghanns, 1983). Taut's Berlin offices, which he shared with Franz Hoffmann, were initially located south-west of the city centre in *Linkstra e*, but later also in *Potsdamer Stra e* (Junghanns, 1983). Both of these locations were within seven to eight kilometres of the new Berlin Botanical Gardens. Additionally, these two locations were also a mere three kilometres from the Borsig *Victoria regia* glasshouse and one to two kilometres from the location of the Old Berlin Botanical Gardens, Schöneberg. It is not known whether either the Borsig or Schöneberg *Victoria regia* glasshouses still existed in 1908. As mentioned above, Korner's 1895 plan for Dahlem considered incorporating the Schöneberg *Victoria regia* glasshouse, which was still at this stage 'relatively new'. Additionally, in the photo of the Borsig Works that was taken around 1900, the Borsig *Victoria regia* glasshouse is visible. Thus, it is proposed that when Taut returned to Berlin in 1908 both the Borsig and Schöneberg *Victoria regia* glasshouses still existed. But once again no documentary evidence can be found that directly links Taut with any of these. However, it is highly likely that Taut had direct knowledge of the glasshouse construction activity at Berlin Botanical Gardens, Dahlem, which, as explained above, contained a *Victoria regia* glasshouse at its very centre. A closer comparison between the *Victoria regia* (both from the perspective of the glasshouses built to cultivate it and from the lily itself) and Taut's *Glashaus* reveals startling and immediate similarities.

As stated above, from about 1860, most *Victoria regia* glasshouses were executed according to a circular or polygonal plan that were covered by flattish curved glazed domes. If regular cuboid-shaped *Victoria regia* glasshouses are excluded, it is clear from the argument presented above that initially, *Victoria regia* glasshouses had circular plans; e.g. the van Houtte/Ortgies (1850) and Borsig (1851) examples. It is also clear that polygonal plans emerged only later; e.g. the Balat (1854) example. In all of the examples presented above, the central component of the plan was always occupied by a large (nearly always circular) tank or cistern that accommodated the *Victoria regia*. Likewise, this central tank was, in most cases, surrounded by a pathway, which was further surrounded by a tank for smaller aquatic plants. The circular planned *Victoria regia* glasshouses can be directly connected to Loudon's conceptual aquarium (1822) and the pioneering smoothed curved glasshouses of W. & D. Bailey. When the plan of the *Glashaus* is compared to that of the circular planned *Victoria regia* glasshouses, similarities are immediately apparent. The overall forms of both buildings were similar; outwardly, both were stand-alone pavilion type buildings, and both had a low squat solid base that contained the pools and mechanical equipment needed to maintain them. Both had a distinct entrance, which rose upwards through the base. The main features of both buildings were their glazed curved domes, which sprang from the base, that were highly faceted. Additionally, both domes had a 'lantern' or 'accumulated apex' at the top of the dome. However, the dome over the *Glashaus* was intended to shed rain, much like Loudon's 1822 proposal. Furthermore, both plans were based on regular polygon/circular arrangements, and both had a deeper central 'pool' to their designs. In the case of the *Glashaus*, the 'pool' could either have been the physical cascade or the oculus that connected the Dome Room to the Cascade Room below.

Certain aspects of the *Glashaus* are reminiscent of particular features of *Victoria regia* glasshouses. The dome of Taut's *Glashaus* had a seemingly curious external diameter of 11.06 metres. However, when this number is considered within the context of the *Victoria regia*, it becomes apparent why Taut would have used it. As mentioned above, the van Houtte/Ortgies' *Victoria regia* glasshouse of 1850 had an overall diameter of 11.03 metres, while Paxton's *Victoria regia* glasshouse (1849–50) had a central tank that was 33 feet, or 10.06 metres, in diameter (Lindley, 1850). Likewise, The Exotic Nursery in Kings Road, Chelsea, had small vases placed on the lip of the central tank, and pendant vases to the underside of the roof. Could these vases not be synonymous with the electric lights that hung in the interior of the *Glashaus'* dome room and the glazed spheres that surrounded the base of the *Glashaus*? Furthermore, the movement of the water, mostly through the use of a small waterwheel, has been identified above as a prominent feature of *Victoria regia* tanks. Could the cascade in the *Glashaus* not be an interpretation, in a more elegant form as Weale (1851) had proposed, of this feature?

However, it could also be proposed that all of the above arguments are still only circumstantial associations.

The *Victoria regia* glasshouse at the Berlin Botanical Gardens, Dahlem, has seven distinct portions to its outer half-circle plan; in contrast, the *Glashaus* had exactly twice this number and so formed a 'full' 14-sided plan. This straightforward analogy is made more tangible when the plan of the *Glashaus* is overlaid onto the Dahlem *Victoria regia* glasshouse. It now becomes evident that the proportions of both are strikingly similar, and both

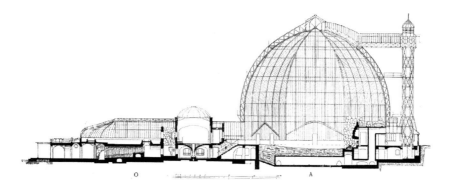

Figure 3.6 A section through the *Victoria regia* (left) and main palm (right) glasshouses at the Berlin Botanical Gardens in Dahlem.

were apparently planned as a series of concentric circles. Of particular interest are the two semi-circular staircases that lead from the lower levels at the Berlin Botanical Gardens upwards to the *Victoria regia* glasshouse's upper terrace; this arrangement is distinctly similar to the interior staircases of the *Glashaus*. The positions of the columns supporting the *Glashaus'* dome align with the positioning of the riser strings of the *Victoria regia* glasshouse. Furthermore, the width of *Glashaus'* interior stairs aligns uncannily with the width of the Dahlem *Victoria regia* glasshouse's upper terrace. This alignment of proportion is again repeated when comparing the highest portion of the *Glashaus'* water cascade with the width of the central pool in the *Victoria regia* glasshouse. The Dahlem *Victoria regia* glasshouse had at its centre an elongated pool, which differs from the strictly circular pool that was common in the post-1860 examples of *Victoria regia* glasshouses. In a similar manner, the *Glashaus* also had an elongated 'pool' (cascade) at it centre.

To enter the Dahlem *Victoria regia* glasshouse, a visitor could proceed from either the lower gardens or the main palm house. This entailed either entering the darker, grotto-like lower floor (if entering from the lower gardens), or down a flight of stairs and then across a brightly lit double-volume space (if entering from the main palm house). Principally, these two routes then converged at a central point that proceeded upwards, originally through a set of curving stairs, to a Swampland glasshouse above with a glazed dome. Once again, this route was distinctly similar to that of the *Glashaus*. In Taut's design, the visitor proceeded up an initial flight of stairs contained in the flared circular base and then entered the building by climbing the semi-circular stairs that led ultimately to the brightly lit dome area above. From here, the visitor progressed downwards using a different set of semi-circular stairs into the darker Cascade Room. Following the cascade downward, the visitor was then directed into the shadowy, more constricted and linear kaleidoscope room, which eventually led to the exit. The original Swampland glasshouse of the Berlin Botanical Gardens has today been replaced by a flat-roofed concrete reception hall, and the spiral staircases have been replaced by a lift. The original Swampland glasshouse had at its centre an oculus, which illuminated the *Brunnensaal* (Fountain Hall) below. The light from the oculus was directed downwards through a small colonnaded structure towards a small circular fountain at the centre of the *Brunnensaal*'s floor. This original arrangement is strikingly similar to the *Glashaus*.

Therefore, it can be argued that the 'inspiration' of the *Victoria regia* glasshouse is highly evident in a number of key features of the 'design' of the *Glashaus*. However, what is still required is the evidence that would establish the correlation of this *Victoria regia* 'inspiration' within Taut's writings. Direct evidence of this can be found in Taut's 1920 film script entitled, 'Die Galoschen des Glucks', and in his 1920 publication *Die Auflösung der Städte*.

In 'Die Galoschen des Glucks', Taut made a direct reference to the *Victoria regia*:

> ...the man leads the youth into a wondrous chamber. Here there are many strange growths, great floating leaves (like victoria regia) and many others. The man takes a curious rod, tickles the growths with its point, and out of the leaves grow houses, yes houses, as sparkling and dream-like as his own, like opalescent domes, butterfly-wing buildings – oh, inexpressible – a fairy-tale city reflected in the water, ravishingly beautiful...
>
> (Whyte and Taut, 1985: 120)

Apart from the direct mention of *Victoria regia*, the above quote refers to houses that 'grow' from giant floating leaves – leaves that are like those of *Victoria regia*. Not just any houses 'grow' from these *Victoria regia*–like leaves, but domed opalescent shimmering houses. The 'Die Galoschen des Glucks' has already been proposed as an analogy of Taut's life up to 1920 – the 'youth' is Taut, the 'man' is Scheerbart and the 'wondrous chamber' is possibly a *Victoria regia* glasshouse. From the extract above, 'as his own' can be interpreted in two ways: it could either be the 'houses' of the 'man' (Scheerbart), or it could also refer to the 'houses' of the 'youth' (Taut). Thus, 'as his own' could refer to Taut's own sparkling dream-like house – a house that grows from 'giant floating leaves'. Could the quote therefore be a retrospective acknowledgment by Taut that the *Victoria regia* served as the direct inspiration for his *Glashaus*?

In *Die Auflösung der Städte*, Taut illustrated what appears to be the 'houses' that grew from the 'giant floating leaves', in an image of 1920 entitled *Die Grosse Blume*. A comparison between the *Die Grosse Blume* and the *Glashaus* reveals some similarities: the overall composition of *Die Grosse Blume* is concentrically planned like the *Glashaus*. The largest leaf had seven distinct portions like the *Glashaus*. Could this largest leaf be proposed as the flared concrete base that surrounded the *Glashaus*? On the largest leaf, a smaller leaf, with a ring of 'columns' to the periphery was also present. Could this smaller leaf be the main body of the *Glashaus* that included the circulation stairs with its ring of reinforced concrete columns? At the centre of this smaller second leaf was a further smallest leaf. This smallest leaf was in turn surrounded by a ring of more delicate 'columns'. Could this be representative of the *Glashaus'* inner dome with the Cascade Room below? Curiously, the *Die Grosse Blume* had a tower-like object that appeared at the periphery of the smaller leaf. While this could immediately be proposed as the dome of the *Glashaus*, it would be problematic because it is not placed at the centre of the leaves.

An alternative explanation for this tower-like object could be that the opalescent, sparkling tower-like structure in reality represented the kaleidoscope that was present in the *Glashaus*. This is probable considering that the tower-like object is illustrated as apparently emitting light. Alternatively, the tower-like structure could have a more direct connection to the story of the *Victoria regia*. On 17 November 1849, the *London News* published an image of Joseph Paxton's daughter Annie standing on a *Victoria regia* leaf. This initial image, demonstrating the phenomenal carrying capacity of *Victoria regia's* leaves, served as the archetype for an act that was often repeated and photographed well into the 20th century. Seen in this light, could the tower-like structure on the 'leaf' be symbolic of this specific *Victoria regia* act?

'Die Galoschen des Glucks' continued:

> …Glow worms suddenly appear and come nearer. Seen from above they are illuminated glass domes. One unfolds and turns into an architectural flower, with a moving light at its base. We seem to fly inside. At the bottom of the flower [is] the shoe library of the Child of Fortune. He is surrounded by box-like compartments… He opens the compartments and examines the shoes… On a glass table in the middle of the room stand the two pairs of lucky shoes… Satisfied, he takes them in his small hands and flies out of his blossom-house…
>
> (Whyte and Taut, 1985: 122)

Victoria regia is most renowned for its massive leaves and gigantic flowers. Startling similarities are evident when a comparison is made between a *Victoria regia* flower and the quote above. *Victoria regia* is pollinated by scarab beetles that belong to the Genus *Cyclocephala*. These Scarab beetles fly into the flower of *Victoria regia* and are captured by the flower, only to be released after a 24-hour period. Are the 'glow worms' that become glass domes that then metamorphose into architectural flowers not the *Victoria regia's* scarab beetles? The flowers of *Victoria regia* are initially a brilliant white, but slowly metamorphose into a pinkish colour over a 24-hour period. The flower of *Victoria regia* is divided into two distinct portions, namely an upper open portion mainly comprising the petals, and a lower enclosed space that contains the reproductive organs.

The upper portion of the flower is comparable to the dome of the *Glashaus*. The geometry of the upper portion of *Victoria regia* flower looks remarkably like the geometry of the *Glashaus* dome. Additionally, the lower portion of the flower, separated by an oculus from the upper portion, has a strong affinity to the Cascade Room of Taut's *Glashaus*, which was also separated from the Dome Room above it by an oculus. The lower portion of the *Victoria regia* flower contains the blooms' reproductive organs and appears as highly 'compartmentalised'. This is comparable to 'box-like compartments' of the 'shoe library' in the quote. Similarly, the 'table at the centre of the room' could be the oculus that was at the centre of the *Glashaus*. Finally, the 'moving light' at the base of the 'architectural flower' could well be the glass spheres that surrounded the base of the *Glashaus*. Therefore, Taut's reference to 'architectural flower' and 'blossom-house' makes a strong, though implicit connection between his *Glashaus* and the *Victoria regia*.

From the discussion of the *Victoria regia* and the *Glashaus* another important aspect becomes evident: the *Victoria regia* was not only a proto-type to be copied, it was also a powerful symbol of prowess that reflected the desires of the client. On the one hand, the *Victoria regia* glasshouse of Ortgies (1850) embodied the distinct commercial aspects of the van Houtte nursery business. Borsig (1851), on the other hand, constructed his glasshouse for profit and advertising; his glasshouse was intended to be a technical prototype that would expose the public to glasshouses, fountains and irrigation equipment of the Borsig Works. Meanwhile, the *Victoria regia* glasshouses constructed at the Berlin Botanical Gardens were meant to be a central attraction, and to implicitly express the national prowess of the emergent German nation. Likewise, the Lyon (1888) glasshouse was intended as a progressive symbol of 'modernity'.

It is clear that the general 'inspiration' of botanical glasshouses was provoked by the specific 'inspiration' of the *Victoria regia*, which in turn can be linked with the central components of the 'design' of the *Glashaus*. 'Inspiration' and 'design' are then linked with the 'poetics' of Taut's writings. The argument outlined above establishes that it is highly likely that Bruno Taut directly referenced *Victoria regia* in his design of the *Glashaus*.

Bibliography

Allen, J. F. (1854). *Victoria regia, or the Great Water Lily of America*. Salem, MA: Dutton and Wentworth.

Banham, R. (1959). The Glass Paradise. *The Architectural Review, 125*(February), 87–89.

Baumol, W. J., Mokyr, J. and Landes, D. S. (eds). (2010). *The Invention of Enterprise: Entrepreneurship from Ancient Mesopotamia to Modern Times*. Princeton, NJ: Princeton University Press.

Benevolo, L. (1978). *Geschichte der Architektur des 19. und 20. Jahrhunderts Volumes 1 und 2*. Munich: DTV.

Biesinger, J. A. (2006). *Germany: A Reference Guide from the Renaissance to the Present*. New York: Facts On File.

Cavendish, D. V. (1999). *The Duchess of Devonshire: The Gardens at Chatsworth*. London: Frances Lincoln Limited.

Chadwick, G. F. (1961). *The Works of Sir Joseph Paxton 1803–1865*. London: The Architectural Press.

Colquhoun, A. (1983). Three Kinds of Historicism. *Architectural Design, 53*(9–10).

Day, J. C. (2005). Characterisation of the luciferase gene and the 5' upstream region in the European glow-worm Lampyris noctiluca (Coleoptera: Lampyridae). *European Journal of Entomology, 102*, 787–791.

Desmond, R. (1995). *Kew: The History of the Royal Botanic Gardens*. London: Harvill Press with the Royal Botanical Gardens, Kew.

Durant, S. (1999). Ferdinand Dutert, Palais des Machines, Paris 1889 *Lost masterpieces*. London: Phaidon Press.

Eggert, G. P. H. (1888). Kaiser Wilhelms Universität Strafsburg- Der Cfarten des Botanischen Instituts. *Zeitschrift für Bauwesen, 4*(6), 199–212.

Ersoy, U. (2008). *Seeing Through Glass: The fictive Role of Glass in Shaping Architecture from Joseph Paxton's 'Crystal Palace' to Bruno Taut's 'Glashaus'*. (PhD), Philadelphia, PA: University of Pennsylvania.

Fay, C. R. (1951). *Palace of Industry 1851: A Study of the Great Exhibition and its Fruits* Cambridge: Cambridge University Press.

Flanders-Darby, M. (2002). Joseph Paxton's Water Lily. In M. Conan (ed.), *Bourgeois and Aristocratic Cultural Encounters in Garden Art, 1550–1850* (Vol. 23). Washington, DC: Dumbarton Oaks

Fontane, T. (1990). *Sämtliche Romane, Erzählungen, Gedichte, Nachgelassenes* (Vol. 2). Munich: Hanser Verlag.

Giedion, S. (1928). *Bauen in Frankreich, Bauen in Eisen, Bauen in Eisenbeton*. Leipzig: Klinkhardt and Biermann.

Giedion, S. (1977). *Space, Time and Architecture: The growth of a New Tradition* (5 edn.). Cambridge, MA: Harvard University Press.

Gloag, J. and Bridgewater, D. (1948). *A History of Cast-iron in Architecture*. London: George Allen and Unwin Ltd.

Goedleven, E. (1997). *De Koninklijke Serres van Laken*. Brussels: Fererale Voorlichtingsdienste.

Handy, M. P. (1893). *The Official Directory of the World's Columbian Exposition, May 1st to October 30th, 1893*. Chicago: W.B. Conkey Company.

Harley, B. and Harley, J. (1992). *A Gardener at Chatsworth: Three Years in the Life of Robert Aughtie, 1848–1850*. Worcestershire: Hanley Swan.

Hartmann, K., Nerdinger, W., Schirren, M. and Speidel, M. (2001). *Bruno Taut 1880–1938: Architekt zwischen Tradition und Avantgarde*. Stuttgart, Munich: Deutsche Verlags-Anstalt DVA.

Hays, C., Chandler, F. and Crane, C. S. (1892). *1492: The World's Columbian exposition, Chicago, 1893*. St. Louis: Passenger Department of the Wabash Railroad Company.

Hennig-Schefold, M. and Schmidt-Thomsen, H. (1972). *Transparenz und Masse: Passagen und Hallen aus Eisen und Glas 1800–1880*. Cologne: DuMont Schauberg.

Hill, A. W. (1915). The History and Functions of Botanic Gardens *Annals of the Missouri Botanical Garden* (Vol. 2, pp. 185–240). St. Louis, MI: Missouri Botanical Garden Press.

Hinckeldeyn, K. and Sarrazin, O. (eds). (1883). *Zentralblatt der Bauverwaltung* (Vol. 15). Berlin: Ernst and Korn.

Hitchcock, H.-R. (1977). *Architecture: Nineteenth and Twentieth Centuries*. New Haven, CT: Yale University Press Pelican History Series.

Hix, J. (2005). *The Glasshouse*. London Phaidon.

Hochstetter, W. (1852). *Die Victoria regia: Ihre Geschichte, Natur, Benennung und Culture*. Tübingen: August Ludwig.

Hooker, W. J. (1847a). *Description of Victoria regia or Great Water-Lily of South America*. London: Reeve Brothers.

Hooker, W. J. (ed.). (1847b). *Curtis's Botanical Magazine* (Vol. 73). London: Reeve, Benham and Reeve.

Huysmans, J. K. (1908). *Certains*. Paris: Plon-Nourrit et cie.

Igleheart, W. M. and White, T. (1893). *The World's Colombian Exposition, Chicago, 1893*. Chicago, IL: P. W. Zeigler & Company.

Johnson, G. and Hogg, R. (eds). (1876). *The Journal of Horticulture, Cottage Gardener and Country Gentleman* (Vol. 30). London: The Journal of Horticulture, Cottage Gardener and Country Gentleman.

Jones-Loyd, S. (1851). *Transactions of the Society of Arts, Manufactures and Commerce*. London: The Royal Society of Arts.

Junghanns, K. (1983). *Bruno Taut, 1880–1938*. Berlin (West): Elefanten Press.

Kitchen, M. (1978). *The Political Economy of Germany, 1815–1914*. London: Croom Helm.

Koch, K. (ed.). (1857). *Allgemeine Gartenzeitung* (Vol. 35). Berlin: Nauckschen Buchhandlung.

Kohlmaier, G. and von Sartory, B. (1986). *Houses of Glass: A Nineteenth-century Building Type*. Cambridge, MA: MIT Press.

Koppelkamm, S. (1981). *Glasshouses and Wintergardens of the Nineteenth Century* (K. Talbot, Trans.). London: Granada Publishing Limited.

Korn, A. (1967). *Glass in Modern Architecture* (D. Sharp, Trans.). London Barrie & Rockliff.

Lack, H. W. (ed.). (2004). *Victoria and Co. in Berlin*. Berlin: Botanisches Museum Berlin-Dahlem.

Lindley, J. (ed.). (1849). *The Gardeners' Chronicle and Agricultural Gazette*. London: Bradbury and Evans.

Lindley, J. (ed.). (1850). *The Gardeners' Chronicle and Agricultural Gazette*. London: Bradbury and Evans

Loudon, J. C. (1817). *Remarks on the Construction of Hothouses, pointing out the most Advantageous Forms, Materials, and Contrivances to be Used in their Construction*. London: Taylor.

Loudon, J. C. (1822). *An Encyclopedia of Gardening; Comprising the Theory and Practice of Horticulture, Floriculture, Arboriculture and Landscape Gardening*. London: Longman, Hurst, Rees, Orme and Brown.

Maciuika, J. V. (2005). *Before the Bauhaus: Architecture, Politics and the German State, 1890–1920*. New York: Cambridge University Press.

Mackenzie, G. S. (1815). On the Form which the Glass of a Forcing-house ought to have, in order to receive the greatest possible quantity of Rays from the Sun. In J.

Banks (ed.). *Transactions of the Horticultural Society of London* (3 edn., Vol. 2, pp. 171–177). London: Horticultural Society of London.

Markham, V. (1935). *Paxton and the Bachelor Duke*. London: Hodder & Stoughton Limited.

McIntosh, C. (1838). *The Greenhouse, Hothouse and Stove*. London: W. S. Orr and Company.

Meyer-Rochow, V. B. (2007). Glowworms: a Review of Arachnocampa spp. and kin *Luminescence, 22*(3), 251–265.

Meyer, G. and Schultze, F. (eds). (1916). *Zeitschrift für Bauwesen* (Vol. 66). Berlin: Wilhelm Ernst unt Sohn.

Moore, T. and Ayres, W. (eds). (1850). *The Gardeners' Magazine of Botany, Horticulture, Floriculture and Natural Science*. London: W. S. Orr and Company.

Morren, C. A. M. (ed.). (1833–8). *L'Horticulteur Belge, Journal des Jardiniers et des Amateurs*. Brussels: V. AD. Stapleaus.

Muthesius, H. (1902). *Stilarchitektur und Baukunst: Wandlungen der Architektur im XIX. Jahrhundert und ihr heutiger Standpunkt*. Mülheim-Ruhr: Schimmelpfeng.

Parent, F. (ed.). (1850). *Journal D'Horticulture Pratique de la Belgique*. Brussels: F. Parent.

Paxton, J. (1850). The Industrial Palace in Hyde Park, *The Illustrated London News*, pp. 385–386.

Pevsner, N. (1976). *A History of Building Types*. Princeton, NJ: Princeton University Press.

Prance, G. (1980). A Note on the Pollination of Nymphaea Amazonum Mart. & Zucc. (Nymphaeaceae). *Brittonia, 32*(4), 505–507.

Renehan, E. (2008). *Dark Genius of Wall Street: The Misunderstood Life of Jay Gould, King of the Robber Barons*. New York: Basic Books.

Roisecco, G. (1972). *l'Architettura del Ferro*. Rome: Bulzoni.

Sala-Newby, G. B., Thompson, C. M. and Campbell, A. K. (1996). Sequence and biochemical similarities between the luciferases of the glow-worm Lampyris noctiluca and the firefly Photinus pyralis. *Biochemical Journal, 313*, 761–767.

Sarrazin, O. and Schultze, F. (1907). Die neuen Pflanzenschauhäuser im Palmengarten in Frankfurt am Main. *Zentralblatt der Bauverwaltung, 43*, 283–287.

Scheerbart, P. (1914). *Glasarchitektur*. Berlin: Strum.

Schrader, D. (2008). *Extraordinary Leaves*. Buffalo, New York: Firefly Books.

Schultze, F. (1883). Das neue Victoria-regia-Haus des Botanischen Gartens in Berlin. *Zentralblatt der Bauverwaltung, 3*(15), 133–134.

Sharp, D. (1966). *Modern architecture and expressionism* London: Longmans.

Sheehan, J. J. (1989). *German History, 1770–1866*. Oxford, England: Oxford University Press.

Skrabec, Q. (2010). *The World's Richest Neighbourhood: How Pittsburgh's East Enders Forged American Industry*. New York: Algora Publishing.

Speidel, M. (2015, 16 January). [Re: Bruno Taut Glashaus].

Squirrel Hill Historical Society. (2005). *Images of America: Squirrel Hill*. Chicago, IL: Arcadia Publishing.

Taut, B. (1920a). *Der Welt Baumeister Architektur-Schauspiel für symphonische Musik* Hagen: Folkwang.

Taut, B. (1920b). Die Galoschen des Glucks. In I. B. Whyte (ed.). *The Crystal Chain Letters: Architectural Fantasies by Bruno Taut and his circle* (pp. 118–122). Cambridge, MA: MIT Press.

Taut, B. (1921). Das Bauen mit Glas. *Qualitat 2, 3/4*, 35–39.

124 Bruno Taut's design inspiration for the Glashaus

Thanos, C. A. (2000, July 6–8, 2000). *The Geography of Theophrastus' life and his Botanical Writings*. Paper presented at the Theophrastus 2000: Biodiversity and Natural Heritage in the Aegean, Eressos, Lesbos.

Thiekotter, A. (1993). *Kristallisationen, Splitterrungen: Bruno Taut's Glashaus*. Basel: Birkhauser Verlag.

Thompson, E. and Galison, P. (eds). (1999). *The Architecture of Science*. Cambridge, MA: MIT Press.

Tschira, A. (1939). *Orangerien und Gewächshäuser, ihre geschichtliche Entwicklung in Deutschland*. Berlin: Deutscher Kunstverl.

Tyler, J. (1986). The Ecology and Conservation of the Glow worm, Lampyris noctiluca (L.) in Britain. *Atala, 12*, 17–19.

van Houtte, L. (ed.). (1850–1). *Flore des Serres et des Jardins de l'Europe* (Vol. 6). Ghent: van Houtte.

Weale, J. (ed.). (1851). *London Exhibited in 1851: Elucidating its Natural and Physical Characteristics; Its Antiquity and Architecture; Its Arts, Manufactures, Trade and Organization; Its Social, Literary, and Scientific Institutions; and Its Numerous Galleries of Fine Art*. London: John Weale.

Whyte, I. B. and Schneider, R. (1986). *Die Briefe der Gläsernen Kette*. Berlin: Ernst, Wilhelm & Sohn.

Whyte, I. B. and Taut, B. (1985). *The Crystal Chain letters: Architectural Fantasies by Bruno Taut and his Circle*. Cambridge, MA: MIT Press.

Wise, M. N. (ed.). (1995). *The Values of Precision*. Princeton, NJ: Princeton University Press.

Wittmack, L. (ed.). (1894). *Gartenflora: Zeitschrift Für Garten und Blumenkunde* (Vol. 43). Berlin: Vereins zur Beforderung des Gartenbaues in den Preussisch Staaten.

www.bgbm.org. (2010). Die Victoria – Victoria amazonica Retrieved 8 March 2013, 2013, from www.bgbm.org/BGBM/PR/zurzeit/papers/victoria.htm

www.jardin-botanique-lyon.com. Les serres du jardin. Retrieved 14 March, 2013, from www.jardin-botanique-lyon.com/jbot/sections/fr/historique/promenades_exotiques_les_serres_du_jard

4 Bruno Taut and the Gothic

4.1 Introduction

This chapter starts with an explanation as to how the Gothic was perceived in Europe after the Enlightenment. It then details how these initial perceptions of the Gothic were subsequently evolved by the Romantics and how this latter thinking became to be associated with the *Deutsche Werkbund's* key personalities and theories. These are then in turn connected to the *Glashaus*, and the outcome, is a grounding of the *Glashaus'* design in thoughts and practices that were directly derived from the Gothic.

4.2 Bruno Taut's Gothic thinking

Gutschow (2005) noted how Taut long professed the need to consider continuing traditions and established archetypes when designing, and the Gothic was the traditional archetype often evident in the wider context of Taut and the *Glashaus*. Paul Scheerbart (1914) mentioned the Gothic in *Glasarchitektur*, and Taut quoted from *Glasarchitektur* when he wrote his 1914 pamphlet 'Glashaus: Werkbund-Ausstellung Köln 1914, Führer zur Eröffnung des Glashauses' ('Glashaus: Werkbund Exhibition in Cologne 1914, A Guide to the opening of the Glasshouse'). Here, Taut quoted Scheerbart in stating that Gothic architecture was the prelude to their new glazed architecture. Behne (1912) wrote his dissertation on Tuscan Gothic church ornamentation and further published 'Die Gotische Kathedrale' in 1914. Taut himself wrote about the Gothic in his 1904 article 'Natur und Baukunst' and again in his later 1914 article 'Eine Notwendigkeit'. Taut also made specific references to particular examples of Gothic architecture, namely Strasbourg Cathedral, in both his 1919 article 'Ex Orient Lux: Aufruf an die Architekten' and in a letter he wrote to the Crystal Chain group on 28 January 1920. In 'Ex Orient Lux', Taut praised Strasbourg Cathedral as having been comparable to the wonders of the Orient, while in the 1920 letter, Taut explained his ecstasy when approaching the Cathedral's bell-tower (Whyte and Schneider, 1986). In *Architekturlehre: Grundlagen, Theorie und Kritik aus der Sicht eines sozialistischen Architekten (Teaching Architecture: Foundations, Theory and Criticism from the perspective of*

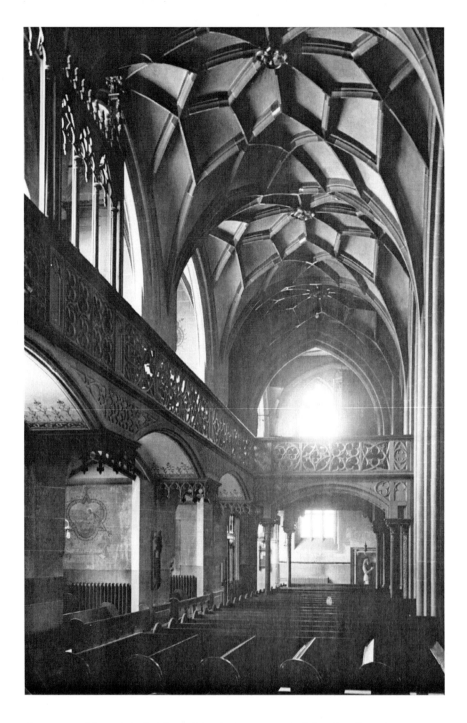

Figure 4.1a The original aisle vaulting in Stuttgart's *Stiftskirche*. Photo by permission of Bildarchiv Stiftskirche Stuttgart.

Socialist Architects), Taut published an image of the western façade of Strasbourg Cathedral (Taut, 1977). In a similar vein, Taut, in his 1904 article 'Natur und Kunst' ('Nature and Art'), also illustrated the central nave of Stuttgart's Gothic *Stiftskirche* (Collegiate Church).

Figure 4.1b The structure of the Dome Room in the *Glashaus*. Photo by permission of Bildarchiv Foto Marburg.

128   *Bruno Taut's design inspiration for the Glashaus*

When Strasbourg Cathedral and Stuttgart's *Stiftskirche* are compared to the *Glashaus*, numerous similarities are immediately apparent. The original vaulting above the south aisle to Stuttgart's *Stiftskirche* was composed of a number of rhombic-shaped facets that, when viewed in plan, assumed a star-like arrangement. Unfortunately, this original vaulting was destroyed in World War Two during the allied bombing raids on Stuttgart. Nevertheless, it was still accessible to Taut in 1904. When the aesthetic of the *Stiftskirche's* original vaulting is compared to that of the structure of the *Glashaus'* dome, they appear as remarkably similar, if not identical. One of the most impressive features of Strasbourg Cathedral is its western rose window, and a comparison between it and the dome of the *Glashaus* reveals similarities. For example, they use the same colours, were centrically planned, and had elaborate structures.

While this direct connection to Gothic exemplars might simplistically answer the question concerning the origins of the *Glashaus*, it still does not fully address the issue. Therefore, significant questions are still unanswered. Why would Taut be interested in the Gothic, and why specifically Strasbourg Cathedral and Stuttgart's *Stiftskirche*? More importantly, what does the Gothic, Strasbourg and the *Stiftskirche* contribute to the discovery of alternative motives and inspirations behind the design of the *Glashaus*?

4.3 *Gotik und Deutsch* (Gothic and German)

In the 19th century, the Gothic cathedral and the medieval conception of society were perceived as symbols of political and national identities, collective memories, traditions and histories. As such, whichever nation could claim the Gothic as its own invention could firmly define its own national identity and gain prominence over others that were likewise attempting to do so. During the Napoleonic period (1799–1815), both the Germans and British saw the Gothic as their own national creation, while the French perceived it as a German creation (Glaser, 2002). In 1772, Johann von Goethe wrote 'Von Deutsche Baukunst' in which he claimed that the Gothic, in the form of Strasbourg Cathedral, was German architecture. In the opening paragraph of this book, Goethe elaborated on his search for a memorial to the designer of Strasbourg Cathedral, Erwin von Steinbach. After searching in vain, Goethe concluded that von Steinbach did not need a memorial, since the magnificent colossus of the Cathedral, '...like trees of God' was more than sufficient (von Goethe, 1772: 2). Goethe then argued that Greek classicism as inherited by the Italians, and as later employed by the French – with its rules of proportions, stark ornament, and use of associated classical columns – were not at all appropriate to the northern European context. Instead, Goethe proposed that they should rather build like von Steinbach by devising an architecture that was rooted in the context of place, people and culture:

Diversify the enormous walls, you should so build towards heaven that they rise like a sublimely towering, wide-spreading tree of God which, with its thousand branches, millions of twigs and leaves more numerous than the sands of the sea, proclaims to the surrounding country the glory of its master, the Lord.

(von Goethe, 1772: 4)

Goethe (1772) then admitted that when he first experienced Strasbourg Cathedral, he was initially influenced by his prior classicism-instilled pre-conceptions of what constituted appropriate architecture. He referred to the building as having been overpowered with applied effects and overloaded with ornament, with a shambolic, crude and unnatural aesthetic. However, these initial perceptions were only fleeting. Goethe then described his surprise at the harmonious experience, dignity and magnificence of Strasbourg Cathedral as one that he was not fully able to explain or identify. He proposed Strasbourg Cathedral as a holistic and soulful experience that embraced the enormous spirit of his 'medieval bothers'. Furthermore, Goethe referred to the 'secret powers' of the Cathedral's towers and the sparkling of the building in the early dawn mist. He continued to describe Strasbourg Cathedral by praising its harmonious masses that were alive with limitless detail, and that mirrored the magnificent work of nature where all things were perfectly formed. Goethe then, with religious zeal, proclaimed:

...thank God ...that this is German architecture, our architecture.

(von Goethe, 1772: 6)

Goethe continued by stating that the only true art was one that became active in people through internal, united, exacting and autonomous emotions, thus creating beauty from within the individual mind. He then stated that the most appropriate source of inspiration for these independent emotions and resultant beauty was to be found in nature, and that the youth were best equipped to express the resultant forms (von Goethe, 1772).

In 'Von Deutsche Baukunst', Goethe was dismissive of other European nations, particularly the French. Undoubtedly, this attitude can be contextualised with the then German search for a unified national identity, and the formative desire of the German peoples to become free of French political control and cultural dominance. Likewise, his thinking also contained associations with German Romanticism – seeking a synthesis of art, literature and science, while similarly looking to the Middle Ages for inspiration on a harmonious and unified society.

The next author to develop Goethe's notions of the Gothic as German was Karl Wilhelm Friedrich Schlegel (Glaser, 2005). In 1806, Schlegel published his *Briefe auf einer Reise durch die Niederlande, Rheingegenden, die Schweiz, und einen Theil von Frankreich* (*Letters from a Tour of the Netherlands, Rhine Regions, Switzerland and Parts of France*). According to Glaser (2005) this work was a nationalistic text. Like Goethe (1772), Schlegel (1806) proposed that Gothic was German because of its connection to the customs, climate and nature of northern Nordic Europe. It is important to note at this point that the concept of 'German' is identical to the term 'Nordic' that is commonly used in both early texts, like Goethe and Schlegel, and later texts. For Schlegel (1806) it was the artistic awareness (*Kunstsinn*) and the artistic commitment (*Kunstfleiss*) of the German people that had created the Gothic through their love of nature and daring imagination. However, unlike Goethe (1772), Schlegel (1806) proposed the unfinished edifice of Cologne Cathedral as the ultimate personification of this Germanic Gothic. Schlegel (1806) even went so far as to dismiss Strasbourg Cathedral as late and decadent Gothic. According to Glaser (2005), this dismissal of Strasbourg Cathedral was, in all probability, a form of misguided patriotism and a protest against French foreign domination, as Strasbourg was then a French city.

At about the same time as Schlegel's (1806) publication, a close friend of Goethe's, Karl Friedrich Schinkel, also had the opportunity to visit Strasbourg Cathedral. In *Reisen nach Italien (Travels to Italy)*, Schinkel climbed the tower of the Strasbourg Cathedral (Schinkel and Riemann, 1979). He detailed this 20 July 1824 visit to the Cathedral as follows: Describing his approach to the Cathedral, Schinkel (1979) told of the 'glorious building' that towered over the medieval city with its transparent, skeleton-like spire. He then detailed how, as his vehicle stopped at the entrance portal to the Cathedral, the enormous mass of the building seemed to rise before him in a bolder and more accomplished manner than that of Cologne Cathedral. Schinkel (1979) then detailed the red sandstone from which Strasbourg Cathedral was constructed, describing it as magnificent and blackened with golden moss, giving it the appearance of a bronze casting. Strangely, he described very little of the interior, other than a mere mention of its lighting being achieved through stained-glass windows. For Schinkel (1979), the delight of a visit to Strasbourg Cathedral, however, lay in climbing the open-work spire that was accessed via a spiral staircase. He ascended from the ground level and arrived at the 300-foot-high platform at the base of the open-work spire:

> Then we climbed the tower to the platform, where an unparalleled overview of Alsace, the Black Forest and the Vosges Mountains, and where you can see the finished tower quite close, a marvel of bold and beautiful design.
>
> (Schinkel and Riemann, 1979: 145)

Continuing to climb the 'octagon' of the open-work spire, Schinkel (1979) found to his surprise that the upper portions of the spire had no abutment. Furthermore, he described the uppermost tip of the spire as a beautiful and unifying mass of stone. The result for Schinkel was that both the ornament and structure effectively became one. For him, this holistic synthesis of form and function was unlike Cologne Cathedral, which he described as having been full of danger and lacking surety. Descending the spire, Schinkel then returned to the platform, which he then described as 'magnificent exposed stone' not only devoted to religious purposes but also to general entertainment. Conjuring up a vision of beautiful evening festivities, with dancing and festivities, Schinkel then described von Steinbach's Strasbourg Cathedral as a true monument. He then departed this 'wonderful place' and descended once again via the spiral staircase to the Cathedral below (Schinkel and Riemann, 1979).

For Schinkel, Strasbourg Cathedral's spire was not, however, the pinnacle of perfection. A day after his visit to Strasbourg Cathedral, Schinkel subsequently visited Freiburg Cathedral. He described the tip of the open-work spire in Freiburg as having the greatest value and beauty, being far more harmonious than the spire of Strasbourg. Like Strasbourg, the open-work spire of Freiburg Cathedral was also accessed via a narrow, spiral staircase. Likewise, Freiburg's spire was described as a hollow, tapered and transparent structure that also started on a square plan and then approximately midway transformed into an octagonal plan, and as it ascended upward, slowly dematerialised before reaching the tip (Schinkel and Riemann, 1979). Freiburg Cathedral was superior because it used far fewer resources during construction. Schinkel then detailed an evening walk to the heights overlooking Freiburg. As with the earlier explanation above of Strasbourg Cathedral within its wider urban context, Freiburg Cathedral was uplifted from the crowd of the medieval city. In the light of the late afternoon, with the sun hiding behind the main spire and with it rays shooting outward, the composition of the image was perfect, according to Schinkel (Schinkel and Riemann, 1979).

With the defeat of Napoleon in 1815 and the supposed removal of French domination, Germans subsequently modified their views of the Gothic. At the Congress of Vienna (1814–15), Europe was divided into a number of spheres of influence, namely, Britain, Prussia, Austria, France and Russia. The Congress, however, made the fundamental error of largely suppressing German nationalist aspirations. Rather, to the detriment of the emergent Prussia, the Congress assumed that the Austro-Hungarians were the dominant 'Germanic' power. The result of the Congress of Vienna was the creation and maintenance of numerous smaller Germanic states. This essentially created a central European buffer between the powers of Russia, Austria and France. As such, political and economic rivalry between Prussia and Austria-Hungary dominated the Germanic landscape until German unification in 1871, with Prussia the eventual victor (Sheehan, 1989).

During this post-Napoleonic period, the Germanic perception of the Gothic evolved into a political symbol of an 'unfinished national project', which shifted focus away from Strasbourg Cathedral and toward the unfinished project of Cologne Cathedral (Glaser, 2005). Authors such as Josef von Görres (1814, 1842) declared Cologne Cathedral as a symbol of unfinished German nationalism, and one that personified German weakness. Von Görres (1814, 1842) therefore urged all Germans to rediscover the 'collective effort' of their medieval ancestors, so as to heal the rifts between Germanic peoples. According to Glaser (2005), von Görres proposed Cologne Cathedral as a symbol of societal transformation and its eventual completion as a further symbol of a strong and united Germany. When work did eventually commence on completing the Cathedral in 1842, the then Prussian king Friedrich Wilhelm IV, declared it to be a symbol of a secular and unified Germany (Nipperdey, 1981). According to Glaser (2005), by 1842, the Gothic as personified in Cologne Cathedral was therefore inextricably bound to German national memory and future unity. However, 1842 was a significant year because it was proven then that Cologne Cathedral was in fact modelled after Amiens Cathedral, essentially making it a French design, and a design of the 'enemy' (Glaser, 2005). Considering that the Gothic was at this stage indivisible from the German nation, the emphasis thus evolved into a stylistic argument. While this argument admitted that the French had invented the Gothic, it argued that the Germans had brought it to its highest perfection. Glaser (2005) cited Franz Theodor Kugler as having propagated this view during the 1840s, who, incidentally, published a monograph on Schinkel in 1842 (www.dictionaryofarthistorians.org).

In the 1840s, archaeological evidence had verified the origins of Gothic as being in Normandy. The French thus faced the difficulty of taking ownership of the Gothic after the end of the Napoleonic era. This was particularly problematic since, then, the French had conceded the Gothic as a German innovation. Initially, the French Revolution regarded the Gothic as a symbol of an oppressive feudal and ecclesiastical past (Glaser, 2005). Strasbourg Cathedral almost lost its spire during this time. The citizens of Strasbourg however crowned the spire with a giant Phrygian cap and thus associated the Cathedral with a group of revolutionaries, *Les Enragés* (The Enraged Ones), and the ideals of the Revolution (Kurtz, 2006). However, when revolutionary fervour had subsided, French perceptions of the Gothic increasingly saw it as symbolic of their national culture, customs, religion and traditions. Much like their German counterparts, the French Romantics in the early 19th century saw medieval Europe as a 'golden age' of heroism and gallantry, fervent Christian faith and unity of ecclesial and royal power. While the Germans saw the Gothic as a symbol of their fledgling national identity and a desire to rid themselves of domination. The French, under the rule of the Bourbons (1815–30) instead saw the Gothic as a part of a decorative style that was intended to revive ecclesial and royal power. With the overthrow of the Bourbons in 1830, the Gothic was again reinvented. However, this time it became a symbol of secular power, the product of the people, inspired by human imagination, and instilled with a spirit of democratic liberty (Glaser, 2005). This later view was personified in Victor Hugo's (1831) publication *Notre-Dame de Paris, 1482*. Viollet-le-Duc (1875) later expanded Hugo's argument by proposing the Gothic as the product of a nationalistic movement against feudalism. As such, for the French, the Gothic personified a struggle against ecclesial, royal and feudal power, while for the Germans it was a symbol of national identity and a longing to rid themselves of French domination (Glaser, 2005).

4.4 The Gothic and the British

The British, like the Germans, had seen the Gothic as a constituent of their national character during the Napoleonic period. However, the British had very early on ceded the origins of the Gothic to the French (Glaser, 2005). Undoubtedly, the British, like their German and French counterparts, saw the Gothic through the lens of Romantic conventions. The British version of Romanticism however had very little connection to nationalism; instead, it sought inspiration in exotic lands, culture and myth. Therefore, in the early 19th century, the British, as the single nation most influenced by the Industrial Revolution, sought refuge in the writing of Wordsworth, Shelley, Keats and Byron (Eastlake, 1872). Gothic Revival architecture can be proposed as the personification of British Romantic thought, with Augustus Welby Northmore Pugin perhaps being the pioneering proponent of the movement (Hill, 2007). In the early 19th century, Pugin and his father published five texts that presented examples of British Gothic Revival architecture. Of these five, *Specimens of Gothic Architecture* comprised the first two volumes, while the last three volumes were entitled *Examples of Gothic Architecture* (1825; 1825; 1838, 1839, 1840). In his later publication, *Contrasts*, Pugin additionally disseminated his thoughts concerning the Gothic ethos and presented the medieval age as one of a pure and unadulterated society when compared to the early 19th century. For Pugin, the society and state of the medieval period was good and therefore its architecture, i.e. Gothic, was also good (Pugin, 1836). Likewise in his subsequent publication, *The True Principles of Pointed or Christian Architecture*, Pugin (1841) resolutely prescribed the features and methods of Gothic Revival architecture:

> It should be honest in its appearance and the building's features should be essential to its proper functioning and construction. Likewise, the building's features and methods of construction should be honestly expressed and judged by the strictest standards of Catholic morality.
>
> (Pugin, 1841)

As a result, Pugin was undoubtedly influential on John Ruskin (Conner, 1978). According to William Morris, while Pugin presented the first wave of the Gothic Revival according to an ecclesiastical Catholic perspective, Ruskin, in a secular manner, later gave it life and spirit (LeMire, 1969). Interestingly, the first of Ruskin's articles was published in *The Magazine of Natural History*, which was edited by John Claudius Loudon, who

134 *Bruno Taut's design inspiration for the Glashaus*

commented to Ruskin's father in 1837 that John Ruskin was undoubtedly the greatest natural genius that he had ever met (Cook, 1911).

In 1849, Ruskin published *The Seven Lamps of Architecture* in which he presented seven 'Lamps', or principles, that all appropriate, or good, architecture should contain: 'Sacrifice' as a symbol of man's love and obedience to God, 'Truth' of construction and materials, 'Power' of architecture through the greatness of nature, 'Beauty' of architecture and ornamentation inspired by nature, 'Life' of the builders and freedom of expression, 'Memory' of culture and context, and 'Obedience' to history and tradition. Ruskin argued that most architecture since the Gothic, and in particular that of the Industrial Revolution, had lost its spirituality and affinity to nature. While Ruskin added nothing new to the debate concerning Gothic Revival, he did however skilfully encapsulate the atmosphere of the period (Curl, 2006). Also interesting is the contention that much of Ruskin's (1849) thinking derived from Archibald Alison's 1790 *Essays on the Nature and Principles of Taste* (Hersey, 1972). Starting in 1851, Ruskin elaborated on his earlier thoughts in *The Seven Lamps of Architecture* by publishing a three-volume set under the title *The Stones of Venice*, in which he (1853) analysed architectural features and details in an effort to establish whether or not they complied with his earlier principles. In the second volume of *The Stones of Venice*, Ruskin (1853) published a number of chapters devoted to the Gothic, of which "The Nature of Gothic" is the most important to this research. Using the Gothic as both a metaphor and physical example, Ruskin proposed that it had six essential characteristics. These, listed in order of importance, were: 'Savageness', 'Changefulness', 'Naturalism', 'Grotesqueness', 'Rigidity', and 'Redundance' (Ruskin, 1853). I will discuss each of these in detail below.

The first and most important, Savageness or 'Rudeness' was more of a metaphor than physical example. Ruskin argued that, historically, the architecture, people and cultures of northern Europe were traditionally seen as barbaric, stern, contemptible, wild and rude. Continuing, Ruskin then stated that the Savageness of northern European architecture, i.e. the Gothic, was a direct result of the physical character, or context, of its place: its rugged, strong and noble people, its forests, its high, ice covered mountains, its shaggy and stout animals, its moss-covered rocks, sombre and moody weather, and grisly landscapes. Contrary to prevailing opinions, Ruskin argued that this Savageness of place, instead of being deplorable, was rather praiseworthy and dignified; it was these very characteristics of place that deserved a profound reverence. Savageness implied a:

> ...look of mountain brotherhood between the cathedral and the Alp... magnificence of sturdy power.
>
> (Ruskin, 1853: 157–8)

He then argued that Gothic architecture's Savageness additionally derived from the higher characteristic of 'religious' principles that were instilled in

Christian men. The men who constructed Roman architecture were mere slaves, with precise and inferior minds; by contrast, the men who constructed the Gothic were noble, imperfect and free-thinking men. In other words, the Gothic was constructed by men freed from sin by Christianity and instilled with independent minds and thoughts. These noble Gothic men, united in a collective endeavour, thus had pleasure in their work; work that, even if it was imperfect, intended to showcase the glory of God. As such, the Savageness of Gothic was also more importantly a mental attitude of a free and independent mind (Ruskin, 1853).

Ruskin started his definition of Changefulness or 'Variety' by stating that where the constituent parts of buildings were alike, then the workmen were undoubtedly utterly enslaved, i.e. they had no Savageness of thought. In contrast, Gothic architecture was designed and executed by workmen who were utterly free and consequently had Savageness of thought, and were capable of perceptual novelty. Changefulness implied that the Gothic broke the prevailing rules of form and rhythm that were established in classical architecture. Through this infringement of prevailing principles, the Gothic therefore created the novel and constantly varying variety of forms of the pointed arch, the grouped column, and tracery. It was thus the irregularity and rich variation of form that expressed the energy of the Gothic and Christian love of variety. However, Changefulness had to be managed, not just in design but also in effect. It was further proposed that if change was too often repeated, it would cease to cause delight; as such, change had to be mixed with a certain degree of monotony. Only having experienced, endured or suffered through monotony could the beholder then experience the ecstasy of change – a process that Ruskin termed 'transparent monotony' (Ruskin, 1853).

The third characteristic of Gothic architecture was Naturalism, or 'Love of Nature', which entailed the realistic and emotional representation of natural facts through design. Naturalism was not the interpretive representation of nature as presented by the ancient Romans; rather, it was an honest recreation that left no need for interpretation. Ruskin contended that the Naturalism that best manifests its true character of the Gothic was to be found in its fondness of representational veracity of vegetation. Not only did the Gothic workman faithfully represent foliage, but he also did it with intense affection and habitual tenderness, therefore being indicative of a more tranquil and gentle existence. Ruskin was careful to dismiss the prevailing notion that the Gothic derived from vegetation, namely '...from the symmetry of the avenues, and the interlacing of the branches' (Ruskin, 1853: 201). Rather, he contended that the Gothic grew into a similarity with vegetation because of the temperament of the builders, nurtured in the context of a harmonious, peaceful society that was as one with nature. The Savage and Changeful expression of vegetation was thus one of the defining features of the Gothic (Ruskin, 1853).

Grotesqueness, or 'Disturbed Imagination', was the fourth of the essential characteristics of Gothic. This element was very briefly defined as the affinity

136 Bruno Taut's design inspiration for the Glashaus

to find enjoyment in the implausible and absurd as well as sublime imagery; it was, according to Ruskin, the '...universal instinct of the Gothic imagination' (Ruskin, 1853: 203). Undoubtedly, this definition can be argued as an extension of a Savage independent mind.

The fifth characteristic of Gothic architecture was Rigidity, or 'Obstinacy'. Rigidity was apparently difficult to define; however, it was tentatively defined as not only being stable but 'actively rigid'. In Ruskin's words, it was that strange power that gave tension to movement; opposition to movement; scattered the most powerful lighting; was seen in the trembling of the lance; and the sparkle of the icicle. As such, tracery and vaulting were rigid, like human bones or tree fibres, where elastic transferral of tension and force was evident in all aspects of the building. Likewise, Gothic *Rigidity* was also to be found in its ornament that projected in 'prickly independence', formed into pinnacles like frozen water, starting as a monster and then metamorphosing into a blossom via a knitted, thorny or writhed branch. However, it was the Gothic workmen who truly made Rigidity 'active' through their independence of nature, strength of will, unyielding purpose, non-acceptance of dictatorial control, and independence of thought (Ruskin, 1853).

The last of Ruskin's six characteristics was Redundance, or 'Generosity'. Redundance essentially revolved around the Gothic notion of humility, which could accept both the complex and simple, and that admitted the crudest of minds as well as the most refined. The Gothic achieved Redundance by masking the work of the inattentive, imperfect and feeble in the endeavour of generation of the unselfish collective through the accumulation of ornament. Likewise, the individual could only comprehend a small part of the universal natural sum, but collectively a community would complete a 'tapestry of traceries' in the Gothic cathedral (Ruskin, 1853).

Essentially, Ruskin's explanation of the characteristics of Gothic can be seen within the most basic of the tenets of Romanticism: the free expression of the intent or will of the artist and a close affinity with nature.

Romanticism and the affinity for the Gothic appeared to have ended in the mid-19th century. This could have been because the ideals of the French Revolution were effectively negated by the dictatorships of Napoleon and the return of the monarchist Bourbons. In the rest of Europe, nobility was likewise reasserting its authority and persecuting democrats. Similarly, in the second half of the 19th century, massive power shifts occurred in Europe, such as the unification of Italy in 1870 and Germany in 1871. The second half of the 19th century was a period of unbridled industrialisation in Europe, in particular Belgium and Germany, and their new-found industrial wealth undoubtedly led to the desire for colonial empires, both of which were subsequently established in the latter half of the 19th century. Industrialisation also resulted in a logical shift towards urbanisation. As such, the reality of the industrial city-slums, pollution, overcrowding, disease and social breakdown led to a redirection from Romanticism toward Realism. However, the new reality of Realism could not fully suppress Romantic tendencies, which ultimately remerged in the artistic eclecticism of the late 19th and early 20th centuries. Movements like the European Art Nouveau and the British Arts and Crafts arguably contained elements of Romanticism. Therefore, in Germany during the first decade of the 20th century, the Gothic and Romanticism re-emerged in the writings of Wilhelm Worringer and Herman Muthesius.

4.5 Wilhelm Worringer

In 1907, Worringer published *Abstraktion und Einfühlung: ein Beitrag zur Stilpsychologie (Abstraction and Empathy: Essays in the Psychology of Style)*. In this document, Worringer developed Theodore Lipps earlier notions of *einfühlungs* (empathy); if people could empathise, or identify, with a work of art, they would logically find it beautiful because of their own sense of delight in themselves. Consequently, empathetic societies produced 'representational art', such as that produced in the Renaissance. Furthermore, 'representational art' meant that these empathetic societies would be confident in their space/time contexts. Conversely, 'abstract art' was derived from peoples who were insecure, anxious, fearful and uncertain of their space-time contexts. 'Abstract art' could be found in the societies of Egypt and Byzantium; likewise, it additionally included primitive and even modern Expressionist art (Worringer, 1907). In the last chapter of *Abstraktion und Einfühlung*, Worringer presented his initial thoughts on northern European 'representational art', i.e. the psychological *Kunstwollen* (artistic will, or 'the Will to Art') inherent in the Gothic. *Kunstwollen* was however not Worringer's creation; rather it was the Austrian art historian Alois Riegl who first developed the term (Riegl, 1893).

Worringer's (1907) initial thoughts concerning the Gothic were later expanded on in his book *Formprobleme der Gothik (Form Problems of the Gothic)* of 1910. Here, Worringer proposed that Gothic architecture was essentially an expression of the *Kunstwollen* of the men who had built the Gothic. In other words, *Kunstwollen* was inherent in the Gothic as a feeling of vitality that manifests as a higher spiritual existence and ultimate salvation. As such, Gothic man created a transcendent Expressionism manifest in stone. However, Gothic man effectively dematerialised stone through creating form that, instead of being expressive of gravity, sought to reverse it, creating an unrestricted upward movement of free and uninhibited forces. By dematerialising it, stone was effectively spiritualised. Therefore, the Gothic form became a living, breathing body that both externalised its inherent longing for spiritual expression and structural reality. This synthesis of structural reality and desire for expression was most evident in the pointed arch, which was the system that ultimately guided the entire aesthetic of the Gothic cathedral. Worringer accordingly proposed that the whole interior effect of the Gothic cathedral was as a result of the pointed arch. From a structural perspective, the pointed arch allowed the vertical expression of a large

138 *Bruno Taut's design inspiration for the Glashaus*

enclosed space. However, from an expressive perspective, the pointed arch further allowed this large enclosed space to create the aspiration of a heavenward verticality.

The 'structure' of columns and vaulting thus became strained sinews that, once freed from material weight, then transcended terrestrial limitations. The column and vaulting likewise became one, with the expressive lines of the vaulting starting at the floor, then transferring up the column shaft and terminating in the dizzying verticality of the ceiling vaulting. This verticality of lithe, living forces was then naturally centred on a vaulting keystone that was as light as a flower. This arrangement therefore created an 'atmospheric space', which was spiritual, incomprehensible and directly affected and grounded in the human senses. But, more than an 'atmospheric space', the interior of the Gothic cathedral was further a 'super-sensuous space', which intoxicated and overpowered the human senses through the experience of unbridled activity. However, Worringer further contended that this 'super-sensuous space' found its ultimate expression on the exterior of the Gothic cathedral. In the towers, all the upward energy, movement and transcendent desires culminated in one final, delivering utterance. According to Worringer, nowhere else were all of the intoxicating, transcendental and ultimately mystical effects of the Gothic cathedral more evident than in its towers. Worringer, while crediting the French with the creation of the Gothic system, stated that it was the momentum or impulse inherent the *Kunstwollen* of the Germanic character that untimely bought it to its fullest manifestation. As such, Worringer proposed that the form of the Gothic was the result of the will and intent of the artists involved, rather than an expression of a wider artistic cycle. Therefore, Worringer made a call for a new abstract art that was drawn from both the intuition and the serrated geometry of the East and the Orient. This art form would transcend the chaos of the modern era through the creation of architecture that reflected order, truth, and spiritual clarity; a new art that was both independent and autonomous, and that was based on an intuitive, emotional and creative artistic awareness of form (Worringer, 1910).

In 1902, Herman Muthesius published *Stilarchitektur und Baukunst*. In this work, arguably all of the prior ideas of Goethe, Schinkel and Ruskin finally found a holistic expression. Furthermore, Muthesius' work, apart from impacting on the 'immediate' past of the Gothic, also connected the wider political, social and economic histories of the 18th and 19th centuries. These socio-economic connections were therefore ultimately more powerful, as they additionally incorporated personalities like Paxton, Borsig and van Houtte. Likewise, Muthesius' work also forcefully resonated into the future.

4.6 Herman Muthesius

Muthesius' association with religious buildings had an early start, because his father was a mason who owned a small construction firm that built country churches and designed church towers. Following his secondary schooling, Muthesius subsequently attended the Friedrich Wilhelm University in Berlin from 1881 to 1883, where he studied art history and philosophy. After a year of military service, Muthesius then enrolled to study architecture at the *Technische Hochschule* (Technical Institute) in Charlottenburg, Berlin. While undertaking his architectural studies, he also worked in the architectural practice of Ende and Böckmann (H. Muthesius, Günther, Posener, Sharp and Muthesius, 1979). The founding director, Wilhelm Böckmann, had travelled to Japan in 1886, and his partner, Hermann Ende, in 1887. During this period, Ende and Böckmann presented a master-plan for Tokyo, along with numerous new government buildings (Lepik and Rosa, 2005). Likewise, from 1887 to 1891, Muthesius was also in Japan, where he supervised contracts for Ende and Böckmann, and completed a number of buildings that included a Gothic Revival church. On his return to Berlin in 1891, Muthesius completed a period of employment with the Ministry of Public Works, while also completing additional studies and travels in Italy. As a result of these studies, Muthesius, in a similar manner as Goethe, Schinkel and Ruskin before him, published his first book *Italienische Reise-Eindrücke (Italian Travel Impressions)* in 1898.

However, prior to this, in 1896, Muthesius was appointed as the German cultural and technical attaché to London. The primary purpose of this appointment was for him to study and report back to the German (Prussian) Government on British technology, art and architecture, and he subsequently published a number of books on the subjects. The first two of these books, *Die Englische Baukunst der Gegenwart (Contemporary English Architecture)* and *Die Neuere Kirchliche Baukunst in England (Recent Religious Architecture in England)*, were both published while he was in Britain, while a third and arguably the most influential book, the *Das Englische Haus (The English House)*, was published after his return to Germany. Also published after Muthesius' return to Germany was the previously mentioned *Stilarchitektur und Baukunst, (Style-architecture and Building-art)* which is the book most relevant to this study.

On his return to Germany, Muthesius was appointed to the German (Prussian) Ministry of Commerce where he was an ardent proponent of the knowledge that he had acquired in Britain; in particular, those lessons acquired from his study of the Arts and Crafts Movement. Muthesius accordingly proposed the integration of craft into all spheres of arts and architecture education, in the attainment of an artistically driven culture for the emergent German industrial society. Once he was released from the Ministry in 1904, Muthesius then continued to advance this goal through the establishment of his own architectural practice, as well as the founding of the *Deutsche Werkbund* in 1907 (Mallgrave, 1994).

In *Stilarchitektur und Baukunst*, Muthesius (1902) made an impassioned plea for the renewal of German culture through the medium of high-quality, industrial goods. However, unlike the British example of the Arts and Crafts

140 *Bruno Taut's design inspiration for the Glashaus*

Movement, which, according to Muthesius, had restricted modern change and was ultimately the preserve of the privileged classes, the German version would be solely aimed at the middle classes and actively embrace modern industrial change. Muthesius therefore envisioned a resultant middle-class art that was to distinguish itself through the fundamental embodiment of *Sachlichkeit* (Objectivity or Reality), or its adjective *sachlich* (practical, functional or pragmatic) (Mallgrave, 1994). Muthesius (1902) contextualised his argument for this new middle-class *sachlich* art within the premise that all the artistic production since the demise of the Gothic was essentially a cacophony of meaningless styles, or *Stilarchitektur*. Nowhere else was the disharmony of *Stilarchitektur* more evident than in the 'mother of the arts', architecture. Consequently, architectural styles like Gothic Revival, Art Nouveau and *Jugendstil* were simple *Stilarchitektur* with no *Sachlichkeit*. To remedy this situation, Muthesius argued that the genuine new forms of 19th-century industrial buildings and new material essence of glass and steel, in particular railway stations and exhibition buildings, offered the solution:

> With the construction of the Crystal Palace at the World Exhibition of 1851, England showed the world the way in exhibition architecture. ... The Crystal Palace was built by the gardener and subsequently knighted Joseph Paxton ... Paxton's singular construction of iron derived from his experience with greenhouses. In his time, the Crystal Palace was hardly considered as architecture, and yet this prototype inspired the architectural phenomena of the following decades: the structural-iron, wide-span hall. This method of constructions was particularly suited to the exhibition buildings of the French World's Fairs. ... Here the most splendid iron architectures were realised at the Paris Fair of 1889, in the form of the great Galerie des Machines and the Eiffel Tower. In comparison, the works of the 1900 Paris Fair can be considered as having represented an embarrassing regression. However, this regression was already anticipated in America. To the astonishments of the world that was expectant of something original, the Americans at the Chicago Columbian Exposition of 1893 produced nothing better than antique masquerading facades that were hung on the iron frames of the exhibition buildings. Despite its enchanting fairy-tale imagery, this regressive production accounted for less than nil...
>
> (Hermann Muthesius, 1902: 41–2)

As such, contained within these railway stations and exhibition buildings were the modern ideas and principles of progressive design. Therefore, these rigorous, logical and scientific buildings firmly embodied the desired *Sachlichkeit* (Mallgrave, 1994). However, what was not evident in the new *sachlich* industrial architecture were the desired supportive social conditions. Like many authors before him, Muthesius (1902) therefore proposed Gothic society as the solution. His version of the Gothic took the Romantic thoughts of authors like von Görres, Pugin and Ruskin and added the Realism of German industrialisation. Like almost all the authors mentioned above, Muthesius likewise argued that the Gothic was the unique creation of northern European peoples, wholly independent of the prevailing classical model. Using this as a starting point, Muthesius then proceeded to add the Realism of context.

Muthesius started this discussion by exposing the modern and wholly national art and architecture, which derived directly from the Gothic in Britain after 1860. The British people had inundated themselves within the new ideas that derived from this concern with the Gothic. The characteristics of this new British art were sound workmanship, reasonableness, and sincerity, while its motive was a genuine and popular local enthusiasm for art. According to Muthesius (1902), the father of this modern British art was William Morris and its propagandist was John Ruskin. However, within continental Europe, a similar situation was not possible because of the prevalence of classical conceptions of beauty that derived from Greece and Italy. To remedy this situation, Muthesius proposed the British-Gothic model as the solution, albeit with numerous modifications. The most significant of these modifications was that while he recognised that Morris' social vision had failed – in that it maintained the status of the ruling classes – he acknowledged that the desirable work, craft and product outcomes of Morris had been achieved within an idealised industrial context (Mallgrave, 1994). On the other hand, Muthesius (1902) proposed to transplant the Gothic version of society into the modern German industrial context. This Gothicised society was explained as a construct during which art and architecture were common cultural property and were thus highly valued. This art and architecture perfectly mirrored the context of its period, and permeated all of its contemporary expressions of life. A unified cultural model of both art and architecture was therefore applicable and evident in all levels of society. And, it was this holistic inclusion of all members of society, especially the middle classes, that would set Muthesius' (1902) Gothicised society apart from the failings of the British model.

A further shortcoming of the British-Gothic model had to do with the instruments of its industrial society, i.e. the machine. Mirroring Ruskin, Muthesius (1902) argued the English Arts and Crafts Movement had overtly condemned machined products because they produced 'false works of art' that ultimately resulted in an undercutting of prices and therefore a decline in quality. Machine production affected the worker, the consumer and the nation. The worker earned less, lost interest in his work, and was 'spiritually injured' because he had to produce inferior articles. The consumer acquired a 'false economy' in which he was obliged to participate in an artificially constructed consumer society through the acquisition of inferior quality goods. (Therefore, the worker became the focus of the consumer's wrath in relation to poor quality goods.) Likewise, the nation was also affected because it had to import expensive raw materials to produce these 'false works of art'.

142 *Bruno Taut's design inspiration for the Glashaus*

But, unlike the English Arts and Crafts Movement, Muthesius proposed that the machine should be actively employed in his new Gothicised society. However, in this new society the machine would not expel cheap mass-produced rubbish; rather, it would produce quality *Sachform* (the undecorated forms or products of *Sachlichkeit*) from which the worker would then assemble into *sachlich* artefacts. These *sachlich* artefacts would more than compensate for any increase in price through a dramatic increase in quality. Additionally, both the worker and consumer would be drawn closer, in that both now would take personal pleasure in crafting and consuming a higher quality artefact. The progress required to bring about this Gothicised society would require that the whole nation acquire an understanding of quality. Therefore, the state, as the ultimate demander of quality in the products that it procured, was to be the teacher (Hermann Muthesius, 1902).

Muthesius' (1902) concern for *sachlich* artefacts extended further than individual machine produced forms; it additionally concerned both the shape of German industrial cities and its constituent architecture. Apart from endorsing both Schinkel as the last notable architect who unified architecture and art and Alfred Messel's Wertheim Department store, Muthesius once again returned to the precedents offered during his stay in Britain. As such, he proposed that the domestic, vernacular-inspired architecture of Richard Norman Shaw held the solution, for the future direction of architecture. In Shaw, Muthesius (1902) saw a simple and natural architecture that derived from the customs and practices of the small towns and rural landscapes of Britain. The resultant architecture that adapted to local needs and conditions was therefore instilled with unpretentious and honest feelings. As such, Shaw's domestic architecture, or 'artistic house', created the only convincing basis for a new artistic culture.

While the conditions for such architecture were available in Britain, they were not yet present in Germany. Thus, Muthesius proposed that if Germans wanted to create the correct conditions, they would have to have exposure to both journals and exhibitions. A further source of inspiration, which was both surrounded by poetry and rich in sentiment, was the rich vernacular tradition present in German rural architecture. Muthesius was also careful to state that the unpleasant architectural character of contemporary German cities, with their collective consumption, false sensibilities and American tempos, was a hindrance in the creation of the desired, natural and healthy artistic condition. This was because an authentic art could only result from authentic *Sachlichkeit* feelings and people born of Germany (Hermann Muthesius, 1902).

4.7 Muthesius and the Deutscher Werkbund

In the late 19th century, Germans realised that they could only effectively compete with established trading nations, in particular Britain, if they offered improved design and vastly superior quality. As such, Muthesius,

Figure 4.2a Bruno Taut's 1904 illustration of Stuttgart's *Stiftskirche*. Photo by permission of the Akademie der Künste.

Figure 4.2b Bruno Taut's 1904 illustration of a *Tannenwald*. Photo by permission of the Akademie der Künste.

Friedrich Naumann and Karl Schmidt founded the *Deutscher Werkbund* in 1907. The initial membership of the Werkbund included 12 individual artists and 12 industrial, or craft, firms (Frampton, 2007). The *Werkbund* promoted the term *Qualität* (Quality), which was a holistic ethos that both embodied the raising of the standards of design and used the finest materials, in combination with the very best of talent. *Qualität* would accordingly bring about the desired cultural reintegration and rejuvenation that Muthesius and his peers so actively sought (Mallgrave, 1994). Between 1907 and 1914, industrial membership of the *Werkbund* grew from 143 to almost 300 (Maciuika, 2005). Considering the diversity of the *Werkbund's* membership, very soon after its establishment, a rift appeared between those that preferred prescriptive or set forms and those that favoured individual artistic free-will forms. These issues came to a head at the Werkbund meeting in 1914, at which Muthesius proposed the production of *Typisierung* (Standardisation) for both domestic and international markets. This was quickly countered by a proposal for artistic individualism from a group led by Henry van de Velde and that included Bruno Taut (Maciuika, 2005). Mallgrave (1994) is correct in arguing that, before 1914, Muthesius never used the term *Typisierung*. Mallgrave further argued that in keeping with Muthesius' earlier thoughts, *Typisierung*, rather than meaning standardisation, instead implied the formation of norms that would have been equally applied to architecture, crafts and industrial products. As such, *Typisierung* can rather be seen as shared conventions of practice, which would have brought about the required harmonious and unified culture that Muthesius desired (Mallgrave, 1994).

As a participant in the wider debate concerning individual versus prescriptive form, Bruno Taut expressed his thoughts as early as 1904 in both 'Natur und Kunst' and 'Natur und Baukunst'. Taut wrote the former while in the employ of Theodore Fisher in Stuttgart. Fisher who was one of the later 12 founders of the *Werkbund* (Junghanns, 1983). In it, Taut stated that the architecture of his time was less about the authenticity of any particular style (*Stilechtheit*), but rather about the free artistic will or power (*freie künstlerische Kraft*) of a 'master', who, without renouncing tradition, created a new architecture from both the technical and aesthetic traits of his present context. This joyful development owed its existence to the fact that a new generation of architects once again studied nature. Stating that he dismissed the idealistic notions concerning the rural village, Taut (1904b) alternatively proposed that the rural village rather had a close and intimate affinity to nature. Not only was the rural village derived from nature, but it also had the same origin as both the forest and the mountain. Taut then proposed that young architects should endeavour to 'feel' the same affinity or connection toward, and with, nature as the rural village. To demonstrate this somewhat vague point, Taut (1904b) illustrated the nave of a Gothic church and a forest (*Tannenwald*) of either fir or pine trees. Taut continued by stating that while the Gothic pointed arch and vaults were not directly

146   *Bruno Taut's design inspiration for the Glashaus*

present in the forest, they were there as the 'free will' interpretations of the architect. This was because the architect could never directly reproduce nature, but only offer a picture, image or interpretation of its glory. To further emphasise his point, Taut then quoted directly from John Ruskin's *The Stones of Venice* (Ruskin, 1880: 353–4):

> We are forced, for the sake of accumulating our power and knowledge, to live in cities, but such advantage as we have in association with each other is in great part counterbalance by our loss of fellowship with nature. We cannot all have our gardens now, nor our pleasant fields to meditate in at eventide. Then the function of our architecture is, as far as may be, to replace these, to tell us about nature, to possess us with memories of her quietness, to be solemn and full of tenderness, like her, and rich in portraitures of her, full of delicate imagery of the flowers we can no more gather, and of the living creatures now far away from us in their own solitude.
>
> (Taut, 1904b: 51)

Taut then concluded 'Natur und Kunst' by describing two drawings that, apart from having direct relevance to the content of his article, were also additionally dedicated to his studies: one of a *Tannenwald* on the outskirts of Stuttgart [Figure 4.2b] and another of the interior of the *Stiftskirche* in Stuttgart (Taut, 1904b)[Figure 4.2a].

Taut's second article, 'Natur und Baukunst', which can be seen as a refinement of the first, further elaborated on nature as a source of inspiration for architecture, in that it offered an extremely delicate sense of space organisation. Taut proposed that the Gothic cathedral triggered in the viewer a sense similar to that of the space formation of nature, but only when viewed as an entirety and in a peaceful and devoted manner. Based on this, Taut proposed that the ultimate role of the architect was to interpret nature and create architecture that unconsciously and involuntarily evoked in the viewer the sense of a natural environment – be it the starry night sky or the mountains. Taut, once again, referred to the two images published earlier in 'Natur und Kunst', stating that while both images were different in their detail, they were essentially the same. Likewise, one image was not directly imitating the other; rather the result was an independent, creative, and natural architecture that was achieved through the architect's 'free will' to imagine space (Taut, 1904a).

From the above explanation of Taut's early writings, it is clear that he was under the influence of a long line of Romantic thought that culminated in Muthesius' *Stilarchitektur und Baukunst*. However, it was not Muthesius who appears as directly influential on these two articles; rather it was Ruskin. Apart from the direct quotation of Ruskin's *The Stones of Venice* in 'Natur und Kunst', Taut's two works are additionally littered with other references to Ruskin, since he refers to *Savageness, Changefulness and Naturalism*.

Likewise, Taut's instance of 'quiet contemplation' in 'Natur und Baukunst' derives directly from Ruskin.

In 1914, Taut published 'Eine Notwendigkeit' (A Necessity). This article can be seen as a later elaboration of Taut's earlier quotation of Ruskin and the Romantics, in that the architecture that best compensated for the loss of nature in the city was embodied in the Gothic cathedral. In 'Eine Notwendigkeit', Taut elaborated on the perceived collaborative effort that was personified in the Gothic cathedral as a building that was the collective endeavour of architects and artists, and, in particular, painters. Taut (1914a) thus called for the construction of buildings where architecture could once again merge with the arts. Taut envisaged a building much like a Gothic cathedral, which would be the 'entirety' of all its artistic endeavours. This entirety, or collective endeavour, was proposed by Taut as a 'secret' or 'great architecture'. Much like the great Gothic cathedrals, Taut stated that the proposed building need not be finished by any one generation. Taut continued that the building must be everything at once, both frame and content, set free from practical demands. Taut proposed a house in which art was to be displayed and kept safe, a building that might contain rooms for all manner of artistic purposes. For Taut, this building was to have been an artistic organism that contained great stained-glass windows, walls in Cubist rhythms, paintings by Wassily Kandinsky and Franz Marc, columns decorated by Alexander Archipenko, and ornament provided by Heinrich Campendonk (Taut, 1914a).

But how does any of the above argument directly concern the actual design of the *Glashaus*? As stated previously, this work primarily seeks to propose alternative explanations for the origins of the *Glashaus*, and this chapter specifically attempts to answer this question in the context of the Gothic. Clearly, the above explanation of the Romantic and Gothic theoretical under-pinnings of the *Glashaus* would therefore firmly position it as a continuation of this process. The most important connection to this process would have been the creation of a building that was an entirety, or collective endeavour, and one that was proposed by Taut (1914a) as a 'secret' or 'great archi-tecture'. Considering the large number of firms, artists and personalities involved, such as the *Deutsche Luxfer Prismen Syndikat*, J. Schmidt and Gottfried Heinersdorf, *Zwieseler und Pirnaer, Eduard Liesegang Fabrik Optischer Apparate*, the Auer Company, Bruno Taut, Paul Scheerbart, Franz Mutzenbecher, Adolf Holzel, etc., it is clearly evident that the *Glashaus* was undoubtedly a 'secret' or an example of 'great architecture'. Furthermore, this quest for a 'secret architecture' clearly resonates with what Goethe (1772) referred to as the 'secret powers' of the Strasbourg Cathedral's towers and the sparkling of the building in the early dawn mist.

However, the above investigation has also exposed certain facts, such as Taut's affiliation to the *Stiftskirche* in Stuttgart, which could be relevant in determining alternative origins for the *Glashaus*. Consequently, these are further avenues worth pursuing.

4.8 Imitating the Gothic masters

From the two images published in 'Natur und Kunst', it is apparent that, for Taut, the Gothic nave of Stuttgart's *Stiftskirche* evoked in him the image, or sense, of being in a *Tannenwald* on the outskirts of Stuttgart. Alternatively explained, the *Tannenwald* served as the original, or natural, inspiration behind the 'free will' conception of the *Stiftskirche*'s nave. In comparing the two images, it is relatively easy to comprehend why Taut would have made this comparison. For example, the overall space organisation of the two is similar in that the space depicted between the two parallel rows of trees could

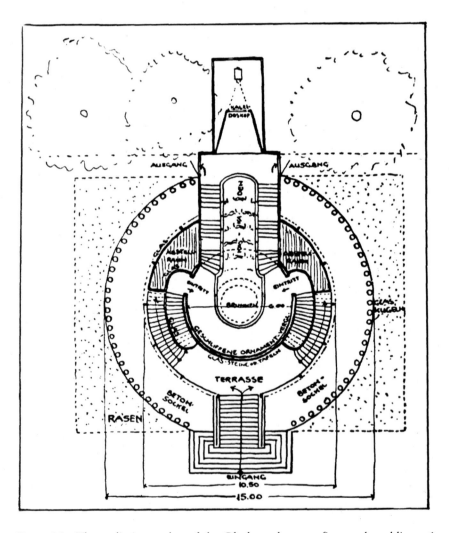

Figure 4.3a The preliminary plan of the *Glashaus* that was first made public on 1 January 1914.

be the volume of the nave, as defined by the two parallel rows of columns; the flared bases of the trees could relate directly to the expanded bases of the gothic columns; the trunks of the trees are clearly the shafts of the church columns; and the top of the trunks could be the column capitals.

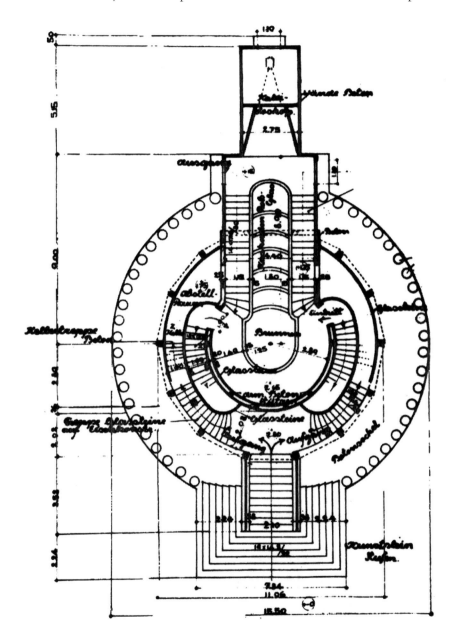

Figure 4.3b The final plan of the *Glashaus* as submitted to the Cologne City Authorities. Photo by permission of Historisches Archiv Köln.

150 *Bruno Taut's design inspiration for the Glashaus*

Furthermore, the high branches of the trees could be the projecting ribs to the underside of the nave's vaulting.

The *Stiftskirche* was constructed according to the *Staffelhalle* (Pseudo-Basilica or Hall-church) principle, which dictated that when viewed in section, the central nave was the tallest portion of the building and that the outermost aisles were not as tall as the innermost aisles. The *Staffelhalle* principle also dictated that the nave should have no clerestory windows. Hänslin Jörg, the architect of the *Stiftskirche's* nave, began working on it in 1433. However, it was not until 1495 that Hänslin's son, Aberlin Jorg, completed the rib vaulting over the nave (Nussbaum, 2000). As stated above, when the original 1495 vaulting is compared to the structure of the *Glashaus'* dome, they appear remarkably similar. This similarity even extended to the point where the dome structure of the *Glashaus* could very well be argued as identical. However, this similarity is not only unique to the *Stiftskirche*. Indeed, the aesthetic of the *Glashaus'* dome could likewise be proposed as similar to that of the naves featured in St. Martin (1421–83) in Amberg, and St. Lamberti (begun in 1450) in Münster. Furthermore, the rib vaulting to the lower aisle of the *Stiftskirche* is proposed as similar to that above the aisle of St. Mauritius (1433–83) in Olmütz. In a letter that Taut wrote in June 1908, he described the architecture of the Alexander Church in Marbach, near Stuttgart, as 'a classical work' (Personal communication with Speidel, 2014). Remarkably, the Alexander Church's architect was also Hänslin's son Aberlin (www.alexanderkirche-marbach.de), and the interior vaulting is almost identical to that of the *Stiftskirche*.

When the general aesthetic of the space organisation inherent in these gothic rib vaults is compared to the dome structure over Taut's 1914 *Glashaus*, it becomes apparent that they are, as Taut would have contended, essentially the same thing. However, while the Gothic rib vaulting, in particular, in Stuttgart's *Stiftskirche,* was undoubtedly influential in Taut's formative thinking for the dome structure of the *Glashaus*, it could be argued as simply a direct imitation rather than a 'free will' interpretation.

A yet unpublished imitation of Gothic thinking is additionally obvious in the *Glashaus*. Gutschow (2005) identified Hendrick Berlage as having been important to the development of 'Eine Notwendigkeit'. This connection was primarily established through Berlage's 1908 *Grundlagen und Entwicklungen der Architektur (Foundations and Development of Architecture)*, which Gutschow (2005) identified as having uncanny parallels to the writing of not only Taut but also Behne. Taut supposedly became aware of this book through Behne, and requested a copy from Behne in April 1913 (Gutschow, 2005: 250). Interestingly, Berlage directly referenced the Gothic in the façade and planning of his *Amsterdam Bersus* (Amsterdam Commodities Exchange) building of 1903. Some historians have noted that Taut had the opportunity to visit the *Amsterdam Bersus* during a trip to Holland in 1912 (Hartmann *et al.*, 2001).

However, new evidence supports the fact that Taut had a copy of *Grundlagen und Entwicklungen der Architektur* three years prior. In 2013, Robin

Rehm published an article entitled 'Nieznany rysunek Brunona Tauta Historia projektu Monument des Eisens (Pomnik elaza) z 1913 roku' ('Bruno Taut's Unknown Drawing. A History of a Design for *Monument des Eisens* (*Monument of Iron*) of 1913'), in which it was revealed that Taut already had a personal copy of *Grundlagen und Entwicklungen der Architektur* in 1910. Aside from this, what is most remarkable about Rehm's (2013) article is the fact that it mentions Taut as having personally drawn over a particular image in the book. According to Rehm, the resultant illustration is a conceptual elevation of Taut's 1913 *Monument des Eisens*, while the original image over which Taut drew was a system that, according to Berlage, was used to proportion Gothic architecture (Rehm, 2013). This Gothic proportioning system was based on multiples of the square root of 2, i.e. 1.41421356. Furthermore, the image that Taut drew over was an isosceles triangle that derived from a system of squares, which were in turn proportioned according to the square root of two.

The most obvious aspect of the *Glashaus'* plan was its central planning, expressed as a number of concentric circles. Curiously, on the plan that Taut and Hoffmann submitted to the Cologne City Authorities, which was dated 25 February 1914, some of these concentric circles had strange overall dimensions, i.e. these dimensions are correct to within one centimetre. For instance, the outer dimension of the 14-column base that supported the *Glashaus'* dome was 11.06 metres, and the inner wall that surrounded the staircases had an inside diameter of 5.78 metres. These strange dimensions are however contrasted with other dimensions that can be considered as conventional. For instance, the overall dimension of the flared concrete base that surrounded the *Glashaus* was 15½ metres, and the outer dimension of the head of the fountain had a diameter of 2.8 metres (Taut, 1914b). However, on the preliminary drawings that Taut made public on 1 January 1914, the dimensions were slightly different in that they were exclusively conventional. For instance, the *Glashaus* dome was noted as having had a diameter of 10½ metres, the flared concrete base that surrounded the *Glashaus* was dimensioned as having been 15 metres, and the inner wall that surrounded the staircases had an inside diameter of 6 metres. Hence, at some point between 1 January and 25 February 1914, numerous changes were made to the *Glashaus'* dimensions.

Bettina Held (1993) contended that construction work to the *Glashaus* had apparently commenced two weeks prior to the issue of the building permit, i.e. two weeks prior to 25 February 1914. Hence, these dimensions were likely applied to the *Glashaus* five to six weeks after 1 January 1914. Thus, the later tendency for dimensional accuracy i.e. on the plan that Taut and Hoffmann submitted to the Cologne City Authorities, would tend to indicate some rapid and yet unknown desire for either exacting mathematical or absolute geometric accuracy. Considering Taut's acknowledged interest in the Gothic, Berlage's prior dictation of a Gothic proportioning system, and Taut's firm connection to prior use of Berlage's proportioning system in the

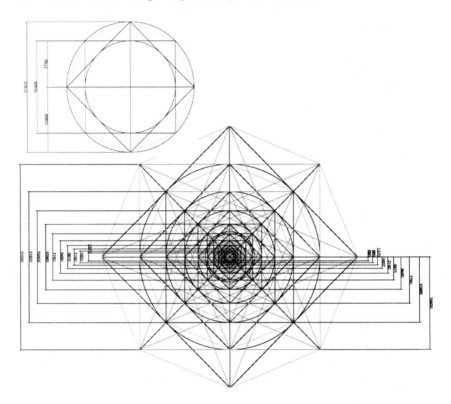

Figure 4.4 The initial 'geometric seed' that was scaled according to the square root of two. Picture by permission of David Nielsen.

Monument des Eisens, it would be logical to attempt to apply Berlage's proportioning system to the *Glashaus*.

Thus, taking the dimension of 15½ metres as a starting point, a square with a breadth and length of 15½ metres was constructed. A second square with identical dimensions was then added. This second square was however rotated 45 degrees along the intersection of the first square's diagonals. An isosceles triangle was then inscribed over these two squares, producing its base from the lower edge of the first square and its height by the most-distant angle of the second square. This process was then repeated to produce a total of four triangles, but with their bases either parallel or at 90 degrees to the first. By connecting the corners of the two squares, a regular eight-sided polygon was then constructed. Furthermore, a circle was additionally inscribed over the two squares and polygon, using the intersection of the squares' diagonals as its centre. This resultant circle therefore also had a diameter of 21.92 metres, i.e. 15½ multiplied by the square root of two. This final figure can be considered as the initial 'geometric seed', which was then scaled

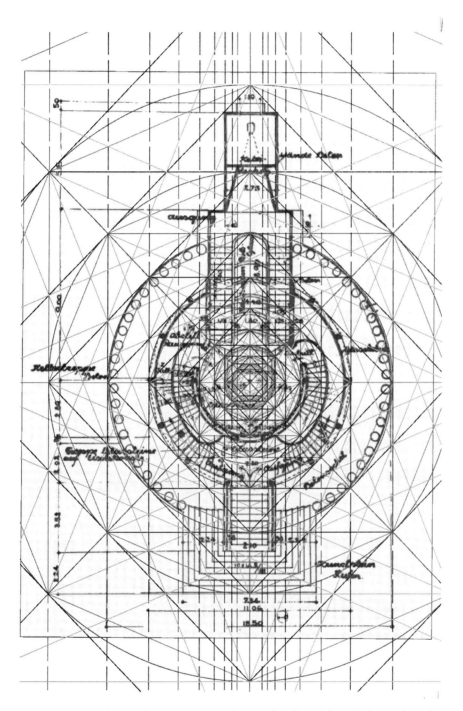

Figure 4.5a Overlaying the 'geometric seed' onto the plan of the *Glashaus*. Photo by permission of Historisches Archiv Köln.

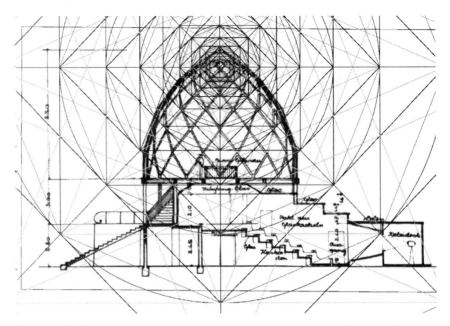

Figure 4.5b Overlaying the 'geometric seed' onto a section of the *Glashaus*. Photo by permission of Historisches Archiv Köln.

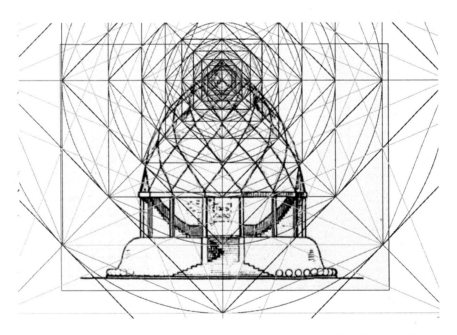

Figure 4.5c Overlaying the 'geometric seed' onto an elevation of the *Glashaus*. Photo by permission of Historisches Archiv Köln.

according to the square root of two, or 1.41421356. This produced a series of proportional 'seeds' that are listed according to the diameter of their associated circles: 0.685, 0.969, 1.370, 1.937, 2.740, 3.875, 5.480, 7.750, 10.960, 15.500, 21.920 metres, etc.

When this final diagram was overlaid and centred on the plan of the *Glashaus* by the author, numerous similarities immediately became evident. The most obvious of the similarities is the almost exact convergence of 'geometric seed' circles with the concentric circles of the *Glashaus* plan. In certain instances, where the circular arrangement of the plan did not coincide with the circles of the scaled 'geometric seeds', another method was used by the author. In these cases, a circle that intersected with the meeting points between the squares and-or the triangles can however be drawn. Certain other key dimensions can likewise be determined if the origin of the 'geometric seed' is moved up and down on the *Glashaus* plan, so that its 'seed' is centred on the intersections of the squares and circles, rather than its centre. Likewise, when the scaled 'geometric seeds' are placed over both the front elevation and the section of the *Glashaus*, immediate similarities are evident.

Therefore, this process proves that Taut used the above described geometric system to finally proportion the *Glashaus*. However, it has to be acknowledged that not all of the dimensions of the scaled 'geometric seeds' are an exact fit with the *Glashaus*' indicated dimensions. This minor discrepancy could in all probability be explained in one of two ways: firstly, Taut's ratio was not the exact square root of two, i.e. 1.41421356, but was rather closer to 1.4. Secondly, Taut could have used the ratio not in a strictly mathematical sense, but rather more as an indicative proportion gained from initial drawing and subsequent scaling of dimensions. This later argument is supported by Berlage's (1908) argument that there were significant variances in Gothic architecture due to the fact that dimensions were gained from geometric drawing and subsequent scaling, rather than pure mathematics.

4.9 Conclusion

As shown above, when Taut's Gothic writings are contextualised, they are clearly part of a much longer tradition of similar practices that revered the Gothic. Clearly, Taut's interest in the Gothic, contained within the powerful metaphor offered by Strasbourg Cathedral, partly derives from the important literary precedents offered by authors like Goethe, Schlegel, Schinkel and Ruskin. However, Taut's interest in the Gothic can also be explained in spheres outside of writing. Taut additionally mirrored the physical acts realised by these personalities, like his description of approaching the Strasbourg Cathedral's spire. Within this wider context, it therefore becomes very clear why Taut would have copied the vaulting of the Stuttgart *Stiftskirche* and Gothic proportion, into the *Glashaus*. By mirroring these acts and keeping the Gothic tradition alive, Taut effectively breathed life into a very important constituent of his developing milieu. Taut was obviously

156 *Bruno Taut's design inspiration for the Glashaus*

connecting the *Glashaus* to tradition and precedent, or reconfiguring the historical conception of the Gothic into his contemporary setting.

Through the connection of a number of progressive clients and products, but principally those of the *Deutsche Luxfer Prismen Syndikat*, to the *Glashaus* endeavour, Taut was transplanting the Gothic collective endeavour and societal transformation into the contemporary ideals of the *Werkbund*.

Bibliography

Behne, A. (1912). *Der Inkrustationsstil in Toscana.* (PhD), Friedrich-Wilhelms-Universität, Berlin.

Berlage, H. P. (1908). *Grundlagen und Entwicklung der Architektur; vier Vorträge gehalten im Kunstgewerbemuseum zu Zürich.* Berlin: Julius Bard Verlag.

Conner, P. R. M. (1978). Pugin and Ruskin. *Journal of the Warburg and Courtauld Institutes, 41*, 344–350.

Cook, E. T. (1911). *The Life of John Ruskin* (Vol. 1). London: George Allen & Company, Ltd.

Curl, J. S. (2006). *A Dictionary of Architecture and Landscape Architecture* (2 edn.). Oxford: Oxford University Press.

Eastlake, C. L. (1872). *A History of the Gothic Revival.* London: Longmans, Green and Company.

Frampton, K. (2007). *Modern Architecture: A Critical History* (4 edn.). London and New York: Thames & Hudson Ltd.

Glaser, S. (2002). *Explorations of the Gothic Cathedral in Nineteenth-Century France.* (PhD), Bloomington, IN: Indiana University.

Glaser, S. (2005). 'Deutsche Baukunst', 'Architecture Française': The use of the Gothic Cathedral in the Creation of National Memory in Nineteenth-Century Germany and France. In C. Cluver, V. Plesch & l. Hoek (eds). *Orientations: Space, Time, Image and Word* (pp. 77–92). Amsterdam and New York: Editions Rodopi B.V.

Gutschow, K. K. (2005). *The Culture of Criticism: Adolf Behne and the Development of Modern Architecture in Germany, 1910–1914.* (Doctor of Philosophy), New York, Columbia University.

Hartmann, K., Nerdinger, W., Schirren, M. and Speidel, M. (2001). *Bruno Taut 1880–1938: Architekt zwischen Tradition und Avantgarde.* Stuttgart, Munich: Deutsche Verlags-Anstalt DVA

Held, B. (1993). Kleine Glashaus – Chronologie In A. Thiekotter (ed.). *Kristallisationen, Splitterungen: Bruno Tauts Glashaus* (pp. 183). Basel: Birkhauser Verlag.

Hersey, G. L. (1972). *High Victorian Gothic: a Study in Associationism.* Baltimore, MD: Johns Hopkins University Press.

Hill, R. (2007). *God's Architect: Pugin and the Building of Romantic Britain.* London: Allen Lane – Penguin Books Ltd.

Hugo, V. (1831). *Notre-Dame de Paris, 1482* (1894 edn.). Paris: L'Imprimerie Nationale Librairie Ollendorff.

Junghanns, K. (1983). *Bruno Taut, 1880–1938.* Berlin (West): Elefanten Press.

Kurtz, M. J. (2006). *America and the Return of Nazi Contraband: the Recovery of Europe's Cultural Treasures.* Cambridge: Cambridge University Press.

LeMire, W. M. (ed.). (1969). *The Unpublished Lectures of William Morris*. Detroit: Wayne State University Press.

Lepik, A. and Rosa, I. (2005). Tokyo-Berlin / Berlin-Tokyo: Architecture, The Berlin-Tokyo connection from late 19th Century to late 1920's (pp. 118–119). Tokyo: Mori Art Museum.

Maciuika, J. V. (2005). *Before the Bauhaus : Architecture, Politics and the German State, 1890–1920*. New York: Cambridge University Press.

Mallgrave, H. (ed.). (1994). *Style-Architecture and Building-Art: Transformations of Architecture in the Nineteenth Century and Its Present Condition*. Santa Monica: The Getty Centre for the History of Art and the Humanities.

Muthesius, H. (1902). *Stilarchitektur und Baukunst: Wandlungen der Architektur im XIX. Jahrhundert und ihr heutiger Standpunkt*. Mülheim-Ruhr: Schimmelpfeng.

Muthesius, H., Günther, S., Posener, J., Sharp, D. and Muthesius, E. (1979). *Hermann Muthesius, 1861–1927*. London: Architectural Association.

Nipperdey, T. (1981). Der Kölner Dom als Nationaldenkmal. *Historische Zeitschrift, 3*(December), 595–613.

Nussbaum, N. (2000). *German Gothic Church Architecture*. New Haven, CT: Yale University Press

Pugin, A. W. N. (1825). *Specimens of Gothic Architecture; Selected from Various Ancient Edifices in England* (3 edn. Vol. 2). London: M. A. Nattali.

Pugin, A. W. N. (1825). *Specimens of Gothic Architecture; Selected from Various Ancient Edifices in England* (3 edn. Vol. 1). London: M. A. Nattali.

Pugin, A. W. N. (1836). *Contrasts, or, A Parallel Between the Noble Edifices of the Fourteenth and Fifteenth Centuries and Similar Buildings of the Present Day; Shewing the Present Decay of Taste*. London: A. Welby Pugin.

Pugin, A. W. N. (1838). *Examples of Gothic Architecture; Selected from Various Ancient Edifices in England* (2 edn. Vol. 1). London: Henry G. Bohn.

Pugin, A. W. N. (1839). *Examples of Gothic Architecture; Selected from Various Ancient Edifices in England* (2 edn. Vol. 2). London: Henry G. Bohn.

Pugin, A. W. N. (1840). *Examples of Gothic Architecture; Selected from Various Ancient Edifices in England* (2 edn. Vol. 3). London: Henry G. Bohn.

Pugin, A. W. N. (1841). *The True Principles of Pointed or Christian Architecture*. London: J. Weale

Rehm, R. (2013). Nieznany rysunek Brunona Tauta Historia projektu Monument des Eisens (Pomnik elaza) z 1913 roku. *Quart, 1*(27), 96–106.

Riegl, A. (1893). *Stilfragen*. Berlin: G. Siemens Verlag.

Ruskin, J. (1849). *The Seven Lamps of Architecture*. London: Smith, Elder and Company.

Ruskin, J. (1853). *The Stones of Venice: The Sea Stories* (Vol. 2). London: Smith, Elder and Company.

Ruskin, J. (1880). *The Stones of Venice: The Foundations* (Vol. 1). New York: John Wiley and Sons.

Scheerbart, P. (1914). *Glasarchitektur*. Berlin: Strum.

Schinkel, K. F. and Riemann, G. (1979). *Reisen nach Italien: Tagebucher, Briefe, Zeichnungen, Aquarelle* (1982 edn.). Berlin: Rutten & Loening.

Schlegel, K. W. F. (1806). Briefe auf einer Reise durch die Niederlande, Rheingegenden, die Schweiz, und einen Theil von Frankreich In H. Eichner (ed.). *Kritische Friedrich-Schlegei-Ausgabe* (Vol. 4, pp. 186–192). Darmstadt: Darmstadt University Press.

Sheehan, J. J. (1989). *German History 1770–1866*. New York and Oxford: Clarendon Press.

Speidel, M. (2014, 24 June). [Re: Glashaus].

Taut, B. (1904a). Natur und Baukust In M. Speidel (ed.). *Bruno Taut: Natur und Fantasie 1880–1938*. Berlin: Ernst & Sohn.

Taut, B. (1904b). Natur und Kunst. In M. Speidel (ed.). *Bruno Taut: Natur und Fantasie 1880–1938*. Berlin: Ernst & Sohn.

Taut, B. (1914a). Eine Notwendigkeit. *Der Strum 4, 196/197*, 174–175.

Taut, B. (1914b). *Glashaus Köln*. (19, A12/4, 25). Historical City Archive, Cologne.

Taut, B. (1977). *Bruno Taut Architekturlehre: Grundlagen, Theorie und Kritik aus der Sicht eines Sozialistischen Architekten* (German edn.). Hamburg: Verlag fur das Studium der Arbeiterbewegung.

Viollet-le-Duc, E-E. (1875). *Dictionnaire Raisonné de l'Architecture Française du XIe au XVIe siècle* (Vol. 2). Paris: A. Morel & Cie.

von Goethe, J. W. (1772). On German Architecture: D.M. Ervini a Steinbach (J. Gage, Trans.). In J. Gage (ed.). *Goethe on Art* (pp. 103–112). Berkley, CA: University of California Press.

von Görres, J. (1814). Der Dom in Koln. In W. Schellberg (ed.). *Joseph von Gorres' Ausgewahlte Werke und Briefe*. Munich: Kosel.

von Görres, J. (1842). *Der Dom von Köln und das Münster von Strasburg*. Regensburg: G.J. Manz Verlag.

Whyte, I. B. and Schneider, R. (1986). *Die Briefe der Gläsernen Kette*. Berlin: Ernst, Wilhelm & Sohn.

Worringer, W. (1907). *Abstraktion und Einfühlung: ein Beitrag zur Stilpsychologie* (3 edn.). Munich: R. Piper and Company.

Worringer, W. (1910). *Formprobleme der Gotik* (2 edn.). Munich: R. Piper & Co. Verlag.

www.alexanderkirche-marbach.de. Die Alexanderkirche. Retrieved 10 November, 2014, from www.alexanderkirche-marbach.de/

www.dictionaryofarthistorians.org. Dictionary of Art Historians. *Franz Theodor Kugler* Retrieved 12 August, 2013, from www.dictionaryofarthistorians.org/kuglerf.htm

5 Conclusion

5.1 Introduction

This study has uncovered some of the original motives and inspirations behind the design of the *Glashaus,* which have been largely overlooked. It has re-established the primary importance of the client–architect relationship between Frederick Keppler and Bruno Taut. Keppler, as the project's client, urged a rigorous and predefined prototype for the design of the *Glashaus.* In turn, Taut, as the architect, developed this stipulation into the *Glashaus* design through his interpretations of the *Victoria regia* lily, in addition to architectural precedents associated with Strasbourg Cathedral and the Stuttgart *Stiftskirche.* The common feature between these sources is a proportioning system based on the Gothic norm of the square root of two.

5.2 Myths, symbols and personalities

Frederick Keppler is thereby reintroduced as a key personality in the *Glashaus* narrative. While in the United States of America, Keppler developed an association with the Luxfer Prism Company, and when he returned to Europe in 1898, as the company's German representative, he sought to diversify and aggressively promote Luxfer's products. In particular, Keppler wished to introduce Luxfer's primary product, Luxfer Prisms, to a European audience and to promote it as a symbol of a progressive modernity. Keppler further refined the key technologies of the Luxfer Company. He introduced simplified glass tiles and a reinforced concrete joining system. Inevitably, Keppler sought a platform to promote these innovative new products. Bruno Taut and the *Glashaus* were chosen to accomplish this task because of the avantgarde character of his architecture.

In striving to attain his goals, Keppler proved highly influential in the development of prototype exhibition buildings displayed at numerous exhibitions. The Luxfer prototype found its ultimate expression in the *Glashaus.* However, the prototype did not emerge in isolation. Rather, it evolved from earlier exhibition buildings, most notably the glazed buildings featured at both the 1893 Chicago and 1900 Paris World Fairs. This study has argued that it was Keppler's personal experience of these earlier exhibitions that drove the development of the Luxfer prototype in Berlin. As the Director of the *Deutsche Luxfer Prismen Syndikat*, Keppler mandated that any iteration of the Luxfer prototype should use Luxfer products as the main building material and that it should showcase these in the best possible manner. To achieve these ends, Keppler further specified that the proposed exhibition building should contain a glazed dome, an elaborate structure to support the dome, spiral staircases, and a cascading fountain.

Considering the comprehensive brief outlined by Keppler, the architect selected for the brief would have few options other than to engage with these highly detailed requirements. This thesis asserts that this is what Bruno Taut did. Yet, Taut also lent an innovative interpretation to the project by introducing the themes and the poetic vision offered by Gothic architecture and the *Victoria regia* lily.

From the Gothic, Taut borrowed the vaulting from the Stuttgart *Stiftskirche*, and applied it to the structure of the *Glashaus'* dome. Likewise, the western rose window of Strasbourg Cathedral had an influential impact on Taut in determining the general planning of the *Glashaus* and the colours of its dome. And in this context, as already mentioned, Taut proportioned the overall *Glashaus* structure according to the Gothic norm using the square root of two.

A further source of symbolic interpretation, if not direct copying, can be derived from the influence of the *Victoria regia lily*. The general appearance and plan of the *Glashaus* is very similar to the post-1860 *Victoria regia* glasshouses, which were executed according to a circular or polygonal plan, which were in turn covered by flattish curved, glazed domes. More specifically, this thesis has shown that the planning of the *Glashaus* drew directly from the *Victoria regia* glasshouse at the Berlin Botanical Gardens in Dahlem.

Taut was aware of the symbols of the Gothic and the *Victoria regia*. As discussed, Hendrick Berlage revealed to Taut the Gothic proportioning based upon the square root of two. In addition, Taut imitated Schinkel's act of climbing the tower of Strasbourg Cathedral, and he was also familiar with the discourse surrounding the Gothic by important figures like Goethe, Schlegel, Ruskin and Worringer.

The dimension of the *Glashaus* dome also suggests prior knowledge of the work of Paxton, van Houtte and Ortgies, who all had an intimate association with the *Victoria regia*. Likewise, Taut's essay 'Die Galoschen des Glucks' demonstrates that he was intimately aware of the anatomy and pollination habits of the *Victoria regia*, and this knowledge is also evident in the physical form of the *Glashaus*.

All the evidence presented here strongly points to the fact that crucial aspects of the *Glashaus* design drew upon the influence and impact of the Gothic and *Victoria regia*. Indeed, their presence is unmistakable and undeniable. Furthermore, this thesis proposes that, despite Keppler's detailed brief, Taut produced a design that imaginatively interwove his interpretations of the

Gothic and the *Victoria regia* into the *Glashaus*. By doing so, Taut achieved something far more significant than the highly circumscribed brief might have originally suggested possible.

5.3 Implications

This thesis is significant because it re-establishes the primary importance of the client–architect relationship in the design of the *Glashaus*.

The research undertaken in this work and the answers it produces pose a number of challenges to conventional wisdom in the study of architectural modernism. First of all, it challenges the accepted assumption that both the modern movement and the *Glashaus* are best understood in terms of a 'clean break' from the past. Clearly, this is not the case, since it has been demonstrated that the *Glashaus*' design drew upon the architecture featured in previous World Fairs, the Gothic tradition, and the glasshouses of the *Victoria regia*. This book thus makes a significant contribution to answering one of the pivotal remaining mysteries surrounding the *Glashaus* design – the unresolved and little-recognised relationship between horticultural glasshouses and modernist architecture.

By reintroducing Keppler within the narrative explaining the origins of the *Glashaus*, this thesis extends Gutschow's earlier contention that the *Glashaus* was a collaborative endeavour between Taut, Scheerbart and Behne. Before this study, the *Glashaus* was regarded as the product of an aesthetic collaboration between its visionary architect Taut and the poet Scheerbart, and promoted through the prism of Expressionism by the writer and theorist Behne. This study has altered that view of the *Glashaus* to include its commissioning client, Keppler. Furthermore, by placing the *Glashaus* within a context based in historical precedent and one that recognises the intention to market Luxfer products, the utopian associations of the *Glashaus* are reduced in favour of recognising the more prosaic and pragmatic immediate concerns that led to the commission in the first place.

Yet, the outcome is that the *Glashaus* is still understood as a collaborative endeavour. The result of this thesis' argument is that the endeavour is now best understood as a relation of four different contributions, with Taut and Keppler being the primary contributors and Scheerbart and Behne being secondary.

By reinforcing the understanding of the *Glashaus* as a collaborative project primarily driven by the desire to promote building materials within a particular architectural vision, this study provides a concrete example that testifies to the original collaborative ideals of the *Werkbund*. The *Glashaus* can therefore be proposed as a *Qualität* object that was achieved through the shared vision of a progressive client and an enlightened architect. Yet, by revealing how Taut freely interpreted the influence of Gothic and *Victoria regia* for the design of his *Glashaus*, this study also underscores Taut's opposing vision for the *Werkbund*; that is, it reinforces his stated opposition

162 *Bruno Taut's design inspiration for the Glashaus*

to Muthesius' proposal for *Typisierung* by revealing his counter-ideal that nonetheless maintains artistic individualism.

5.4 Conclusion

This study has established that many of the diverse motives and inspirations behind the design of the *Glashaus* can be traced back to its unique client–architect relationship. As its client, Keppler dictated a highly specific prototype for the design of the *Glashaus*. In turn, Taut, as the project's architect, developed this prototype into the *Glashaus* by using the aesthetic and design precedents of the *Victoria regia* lily and the Gothic aesthetic. The result is an account that re-establishes some of Banham's (1959) 'prophetic ancestry' of modern architecture by introducing yet unexplored personalities, myths, and symbols that were associated with the *Glashaus*.

Bibliography

Banham, R. (1959). The Glass Paradise. *The Architectural Review, 125* (February), pp. 87–89.

Index

abstract art 137
Adanson, Michel 91
Albert, Prince 89
Alexander Church 150
Alison, Archibald 134
Allen, J. F. 79
Alpine Architektur (Taut) 77
American 3-Way Prism Company of Philadelphia 11
American Luxfer Prism Company 15
Amiens Cathedral 132
Amsterdam Bersus (Amsterdam Commodities Exchange) 150
Association of German Bridge and Steel Fabricators 20
Association of German Steelworkers 20
Auer Company 25

Balat, Alphonse 86, 109
Banham, Reyner 68; 'The Glass Paradise' 1–2
Banks, Sir Joseph 91
Basquin, Olin H.: appointment to Luxfer Prism Company 12, 15; development of mathematical formulas 12–13; invention of prismatic glass 13, 58; return to America 17
Behne, Adolf 6; collaboration on *Glashaus* 3; dissertation 125; Expressionism 3
Belfast Botanical Gardens 94
Berlage, Hendrick 150, 151, 151–2, 160
Berlin aquarium 89
Berlin Botanical Gardens 87, 92, 102, 109–11, 112–14, 115; influence on *Glashaus* design 117–18; relocation to Dahlem 112–14
Berlin Central Hotel 88

Berlin Palace 85–6
Beuth locomotive 108
Bicton Gardens 92
'The Big Flower' (Taut) 69
Birmingham botanical gardens 92
Boari, Adamo 16
Böckmann, Wilhelm 139
Boden Luxferprismen mit Betonrippen 21
Boerhaave, Herman 83, 91
Bonafede, Francesco 91
Borsig Gardens 107, 108
Borsig, Johann Friedrich August 87, 106–7, 107–8, 120; steam engine business 107
Borsig Villa 87, 106–7, 107–8
Borsig Works 106–7, 108, 115, 120
botanical gardens: associated with winter gardens 90–1; Belfast Botanical Gardens 94; Berlin Botanical Gardens 87, 92, 102, 109–11, 112–14, 115, 117–18; Birmingham botanical gardens 92; Brussels Botanical Gardens 94; Copenhagen Botanical Gardens 112; Frankfurt Botanical Gardens 113; Hamburg 106; horticultural gardens 90–1; Philadelphia Botanical Gardens 113; Royal Botanical Gardens (Kew) 94, 100–1, 104; university-associated gardens 90–1; University of Leiden 109; *Victoria regia* glasshouses 96; winter gardens 90–1; Zürich Botanical Gardens 106
Botanical Gardens (Hamburg) 106
Botanical Gardens (University of Leiden) 109
Bouché, Carl Freidrich 87, 102, 108
Bourbons 132, 136
Braun, Professor Alexander 102

164   *Index*

Bretton Hall 92
Britain: and the Gothic 133–7; Gothic Revival architecture 133, 134; Romanticism 133, 136, 136–7
British Arts and Crafts 137, 141
British Luxfer Prism Syndicate 15
Bruckmann, Wilhelm 71, 76
Brudern Ház (Brudern) 19–20
Brunel, Isambard 29
Bruno Taut and Paul Scheerbart's Vision: Utopian Aspects of German Expressionist Architecture (Haag Bletter) 2
Bruno Taut and the Architecture of Activism (Whyte) 3
Brussels Botanical Gardens 94
Brussels International World Fair (1910) 18
Burton, Decimus 94

Carnegie, Andrew 113
Cascade Room, *Glashaus* 23, 24, 59, 77; ceiling 23–4; darkness of 24
Castan, Gustav 46
Castan, Louis 46
Caus, Salomon de 82
ceiling, *Glashaus*: Cascade Room 23–4; *Goldsmalten* 24
Centennial Exposition (Philadelphia, 1876) 35–9; Agricultural Hall 36–7; Arkansas building 38; Crystal Fountain 36; Horticulture Hall 37, 38–9; Hydraulic Basin 36, 58; Machinery Hall 36; Main Exhibition Hall 35–6, 38; Memorial Hall of Art 37; Moorish Pavilions 38–9; Pennsylvania Educational Hall 38; Tunisian Coffee House 38
Chadwick, G. F. 29
Champ Du Mars 39
Chicago Architectural Sketch Club 17
Chicago skyscraper 11
'The Child of Fortune' *see* 'Die Galoschen des Glucks'
Ciré, A. 26
Cobb, William 96
Collamore, Peter 11
Cologne Cathedral 130, 131, 131–2
Cologne City Authorities 151
Colquhoun, Alan 68
Columbus, Christopher 43
commercial prisms 14
Compagnie Transatlantique 41
Condie-Nealle Glass Company of

St Louis 11
Congress of Vienna 131
Conrad Loddiges 92
conservatories 81–2
Contemporary English Architecture (Muthesius) 139
Copenhagen Botanical Gardens 112
Copenhagen palm house 95
Crew, Professor Henry 16; development of mathematical formulas 12–13; invention of prismatic glass 13, 58
Crown Glasshouse 109
Crystal Chain Letters 71, 73
Crystal Chain Letters: Architectural Fantasies by Bruno Taut and His Circle (Whyte) 3
Crystal Palace 27–30; atmospheric effect 69; Crystal Fountain 27–9; relocated to Sydenham 29; Water Temples 29–30, 58
Culture of Aquatics and Orchids 103, 106
The Culture of Criticism: Adolf Behne and the Development of Modern Architecture in Germany, 1910–1914 (Gutschow) 3
Cupola Room 72, 75
cut prisms 13–14
Cyclocephala scarab beetle 78, 80, 119

Dahlem glasshouse complex 112–14, 115, 117–18
Dahlem palm house 95
Darley Dale conservatory 99
Das Englische Haus Das (Muthesius) 139
Desmond, R. 101
Deutsche Luxfer Prismen Syndikat 10–11, 15, 17–18; Building Trade Exhibition 18; domed building 18–19; and the *Glashaus* 21–5
Deutscher Stahlwerks-Verband 20
Deutscher Werkbund 142–7; holistic ethos of quality 145; rift in membership 145; Taut's rural village 145–6
Diamant (1910) 18–19
Die Auflösung der Städte (Taut) 118
Die Englische Baukunst der Gegenwart (Muthesius) 139
'Die Galoschen des Glucks' (Taut) 69, 71–8; cathedral tower 73; clogs 77–8; growing house 71, 72; 'happy people' entering the 'city of flames'

75–6; industrialisation, impact of 72; landing airship 76; peculiar rod 75; radiant cathedral 76, 77; rebuilding the Alps 76, 77; reintroduction of nature 72; representation of Scheerbart 72; *Victoria regia* reference 75, 118, 119; vision 71–2
Die Grosse Blume (Taut) 69, 118–19
Die Neuere Kirchliche Baukunst in England (Muthesius) 139
Die Stadtkrone (Taut) 77
Die Weltbaumeister (Taut) 77
Dion, Henri de 39
dome, *Glashaus*: drawing for building approval 21; floor 23; influence of *Stiftskirche* 150, 160; multi-coloured 22, 78, 160; reduction in structural size 21–2; reminiscent of *Victoria regia* glasshouses 116; similarities to other buildings 150; simplified glass tiles 21, 25; triple-glazed 22
Dome Room 5, 7, 21, 23; brightly lit 24; lighting 24–5
d'Orbigny, Alcide 79
Douillier, Nicholas Facio de 91
Dutert, Ferdinand 90

East End (Oakland) 113
Edison Electric Company 49, 50
Edition Company 42–3
Eduard Liesegang Fabrik Optischer Apparate 59
Eggert, Georg Peter Hermann 112
Eichler, Professor A. W. 109–10
Eiffel Tower 41
'Eine Notwendigkeit' (A Necessity) (Taut) 147
Elector Palatine 82
electro-deposition 21
electro-glazing 14
Ende, Hermann 139
England Architect and News Record, The 16
Engler, Professor Adolf 112
English House, The (Muthesius) 139
Ersoy, Ufuk: atmospheric effect of Crystal Palace 69; literary sources 68; similarities between Crystal Palace and the *Glashaus* 68–9
Esposizione pubblica dei prodotti dell'industria 26, 27
European Art Nouveau 137
Examples of Gothic Architecture

(Pugin) 133
exhibition buildings 25–7
Exhibition of the Industry of All Nations (New York, 1853) 30–1, 58
Exhibition Palace (1862) 31–2, 58
The Exotic Nursery 101, 116
Exposición Universal 41
Exposition Internationale d'Anvers 41
Exposition Universelle de Paris (1867) 32–3; Exhibition Palace 32–3
Exposition Universelle de Paris (1878) 39–41, 58; *Le Grand Ballon* (Grand Balloon) 40–1; *Palais du Champ de Mars* 39, 40; *Palais du Trocadéro* 39, 58; *Pavillonde la ville de Paris* 39
Exposition Universelle de Paris (1889) 41–3, 58; *Champ de Mars* 41; dome 41; Edison Company 42–3; electrical lighting 42–3; *Galerie Desaix* 41; *Galerie des Machines* 41; *Les Fontaines Lumineuses* (Luminous Fountains) 42; *Palais des Arts libéraux* 41; *Palais des Expositions diverses* 41
Exposition Universelle de Paris (1900) 51–8; Art Nouveau style 51, 57; *Chateau d'eau* 52–3, 59; influence on the *Glashaus* 59; main venue 51–2; Palace of Electricity 53; *Palais de l'Horticulture* (Horticulture Building) 57; *Palais Lumineux* (Luminous Palace) 55–7, 59; *Salle des Fêtes* 57; *Salle des Glaces ou Salle des Illusions* 53–5, 59; Triumph of Electricity 52–3; Water Palace 52
Expressionism 1, 3, 4; and Adolf Behne 3

factory prisms: factory prisms 14
Falconnier, Gustav 49, 56–7
Fay, C. R. 75, 98
Ferris, George W. G. 44
Fiedler, August 45
Finsterlin, Herman 71
Fintelmann, Axel 112
First International Exhibition of Electricity 41
Fisher, Theodore 145
Fleury, Charles Rohault de 95
Flinn, J. J. 45–6
Floor of Luxfer Prisms with concrete beams 21

166 *Index*

Flore des Serres et des Jardins de l'Europe 105, 106
fountain, *Glashaus* 59
Fowke, Captain Francis 31
France: claims invention of the Gothic 132; expositions 26; French Romantics 132; international exhibitions 26; symbolism of the Gothic 132–3; *see also Exposition Universelle de Paris* (1867); *Exposition Universelle de Paris* (1878); *Exposition Universelle de Paris* (1889); *Exposition Universelle de Paris* (1900)
Franco-Prussian War 33, 35
Frankfurt Botanical Gardens 113
Freiburg Cathedral 131
French Revolution 132, 136
Fresnel, August 12
Frick, Henry 113

Galerie des Machines 90
'The Galoshes of Fortune' *see* 'Die Galoschen des Glucks'
Gautier, A. 57
German Garden City Movement 72
German Romanticism 129
Germany: claims invention of the Gothic 128, 130; exhibition pavilions 25–6; German Romanticism 129; Herman Muthesius 138–47; Johann von Goethe 129; Karl Wilhelm Friedrich Schlegel 129–30; search for a national identity 128, 129; unification 131, 132, 136; Wilhelm Worringer 137–8
Gewerbeschule 107
Giffard, Henry 40
Glasarchitektur (Scheerbart) 72, 115, 125
Glaser, S. 129–30, 132
Glashaus: central planning of concentric circles 151; collaborative project 161; following an established prototype 61–2; proportioning system 151–5, 160; similarities and influence of World's Expositions 58; style 58
'Glashaus: Werkbund-Ausstellung Köln 1914, Führer zur Eröffnung des Glashauses' (Taut): promotion of the *Glashaus* 10
Glas Palast 90, 110–11

Glass-blocks 21, 23
Glass Building Blocks 49
glasshouses *see* horticultural glasshouses
Glass Menagerie 89
Glass Palace 110–11
Glassteine 21
Glassteine und Eisenbeton 23
glass tiles: floor of dome 24, 25; Luxfer Prisms 13, 18, 25; simplified 21, 25
glazed architecture: historicist perspective 68
glazed cladding 69
glazed greenhouses 83–5
Glen Cove Company 38
Global Master Builder, The (Taut) 77
glow-worms 78
Goethe, Johann von 128–9
Goldsmalten 24
Gothic Architecture (Pugin) 133
Gothic Europe 1–2
Gothic Revival architecture 133, 134
Gothic, the: and Britain 133–7; Changefulness/Variety 135; and France 132–3; and Germany 128–33; Gothic Revival architecture 133, 134; Grotesqueness/Disturbed Imagination 135–6; Herman Muthesius 138–47; influence of style on *Glashaus* design 148–55; *Kunstwollen* 137, 138; metaphors and physical examples 134–6; Naturalism 135; pointed arch 137–8; Redundance/Generosity 136; Rigidity/Obstinacy 136; Savageness/Rudeness 134–5; symbolism of Gothic cathedrals 128; Taut's Gothic thinking 125–8; Wilhelm Worringer 137
Gould, Jay 114
Grange Manor House 85
Great Conservatory (Chatsworth) 86, 87, 94; *Victoria regia* lily 105
The Greater Conservatory (Mountain Park) 94
Great Exhibition of the Works of Industry of All Nations, The (London, 1851) 27–30, 58; Building Committee 33; triumphal expression 89
Great Palm House 108
Greenhouse, Hothouse and Stove, The (MacIntosh) 84
greenhouses 81, 83–5

Greenough, Henry 31
Gründerkrach 35
Grundlagen und Entwicklungen der Architektur 150–1
Gutschow, Kai 150; on Adolf Behne 3–4; collaboration on *Glashaus* 3; the Gothic 125; *Monument des Eisens* 20

Haag Bletter, Rosemarie 2–3
Haeneke, Thaddäus 79
Hasenauer, Carl von 33
Haussmann, Georges-Eugène 32
Healy, E. C. 40
Heinz, Henry 113
Held, Bettina 151
Herrenhausen Gardens 101, 101–2, 106
Hix, J. 82, 83, 84, 85, 92, 95, 101, 114
Hoffmann, Franz 115
Hooker, William 100
horticultural gardens: associated with botanical gardens 90–1
horticultural glasshouses 80–2; association with mobility 86; conservatories 81–2; control over nature 80; glazing 83–4; greenhouses 81; innovation during industrial revolution 84; inspiration for *Glashaus* 115; Leiden University 83–4; nature-as-art 81; orangeries 81, 82–3; palm houses 94–6; palms 84; preserving nature 80–1; private winter gardens 85–7; public winter gardens 87–90; purpose-built 83; rapid development during 19th century 84–5; and wealthy industrialists 86; winter gardens 82; *see also Victoria regia* glasshouses
Hugo, Victor 132

Ikelaar, Leo 3
Indian Villa 86
industrialisation 27, 72, 136; in Prussia 107
Industrial Revolution 133
International Cotton Exposition 41
International Exhibition in Antwerp 41
Iridian prisms 13, 14, 15

Jackson Park 43
Jacobsen, J. Carl 87, 88
Jacquard, Joseph 26
Johnson, R. 44, 50–1

Jones-Loyd, S. 98
Jörg, Aberlin 150
Jörg, Hänslin 150
Junghanns, Kurt 3
Jupiter Prism Company of Davenport 11

kaleidoscope, *Glashaus* 59, 77
Keppler Crystal Ceilings 22
Keppler, Frederick 10–11, 16–18; appointment to Luxfer Prism Company 17, 60, 159; business acumen 17, 60; early years 16–17, 60; familiarity with Crew/Basquin products 60; formulating prototypes for Luxfer 61, 159, 160; influence in development of prototype exhibition buildings 159–60; patents 18; relationship with Taut 6; visiting Sydenham Crystal Palace 61; visiting the World's Colombian Exposition (1893) 60
Keppler Glass Constructions 22
Keppler System: patent 18; staircases, *Glashaus* 22–3
Kibble Palace 88
Kingdom of Sardinia 26
Knight, E. H. 40
Knight, T. A. 91
Koerner, Alfred 95
Kohlmaier, G. 82, 83, 84, 86, 87, 88, 89, 114
Koppelkamm, S. 81, 82, 83, 84, 92, 94
Korn, Arthur 68
Korner, Alfred 112, 112–13, 115
Kram, Carl 71, 76–7
Kristallisationen, Splitterungen: Bruno Taut's Glashaus (Thiekotter) 3
Kroonserre 109
Krüger-Passage 19, 20
Kugler, Franz Theodor 132
Kunstwollen 137, 138

Laeken 86
Lampyris noctiluca 78
Lanyon, Charles 94
Le Baron Jenny, William 48
Leeds General Hotel 88
Leiden University 83, 109
Leipzig Exhibition (1913) 19–20
Le Play, Pierre Guillaume Frédéric 32
L'Exposition publique des produits de l'industrie française 26
L'Horticulture Belge 106

168 Index

Libby Glass Company 47
Linnaeus, Carl 91
London International Exhibition on Art
    and Industry (1862) 31–2, 58;
    Exhibition Palace 31, 32
Long Depression 35
Lord and Burnham 114
Lord St. Vincent 92
Loudon, John Claudius 91–4, 103–4,
    133–4; aquarium 103–4, 116;
    flattened semi-dome 92, 103–4; iron
    sash bar 92
'The Lucky Shoes' (Taut) 69
Lutter, Paul 20
Luxfer Österreichische Glas und
    Eisenbau Geschäft, MBH 15
Luxfer Prism Company 11, 12;
    appointments of Crew and Basquin
    12; competition 16; exhibiting
    products 18–20; foreign branches
    15; patents 13; publication of
    formulas 12–13; success of 15
Luxfer Prisms 11–16; architectural
    products 12; Canopy 15;
    commercial prisms 14; cut prisms
    13–14; factory prisms 14; fire-proof
    glazing 17; Forilux 14–15, 15;
    frames 14–15; glass tiles 13, 18;
    invention 11–12; Iridian prisms 13,
    14, 15; Major Prisms 15; marketing
    12; Minor Prisms 15; origins 11;
    patents 11–12; products used in
    Glashaus 10; scientific merit
    established 12–13; Window Plate
    14, 15
Lyndhurst Estate 114
Lyon Glasshouses 111, 120

MacIntosh, Charles 84, 91
Mackenzie, Sir George 91–2
Mackolite Fireproofing Company 17
Mackolite Plaster Board Company 17
Magazine of Natural History, The
    133–4
Major Prisms 15
Mallgrave, H. 145
Maquet, Henri 86
McCabe, James 37
McLean, R. C. 16
Mietskasernen 72, 76, 77, 112
Minor Prisms 15
Moabit Villa 87, 106–7, 107–8
Modern Architecture and
    Expressionism (Sharp) 2

Möhring's pavilion 25
Monument des Eisens 20, 25
Morren, Charles Francois Antoine 106
Morris, William 133
Museum of Natural History (Paris) 95
Muthesius, Hermann 69, 138–47;
    appointment as German cultural and
    technical attaché 139; appointment
    to Prussian Ministry of Commerce
    139; background 138–9; and the
    Deutscher Werkbund 142–7;
    envisions middle-class 140; machine
    production 141–2; national
    understanding of quality 142;
    proposes British-Gothic model
    140–1; proposes modern industrial
    buildings 140; unified model of art
    and architecture 141

Napoléon I 128, 131, 132, 133, 136
'Natur und Baukunst' (Taut) 146
'Natur und Kunst' (Taut) 145, 146, 148
Naumann, Friedrich 145
Neotropical *Nymphaeaceae* 78
Neumann, D. 18, 20, 22–3
Neumann, Dietrich 6
New York: glasshouse complex 96
New York Crystal Palace 30–1
Ny Carlsberg Glyptotek 88–9
Nymphaea gigantean 106
Nymphaea Ortgiesiano-rubra 106

Oakland (East End) 113
Oddos, M. 111
Old Brussels Zoo 109
Olmstead, Frederick Law 43
orangeries 81, 82–3
Orient 1–2
Ortgies, Karl Eduard 99, 103, 104–5,
    106, 116, 120
Osler Glass Company 27
Osztrák-Magyar Luxfer Prizma Gyár,
    KFT 15, 19

Padua 91
Palais du Champ de Mars 39, 40
Palais du Trocadéro 39, 58
palm houses 94–6; curved roofs 95
palms 84
Parisian Glassware Company 49
Paul Scheerbart's Briefe von
    1913–1914 an Gottfried
    Heinersdorff, Bruno Taut und
    Herwarth Walden (Ikelaar) 3

Paxton, Joseph 27, 29, 68; dedicated glasshouse for *Victoria regia* lily 73, 75; experiments with *Victoria regia* 98; purpose-built glasshouse 97–8, 99; ridge-and-furrow system 98, 99; *Victoria regia* lily 69, 73; *Victoria regia* seedling 97
Pennycuick, James G. 11; patents 11–12
Pettit, Henry 35
Philadelphia Botanical Gardens 113
Phillips, Henry 89
Phipps Conservatory 113, 113–14
Phipps, Henry 113
Phoenix Glass Works 49, 50
polygonal plans 109
Ponsin, J. A. 55, 56
Prange, Regine 4
Preu ische Gewerbeförderung 107
prismatic glass 11; invention 13
prisms *see* Luxfer Prisms
private winter gardens 85–7
Prussia 107, 131
Public Exhibition of Industrial Products 26, 27
Public Exposition of French Industrial Products 26
public winter gardens 87–90; Berlin aquarium 89; *Flora* 88; *Galerie des Machines* 90; *Glas Palast* 90; Glass Menagerie 89; hotel foyers 88; *Jardin d'Hiver* 88; peoples palaces 89; Zoological Conservatory 89
Pugin, Augustus Welby Northmore 133

Qualität (Quality) 145

Radiating Light Company 11, 12
Rand McNally and Company 48
Ravené, Louis Fredric 87
Realism 136–7
Recent Religious Architecture in England (Muthesius) 139
Rehm, Robin 150–1
representational art 137
Richards, W. C. 30
Riegl, Alois 137
Roezl, Benedikt 103
Romanticism 133, 136, 136–7
Rothe, Tyge 95
Royal Botanical Gardens (Berlin) 87, 92, 102, 109–11, 112–14, 115; influence on *Glashaus* design 117–18; relocation to Dahlem 112–14

Royal Botanical Gardens (Kew) 94, 100–1, 104
Royal Botanical Society 88, 94
Royal Dublin Society (RDS) 94
Royal Glasshouses 86
Royal Panopticon of Science and Art 46–7
Ruskin, John 133–6, 146, 147; Changefulness/Variety 135; Grotesqueness/Disturbed Imagination 135–6; Naturalism 135; Redundant/Generosity 136; Rigidity/Obstinacy 136; Savageness/Rudeness 134–5; *The Seven Lamps of Architecture* 134; *The Stones of Venice* 134
Russell, Scott 33

Sachform 142
sachlich art 140, 142
San Francisco: palm house 96
Sang, Frederick 31
scarab beetles 119
Scheerbart, Paul 1, 2, 3, 4, 6; Berlin Botanical Gardens 115; the Gothic 125; introduction of Taut to glasshouses 72
Schinkel, Karl Friedrich 130–1
Schlegel, Karl Wilhelm Friedrich 129–30
Schmahl, Henrik 19
Schmidt, Karl 145
Schola Medica Salernitana 90
Schomburgk, Robert 79
Schönbrunn glasshouse (Vienna) 95
Schultze, F. 111
Schulze, Konrad Werner 68
Schuster, Georg Heinrich 101
Schwarzmann, Herman J. 37
Seeing Through Glass: The Fictive Role of Glass in Shaping Architecture from Joseph Paxton's Crystal Palace to Bruno Taut's Glashaus (Ersoy) 68
Semi-prism Glass Company 11, 12
Seven Lamps of Architecture, The (Ruskin) 134
Sharp, Dennis 2, 71
Shaw, Richard Norman 142
Shepp, J. W. 48
'The Shoes of Fortune' *see* 'Die Galoschen des Glucks'
Société d'encouragement pour l'industrie nationale 26
Société Luxfer 15

170 *Index*

Society for the Encouragement of National Industry 26
Solar Prism Company of Cleveland 11
Speidel, Manfred 3, 4, 73
Spiegelglas (Plate glass) 21
Spruce, Robert 79
Staffelhalle 150
staircases, *Glashaus* 22–3
Steinbach, Hugo 20
Stiftskirche (Stuttgart) 128, 148–50
Stilarchitektur und Baukunst (Muthesius) 139–40, 140
St. Lamberti 150
St. Martin 150
St. Mauritius 150
Stones of Venice, The (Ruskin) 134, 146
Strahan, E. 34
Strasbourg Cathedral 73, 125–8, 129, 130–1, 132
Sydenham Crystal Palace *see* Crystal Palace
Syon House 94, 99

Tannenwald 148
Taut, Bruno: architectural flower 79; architecture merging with the arts 147; glazed cladding 69; imitating the Gothic masters 148–55; rural village 145–6
Thiekotter, Angelika 3, 21, 78
Tiffany Glass and Decorating Company 49
Trade Promotion Institute of Prussia 107
Trade Schools 107
Träger-Verkaufs-Kontor Firma 20, 26
Transatlantic Company 41
Treppe Glassteine auf Eisenkonstru 21
Trocadéro Palace 39
True Principles of Pointed or Christian Architecture, The (Pugin) 133
Turner, Richard 94, 100
Typisierung 145

Über-fangglas (conical glass) 21
Umfang Glas (circumference glass) 21
Universal Exposition (Barcelona 1888) 41
Universal Exposition of the Colonies in General Exports 41
Urban, Ignatz 112

van de Velde, Henry 145

van Houtte, Louis Benoit 102–3, 105–6; gardening school 105–6
van Houtte Nursery 102–3, 105, 106, 108–9, 116, 120
vault lighting 11
Venice-Murano Glass Exhibit 49
Verband Deutscher Brücken-und Eisenbaufabriken 20
Victoria regia glasshouses 96, 97–8, 99–112; Balat glasshouse 109; Berlin Botanical Gardens 102, 109–11, 112–14; Borsig 107–9; Botanical Gardens (University of Leiden) 109; circular 116; continental 101–12; Copenhagen Botanical Gardens 112; East End (Oakland) 113; Frankfurt Botanical Gardens 113; *Glas Palast* (Glass Palace) 110–11; Herren-hausen Gardens 101–2, 106; inspiration for *Glashaus* 116; Lyon 111; Ortgies' glasshouse 103, 104–5; Philadelphia Botanical Gardens 113; polygonal plans 109, 115–16; Strasbourg Botanical Gardens 111–12; van Houtte Nursery 102–3, 105, 106, 108–9
Victoria regia lily: beauty of 79; breaking the surface of water 79; and Bruno Taut 69, 73, 78–80; designers desires of clients 120; European cultivation of 97–9; flowering 79–80, 119–20; glasshouses for 73–5, 97–8; influence on *Glashaus* design 119–20, 160; initial buds 99; initial flowering 97; Joseph Paxton 69, 73, 98; ponds for 97; Royal Botanical Gardens (Kew) 100–1, 104; scarab beetles 78, 80, 119; seedling 97, 99; similarities with *Glashaus* 80; structure 79; underside 79
Vienna *Weltausstellung* (World Exhibition) 33–5; global financial problems 35; *Rotunde* 33–5, 58
Villa Berg Conservatory 86
'Von Deutsche Baukunst' (Goethe) 128, 129
von Goethe, Johann 128–9
von Görres, Josef 131–2
von Sartory, Barna 114
von Steinbach, Erwin 128

W. & D. Bailey 92
Wailly, G. 54

Index 171

Walton, W. 58
Washington, George 30–1
Washington Glass Company 36
Water Lily House 100
Water Temples 29–30
Wendland, Heinrich Ludolph 101
Werkbund *see* Deutscher Werkbund
Werkbund Exhibition (1914) 1, 21, 22
Whyte, Iain Boyd 3; translation of
  Taut's letters 71, 73, 75
Wilhelm IV, King Friedrich 132
Wilson, Joseph 35
Winslow, William 14
winter gardens 82; association with
  botanical gardens 90–1; private
  85–7; public 87–90
World Expositions: Centennial
  Exposition (Philadelphia, 1876)
  35–9, 58; Exhibition of the Industry
  of All Nations (New York, 1853)
  30–1, 58; *Exposition Universelle de
  Paris* (1867) 32–3; *Exposition
  Universelle de Paris* (1878) 39–41,
  58; *Exposition Universelle de Paris*
  (1889) 41–3, 58; *Exposition
  Universelle de Paris* (1900) 51–8,
  59; Great Exhibition of the Works of
  Industry of All Nations, The
  (London, 1851) 27–30; London

International Exhibition on Art and
  Industry (1862) 31–2, 58; Vienna
  Weltausstellung (World Exhibition)
  33–5, 58; World's Colombian
  Exposition (Chicago, 1893) 13,
  43–51, 58–9
World's Colombian Exposition
  (Chicago, 1893) 13, 43–51; Art
  Glass 49; Electricity Building 50;
  Electric Tower 49–50; Fisheries
  Building 50; Gallery of Fine Arts
  50–1; glasshouses 48–9;
  Horticulture Building 48, 58;
  influence on the *Glashaus* 58–9;
  Lagoon 43; Manufactures and
  Liberal Arts Building 49, 50;
  Midway Plaisance 43–4, 47–8, 49;
  Mirror Maze 46; Moorish Palace
  45–6, 58; North Pond 43; South
  Pond 43; Texas Building 49; *Victoria
  regia* lily 114; White City 43
World's Industrial and Cotton
  Centennial Exposition 41
Worringer, Wilhelm 137–8
Wright, Frank Lloyd 14, 16

Zoological Conservatory 89
Zürich Botanical Gardens 106
Zwieseler und Pirnaer 24